THE DUMFRIES BOOK OF DAYS

DAVID CARROLL

The History Press

For Willow

ACKNOWLEDGEMENTS

It would not have been possible to compile this book without drawing extensively on our local newspapers, past and present, including the *Dumfries and Galloway Courier*, the *Dumfries and Galloway Courier and Herald*, the *Dumfries Weekly Journal* and the *Dumfries Times*. I am particularly grateful to Kenny Barr, editor of the *Dumfries and Galloway Standard*, for allowing me to include material published in that newspaper. Idiosyncrasies of sentence construction, punctuation, spelling, capital letters etc. contained in the original texts have been preserved here wherever these do not compromise meaning or understanding.

Note: The formerly two separate burghs of Dumfries and Maxwelltown were only amalgamated in 1929. For the purposes of this book, however, I have treated them as a single entity throughout.

First published 2014

The History Press
The Mill, Brimscombe Port
Stroud, Gloucestershire, GL5 2QG
www.thehistorypress.co.uk

British Library Cataloguing in Publication Data.
A catalogue record for this book is available from the British Library.

ISBN 978 0 7524 6474 9

Typesetting and origination by The History Press
Printed in India

— January 1st —

1649: 'Total abstinencey was by no means insisted upon by the [Kirk] Session, but they earnestly strove to prevent the immoderate use of intoxicating drinks, and to abolish or check all social practices which encouraged rioting and carousing ... On this day, the following resolution was minuted: "The Sessioune, resenting the great dishonour done to the Lord by sundry persons in the burgh not only abusing the creatures to excess of riot thro' drinking healths, but likewise in the height of their cups do calle for the drummer to beat the drum to them at every health, do henceforth discharge the drummer to answer any persone whatever in such ungodly demands under the paine of inflicting upon him the sharpest measure of kirk discipline, and extruding him from his place withal."' (McDowall, William, *History of Dumfries* (2nd Edn., 1873))

———

1805: On this day, The *Dumfries Weekly Journal* informed its readers of 'New Malt, East Kent and Worcester Hops, also a quantity of October brewed Ale and bottled porter, fit for immediate use; all of which are of the very best quality. Apply to James McNeil, Baker and Brewer, Dumfries.'

— January 2nd —

1810: On this day, a notice appeared: 'John Crosbie, merchant, St. David's Street, takes the present opportunity of informing the Public, that it has been the practice of a great many for some time past, in not paying the dues that are liable to be paid at the Three Ports of this place, viz. Townhead, Lochmabengate and Kirkgate. – It is therefore particularly requested, that all Goods exported or imported at any of the said Three Ports, such as spirits, wine, oil, tar, iron, butter and cheese, and all corded packs, and other merchandise, together with all kinds of grain, potatoes, roots and fruits, must be paid to the person who collects at any of the said Three Ports; and no exemption whatever shall any pretend in taking grain to the Town's Mills, which are as liable to pay as shipping the same, or bringing it to market.

J.C. is willing to contract with gentlemen, farmers, carriers and others, by the year, for all custom which they are liable to pay at the said Three Ports, together with the Weigh-house dues for butter, cheese, fish &c. – Tickets will be given to each who agrees to the same. – John Crosbie, Merchant.' (*Dumfries Weekly Journal*)

⁓ January 3rd ⁓

1872: On this day, the *Dumfries and Galloway Standard* reported the New Year festivities at the town's Poorhouse: 'A most abundant and well-cooked dinner of roast beef, roast mutton, and plum pudding was served, to which the inmates present did ample justice. Nearly a dozen aged and frail persons, who were unable to be downstairs, were served in their rooms. The manner in which the dinner was cooked and served reflected the highest credit on Mr. and Mrs. Robertson, the indefatigable master and matron of the Poorhouse. Each adult was then served with a quantity of tea and sugar; the men in addition receiving some tobacco, and the children each a small book and some confections.'

The party was also in full swing at Muirhead's Hospital, where 'the old men and women, together with the boys who are cared for in this institution, sat down to a well-furnished table on Monday at two o'clock ... beer being supplied to the old people by Mr. Napier, Brewer.' Meanwhile, at the Industrial School 'the inmates had their usual New Year's dinner, provided by a number of friends. About seventy of the children assembled at noon in the dining-room [and] partook of a very substantial repast.'

— January 4th —

1825: On this day, the following announcement appeared in the *Dumfries Weekly Journal*: 'The Public are respectfully informed that the old "Robert Burns" Coach, to be driven through by one coachman, will start from the Dumfries and Galloway Hotel, Dumfries, every lawful night – on Mondays, Wednesdays and Fridays, at four o'clock precisely in the afternoon; on Tuesdays, Thursdays and Saturdays, at half-past five; and from Mr. Donald's "King's Arms Inn", Carlisle, every lawful night at four o'clock.

By this arrangement, passengers who arrive in Carlisle by the Whitehaven and Newcastle coaches can be forwarded soon after their arrival, and thus obviate the delay and expense of remaining all night in Carlisle. To passengers wishing to travel to Glasgow or Edinburgh, this coach will afford a great accommodation, as they will have the advantage of a night's rest at Dumfries, and will be forwarded from thence at eight o'clock the next morning; whereas by remaining in Carlisle all night, they must be under the unpleasant necessity of rising at three o'clock, which, in a cold winter morning, is not so agreeable as being snugly accommodated with a warm bed till seven o'clock, with plenty of time for an excellent breakfast.'

— January 5th —

1830: On this day, the *Dumfries Weekly Journal* reported that 'on the forenoon of Sunday last, a young man who had been imprisoned … upon a charge of poaching, made his escape in the following curious and somewhat extraordinary manner. When he and four other prisoners were let out of their cells to attend divine worship in the chapel attached to the jail, he contrived to elude the observation of the turnkey, and having got on the top of a dunghill placed against a wall in the yard, he excavated the lime from various parts of the wall, which served him as a ladder, and having got upon the top of the wall, which is nearly 20 feet high, he dropped into Buccleuch Street and fled. Provost Frazer, as soon as he was informed what had happened, sent an express to Langholm, the place of the prisoner's nativity, to which it was supposed he had gone. At 10 o'clock the prisoner was apprehended in the streets of that place. He was immediately handcuffed and, being kept in custody during the dead hours of the night, he was afterwards placed in a cart, attended by two officers, who arrived with him here in the afternoon, and again placed him in jail.'

— JANUARY 6TH —

1909: On this day, the *Dumfries and Galloway Standard* reported that 'old age pensions were paid for the first time at Dumfries Post Office on Saturday, and there was a steady stream of callers all forenoon. Army pensions were payable on the same day, and in consequence the Post Office officials, upon whom the duty of paying the pensions fell, had a busy time. The work was increased by a considerable number of the pensioners not being able, owing to frailty, to sign their name … A good many were so feeble that they had to be assisted forward to the counter, and others who were unable to walk to the Post Office had their pension paid to friends, who acted as agents for them. All were evidently grateful for the pension, and the officer who handed over the money was rewarded by a cheery "thank ye, sir." On Saturday, pensions were paid at the General Post Office to 111 persons … Up to yesterday, 136 had received pensions at the head office, and there were paid at the town sub-offices the following: Queen Street, 18; St. Michael Street, 20; Milldamhead, 25 – altogether 199. The total number of pensioners in Dumfries and Maxwelltown is 221.'

─ January 7th ─

1950: On this day, the *Dumfries and Galloway Standard* recorded that 'the report submitted to the Town Council at its last meeting on housing progress (or lack of it) in Dumfries since the war makes sad reading. Since 1944 ... only 270 permanent houses have been completed along with 304 temporary and other houses. That is an average of 54 permanent houses each year, which cannot be regarded with the smallest degree of satisfaction. Every Councillor knows that when it is learned that a Council house is about to be let, there are scores of applicants. We know of one case where a house was let in Lincluden to a family whose name had been on the waiting-list for fourteen years. Even before the war, when the building of houses was not beset with so many difficulties as now, the demand for houses greatly exceeded the supply, and since that time two new factories have been established in the neighbourhood.

The Council is really not to blame for what is a truly lamentable state of matters. It was the Government who bungled the business of housing so dreadfully that protests have been and are being made all over the county.'

— JANUARY 8TH —

1781: On this day, the following warning appeared in the *Dumfries Weekly Journal*: 'The Magistrates and Council considering that ... there have been many chimneys within this borough on fire, many of which have greatly alarmed and frightened the inhabitants, and others threatened ruin either to the tenement to which the chimneys belonged, or to the neighbouring tenements; and all of which have been occasioned by not ... keeping such chimneys sufficiently clean; to prevent which, in time coming, it is enacted and ordained by the Magistrates and Council, that hereafter if any chimney within this borough be set on fire purposely, or take fire accidentally, so as the flame burns out at the top, the possessor or occupier of the tenement, lodging room or apartment, to which such chimney belongs shall forfeit and pay the sum of FIVE SHILLINGS to the Town Treasurer.

The Magistrates and Council prohibit any persons from throwing out any ashes, the fire in which has not been quite extinguished; from keeping peats or any other kind of firing near any fireplace; from carrying live coals from one house to another, without they be duly covered; from carrying lighted candles without a lanthorn, into any barn, stable, storehouse or outhouse, where there are combustibles.'

— JANUARY 9TH —

1845: On this day, it was reported that 'the Dumfries Soup Kitchen, which was opened on Saturday last, is again in full operation, and will continue ministering to the wants of all and sundry, but particularly the industrious deserving, suddenly thrown out of employment, so long as the Managers consider such an application of the public bounty alike merciful and desirable. At a Meeting of the Committee held on Friday last, arrangements were formed for the most careful supervision on the part of the Distributors, prudence gathered from experience, in the numerous Purchases made, and economy the most rigid in every department, so as to render the Charity the medium of the greatest possible amount of public benefit. Since the storm set in on the 4th current, numerous Labourers have been necessarily thrown idle; hence the necessity of commencing operations nearly a fortnight earlier than usual; but the Committee will watch the course of the weather, in connection with the certainty or prospect of outdoor Labour, and thus economise the Fund placed at their disposal, so as to render any Balance remaining equally efficient in its applications on future occasions.' (*Dumfriesshire and Galloway Herald and Register*)

~ JANUARY 10TH ~

1833: On this day, it was reported that '… while walking along Irish Street on Friday last, near to the brewery of Mr. Corson, we were much surprised to see a horse yoked to a cart dart from Mr. Corson's entry, clear the corner, gallop along Irish Street and Buccleuch Street, past the Post Office where the animal was stopped. What renders the occurrence more singular still is, that the farm servant in charge of the horse, when he found him breaking off, seized him by the nostril with one hand and the loose rein with the other, and bravely hung on and brought the animal up by his own strength alone. The servant had incautiously taken off the blinders, for the purpose of feeding the horse; a practice which has led to numberless serious accidents, and cannot be too severely reprobated.' (*Dumfries Times*)

1837: On this day, 'some half-a-dozen gentlemen met at the house of Mr. David Beveridge, and originated the Dumfries and Maxwelltown Total Abstinence Society. Mr. Broom, its first president, Mr. Beveridge, Mr. John McIntosh, Mr. David Halliday, Mr. William Gregan, and Mr. William F. Johnstone, were among its earliest and most active members. There were no fewer than 1,500 names on its roll in January 1838, and at one time the number reached at least 2,000.' (McDowall, William, *History of Dumfries* (2nd Edn., 1873))

~ JANUARY 11TH ~

1881: On this day, it was reported that 'after the dog show in Dumfries had concluded on Saturday, the highly-commended Pomeranean dog, "Di", belonging to Miss M. J. Payne of Castle Douglas, was taken to the railway station, but at the entrance it slipped its collar, and made off along the Annan Road. After "taking a thocht", the animal wheeled … and reached home between three and four o'clock on Sunday morning. He had never travelled the road before.' (*Dumfries and Galloway Courier*)

1899: On this day, the following letter was printed in the *Dumfries and Galloway Courier and Herald*: 'Dear Sir – As an old Dumfries boy, I take the liberty of sending you our local paper, the "Rhodesian Times", giving a full report of our Caledonian banquet held last St. Andrew's Night … one of the best I have ever attended in Africa. This is saying a good deal for Salisbury … and certainly reflects great credit on the Salisbury Caledonian Society. We have a great number of Scotsmen here – about 200 – and, strange to say, I am the only Dumfries boy among the lot. This is rather peculiar when one remembers that both Cape Colony and the Transvaal are simply alive with Dumfriesians.'

— January 12th —

The following items appeared in the *Dumfries and Galloway Courier* on this day:

1813: It was reported that 'the young woman whom we formerly noticed as having been severely scorched at the Old Crown Inn, after languishing for some time died at the infirmary. Before her death, she was delivered of a living infant, whose mortal existence, however, terminated in the short period of twelve hours, the mother having only been in the sixth month of her pregnancy.'

1813: An article which reported that 'the cook in a family in this town had one of her fingers torn fairly off, by the machinery of a jack which she had just been winding up. We are happy to hear that she seems to have suffered little inconvenience from this shocking accident.'

1875: 'Distribution of Coals to the Poor – On Friday and Saturday last, fifty tons of coals were distributed to the necessitous poor of Dumfries. The coals were purchased from the Crocket Charity, being the interest of a sum of money left by the late Mr. Crocket to be applied for behoof of the poor. Other distributions from the same fund will be made on an early day. Three trucks of coals have been ordered for the poor of Maxwelltown, to be paid for by the voluntary subscriptions of the Coal Fund.'

~ January 13th ~

1779: On this day, 'at Dumfries, in a General Meeting of the Commissioners of Supply for the county of Dumfries, called by their Convener: the meeting, taking into their most serious consideration the late Act of Parliament for relieving Papists in England, from the penalties and disabilities enacted by the statute of King William, and that it has been proposed to bring in a Bill of the same tendency for Scotland; and being justly alarmed at the dreadful consequences of the further increase of so intolerant and oppressive a religion, which has so often endangered our liberties, civil and religious; they think themselves called upon to oppose such extension, and the more, as the statutes at present in force against Papists in Scotland appear much milder than those lately repealed in England, and have very seldom been carried into execution, and never with rigour. With this the Meeting are not dissatisfied, being utterly averse to persecution for matters of private opinion; but they cannot approve of the repeal of these statutes, which they consider as a wise precaution against the dangers so uniformly flowing from the political principles of that sect, and the horrid attempts of its Priests and followers. – Thos. Goldie, Clerk.' (*Dumfries Weekly Journal*)

~ JANUARY 14TH ~

1933: On this day, the *Dumfries and Galloway Courier and Herald* railed against a plan to alter one of the town's most distinctive buildings: 'We join emphatically in the protest against the proposal to break down part of the fabric of the Midsteeple for the purposes of a showroom for the burgh Electricity Department. This is a sheer outrage, excusable on no ground whatever ... To break into the fabric in order to insert what is called a "modern front" for a showroom would be to destroy irretrievably the characteristic lines and design of the building and to render it an intolerable offence alike to the historic and artistic eye. For Dumfriesians everywhere the Midsteeple stands as the centre and symbol of many cherished associations, and they will deeply resent such tampering with it as is proposed. The Midsteeple has stood as we know it for about 230 years, and it does seem an act of impertinence as well as vandalism ... If the Committee must have a showroom and "modern front", let them look elsewhere for it and leave the Midsteeple alone. We hope the community will put a stop to this projected vandalism.'

— January 15th —

On this day, the following items appeared in the *Dumfries Weekly Journal*:

1778: 'At the New Assembly Room, Dumfries, Mr. Dinwiddie will give a lecture on Experimental Philosophy. The various properties of Air will be demonstrated by a large collection of the most useful and entertaining experiments on the Air-Pump, Condensing Engine, Barometer, Wind-Gun &c. These experiments will not be repeated this season.'

———

1799: The Second Corps of Royal Dumfries Volunteers were inspected by Colonel Auriel, of the Oxfordshire Dragoons, agreeable to the orders of the War Office, when they went through their various manouevres and firings much to the satisfaction of the Colonel.'

———

1799: 'The "Motley", under Captain Cunningham, is arrived at the foot of our river, from Gottenburg, with a cargo of iron and deals for Mr. James Crosbie of this town. This vessel has had a tedious passage, and was almost taken by a French privateer.'

———

1845: A sale of 'Guano, by Auction was announced. The fine Brig "Columbine", daily expected in the Nith, will be brought as near to Dumfries as the depth of the water will permit, and her Cargo, which is of the finest quality, will be delivered from the ship's side, thus affording the purchasers the highest possible guarantee of the perfect purity of the article.'

~ January 16th ~

1810: On this day, 'the Council received from the County Commissioners copies of a bill prepared by them and the Commissioners of the Stewartry, for improving the navigation of the river, and the police regulations of the burgh. Hitherto the Council had been the Neptunes of the Nith; and now these other bodies desired, by virtue of a new legislative trident, to acquire dominion over its waters and also sought to intermeddle with the internal affairs of the town. The Provost, Mr. Robert Jackson, was not of a temper to tolerate such assumptions; and in resisting them he was backed by nearly all the Councillors. A conference was brought about ... but as the county authorities stood out for "the bill and the whole bill", those of the town ... prepared a bill of their own based on their existing Tonnage, Ale-Duty, and Police Act, passed in 1787, and which had almost run its course.

Both parties made preparations for a Parliamentary campaign, but no real battle ensued. A technical flaw in the burghal measure having endangered its success, its promoters were induced to withdraw it ...' (A later modified bill was subsequently introduced.) (McDowall, William, *History of Dumfries* (2nd Edn., 1873))

~ January 17th ~

1826: On this day, the following report appeared in the *Dumfries and Galloway Courier*: 'Yesterday morning, the body of a new-born male infant was discovered by a boy of this town, lying in the river opposite the Moat, and was carried to the Council Chamber for dissection. It was full grown, and appeared to be alive. No marks of violence were upon the body. It is probable that its unnatural mother had effected its murder upon the night of Saturday, for, in the course of Sunday, several boys, while strolling along the river, perceived a small white object at the place where it was found; but supposing it to be only a drowned cat, they passed it without any attention.'

1826: Also on this day, the same newspaper noted that, 'The "Jessy" of Dumfries is again afloat. This will remind many of our readers of the unfortunate destruction by fire, off Whitehaven, a few months ago, of the Brig "Jessy" of this port, on her voyage to America, with a valuable cargo – an event which certainly called forth more of the public sympathy and regret than anything of the kind we ever witnessed. It now gives us unqualified pleasure to understand that our enterprising townsmen, Messrs. John and George Thomson, have launched at Le Etang, a very fine vessel, which, in compliment to Mr. John Thomson and his family, has been again named the "Jessy of Dumfries".'

— January 18th —

1865: On this day, the following report appeared in the *Dumfries and Galloway Standard*: 'On a recent market-day, a huge Galloway bull, that was being driven to one of the Dumfries auction-marts from a distant part of the Stewartry, made some strange detours before it reached its journey's end. At the door of the Maxwelltown Provision Store in Galloway Street, the animal stopped for a moment, and … strode boldly in, to the no small dismay of those who had charge of the premises. Receiving anything but a cordial welcome, the beast retired quietly, and then popped its black shaggy head into the next door, "going thither", people said, "to get its portrait taken"; for, true enough, it was in the direct way of entering Mr. Forsyth's photographic establishment. The intruding monster was in the midst of glass cases filled with portraits, and other fragile objects, and a toss or two of its head, a single caper with its heels, would have spread destruction all around. However, before it had leisure to make itself familiar with the many strange articles that met its view, it experienced a violent tugging at the tail, and backed out as if it had been trained to such a retrograde motion.'

~ JANUARY 19TH ~

1813: On this day, it was announced that 'there will be an Assembly on Thursday for the Benefit of such poor distressed families as receive no parochial relief. As the Rev. Drs. Scot and Duncan have agreed to make a distribution of the proceeds arising from the Charity Ball, among the different necessitous objects that are within their knowledge, it is hoped that the Humane of the town will come forward on this occasion, whether they are able to attend in person or not.' (*Dumfries Weekly Journal*)

———

1875: On this day, it was reported that 'the Nith has been heavily flooded, and very few of the gravid salmon collected below the Caul have been able to get over that obstacle … But a number must have got up, as we hear they are swarming in the upper reaches of the river. Large crowds of people daily assemble to watch the movements of the fish, but nothing has been done as yet to facilitate their upward progress. A very slight indentation in the ridge of the Caul near the steps would be sufficient, but after the recent heavy outlay by the town on the repair of that structure, the Council are not likely to initiate the required improvement.' (*Dumfries and Galloway Courier*)

~ January 20th ~

1663: On this day, 'the Councill admitted Mr. Matthew Richmond to be schoolmaster of this burgh and precentor of the church and clerk to the Session, during their pleasure, who is to have from the town one hundred pounds Scots money of pension yearly, and to have the benefit of quarter wages, as was peyed to Mr. William M'Jore, and to have the benefit of proclamations, baptisms, and burialls, and Candlemas nixt to be his entrie to the said offices.'

Richmond had been obliged to sign what was described as an 'offensive oath of allegiance'. This referred to an Act passed by King Charles II in 1661, 'requiring all magistrates, councillors, ministers, and other persons of trust to take an oath of allegiance to himself'. For some reason, Matthew Richmond was dismissed from the school and expelled from the burgh within a year or so, although he did receive some small compensation when 'the counsell having taken to consideration the petitioune of Mr. Matthew Richmond they appoynt the thesaurer to give unto him as a gratuity seeing he is now put from the scooll and is to remove from this place the soume of Twenty five punds Scotts…' (Mackie, Charles, (Ed.), *Dumfries and Galloway Notes and Queries* (1913))

— January 21st —

1846: On this day, this report appeared in the *Dumfries and Galloway Standard*: 'A few days ago, we had the pleasure of seeing a new kind of glass, invented by our talented townsman, Mr. W.C. Aitken. It is a metallic glass, and can have any colour imparted to it. It also has the great advantage of being as little liable to fracture as metal itself. Mr. Aitken … lately constructed a bedstead of this material for the celebrated liliputian, General Tom Thumb, and intends, we understand, to employ it in the manufacture of still bulkier articles of furniture. We lately saw in this town a pair of brackets for looping up curtains designed and made by Mr. Aitken, and ornamented with flowers of this new glass. They are true to nature in colour and design, and are therefore immensely in advance of the old eyesore patterns. The press has already praised Mr. Aitken highly for his improvements in the art of moulding, and the Art Union of London sums up his merits in this well-earned compliment: "Thus, in lieu of an object in no way pleasing, we have an object beautiful and refreshing, an adornment to our rooms, perpetually repaying its cost by giving us pleasure. The merit of this design belongs to Mr. Aitken."'

⟶ JANUARY 22ND ⟶

1828: On this day, the *Dumfries Weekly Journal* reported recent severe disruption to road transport, following heavy snowfalls: 'The London Mail was two-and-a-half hours late, and the Edinburgh Mail Coach stuck in the snow on this side of Noblehouse, when the guard took to horseback until he reached Crook, from whence he and the mail-bags were forwarded in a post-chaise, and reached Dumfries about a quarter-past nine instead of half-past three. The Portpatrick Mail was delayed five hours, viz. from four till nine, waiting upon the Edinburgh Mail, and although it did not arrive till a quarter of an hour after the despatch of the Port Mail, Mr. Fraser the mail contractor, with great alacrity, sent off a person on horseback to stop her, which he did about the five mile stone, and the bags were forwarded by another person on horseback as soon as they could be got ready. The Glasgow Mail Coach did not reach Dumfries till a quarter past ten, with six horses, being nearly five hours beyond her usual time. On Friday, the Edinburgh Mail did not reach Dumfries till half-past five, and the Portpatrick Mail … was despatched immediately afterwards. Since then they have arrived tolerably regularly, though perhaps a little later than usual.'

⟶ January 23rd ⟵

1839: On this day, the *Dumfries Times* reported that as Dumfries had recently been visited by a hurricane, the town council had convened a special meeting to consider 'the general devastation of the Town's property, especially the damage done to the New and Old Churches, Midsteeple and milns. The Provost suggested that a thorough survey should be obtained of the state of the whole of the public buildings and Council property, and a detailed report obtained therefrom, not by any tradesman connected with the Council, who might be suspected to have some interest in the matter, but by a neutral qualified person.

Mr. Crombie said he thought the proposal a proper one, and necessary in so extreme a case; for certainly he had never seen the Old Steeple, Burgh Buildings, the town property, and town generally, in half so dilapidated a state. The steeple of the Old Church, however, he did not think so dangerous, as he knew from its peculiar construction, and being bound with iron, that it was not likely to fall. Still, he thought it ought to be taken down and rebuilt, but this could only be done by the proper erection of a sufficient scaffold; and this ought not to be attempted till the good weather in May or June.'

— January 24th —

1900: On this day, the *Dumfries and Galloway Courier and Herald* reported the following mysterious death: 'Yesterday afternoon, between four and five o'clock, a young man was observed to stagger and fall in English Street … He was immediately assisted into the harness-room of Mr. Irving's posting establishment, but despite the application of restoratives, he expired in a few minutes. The unfortunate young man, who was a stranger in the town, had been residing for the last fortnight with Mrs. Dooley in English Street, to whom, however, he never mentioned his connections further than a remark that his parents were English. He seemed to have no occupation, and was not in search of work, but spent his time in wandering about the town and neighbourhood. Yesterday forenoon he went out as usual about 11 o'clock, and had been seen several times during the day about Queensberry Square, where he had exhibited to some young fellows an empty unlabelled poison bottle, which, however, was not found in his possession after his tragic death. He was well-dressed, wearing a dark grey tweed jacket with brownish tweed trousers, and being tidily attired he seemed in no pecuniary difficulties.'

~ January 25th ~

1859: On this day, Dumfries celebrated the centenary of Robert Burns's birth, and the day was marked by 'a series of fetes and banquets such as was never seen before in the burgh or the Border-land – or, rather we should say, in North Britain – and wherever the sons of Scotia congregate, throughout the world … Little did those Dumfries gentry who deliberately gave Burns the cold shoulder, on a memorable autumnal evening in 1794, suppose that, sixty-five years afterwards … the streets down which they proudly passed would be trophied with garlands, and eloquent with sweet sounds, in honour of the man whom they affected to despise. The old burgh florid with decorations natural and artistic; a great outdoor demonstration, addressed by Mr. Washington Wilkes; a magnificent procession; two dinners – one in the Assembly Rooms, presided over by Dr. W.A.F. Browne, the other in the Nithsdale Mills, where about a thousand persons assembled – Mr. Mundell of Bogrie in the chair – Mr. John Hamilton, of the 'Morning Star', giving in eloquent terms the 'immortal memory'; these were the chief, but not by any means the sole features of the centenary celebration in Dumfries. It was in every respect worthy of the town where Burns lived and breathed his last, and where his ashes lie.' (McDowall, William, *History of Dumfries* (2nd Edn., 1873))

– January 26th –

1779: On this day, it was reported that 'the Magistrates and Council of Dumfries have resolved to let the Cleaning of the Streets, and Dung arising therefrom, for one year after Candlemas next. The town at present pays six pounds yearly to the persons employed, besides furnishing besoms, and allowing them the whole profit of the Dung, which must be considerable; but as there has been much reason to complain that the streets have not been properly cleaned, they wish to enter into a new bargain with any one, two, or more persons, who will undertake the same, and engage to keep them properly clean. Any person or persons who are willing to undertake this business may give in their proposals to the Town Chamberlain immediately.' (*Dumfries Weekly Journal*)

1916: Also on this day, the *Dumfries and Galloway Standard* printed the following stern wartime warning: 'It must be clearly understood that the recent removal of the Restrictions on Hay does not in any way release any individual from such Agreement or Contract as may have been entered into with any of the Purchasing Officers; neither does it give any such individual the right to use, remove, sell, or otherwise dispose of Hay, which by virtue of the Contract entered into will become the property of H.M. Government.'

⁓ January 27th ⁓

1778: On this day, the following stirring call to arms was printed in the *Dumfries Weekly Journal*: 'If there are any clever young men, whose bosoms glow with military ardour, and wish to serve their King and Country, they will find an opportunity to exercise their talents, by just now enlisting with Mr. Heron of Heron (a Justice of the Peace), to serve in a new corps that is to be levied, to assist His Majesty in punishing his rebellious subjects in America, and to prevent their native Country from losing any part of the dominions belonging to it, or from forfeiting any part of the honour that Great Britain so justly acquired in the last War; which was entered into chiefly in the defence of these ungrateful colonies, who are now bidding defiance to the laws which reared, and the arms which formerly protected them. Such ingratitude deserves the severest punishment; and it is hoped there are among us young men of sufficient spirit to assist in giving that punishment.

To such, Mr. Heron hereby offers Ten Guineas of Bounty-Money, with other gratifications usually given to soldiers. God Save King George.'

— January 28th —

1641: On this day, the Kirk Session passed an edict, under the terms of which '… every gentleman absent from church was made liable to a fine of thirty shillings for each day's absence; a burgess committing the same offence had to pay twelve shillings, and a servant five. All the Incorporated Trades had seats assigned to them in the gallery of the parish church; and three years before the … resolution was adopted, the Session, taking into account the absenteeism of which many were guilty, "especially wrights and masons", intimated that they must be more punctual in their attendance on peril of losing their sittings.' (McDowall, William, *History of Dumfries* (2nd Edn., 1873))

1806: 'J. Beverley begs leave to return his grateful acknowledgements to his Friends, for the liberal encouragement he has met with since he commenced business at the "George Inn"; and now informs them that in future he will charge only ONE SHILLING a mile for Posting, in place of ONE SHILLING AND THREE PENCE, the usual charge in the country. J.B. assures those who may honour him with their support, that they shall have excellent accommodation, and that good Horses, comfortable Chaises, and careful Drivers will at all times be ready on the shortest notice.' (*Dumfries Weekly Journal*)

⊸ January 29th ⊸

1834: On this day, 'a case came before the Weekly Committee of the Infirmary … which the Magistrates would do well to give heed to. We allude to a man from Kelton, a lunatic and deaf and dumb (a more terrible combination of calamities can hardly be contemplated), who was admitted to the asylum on Saturday … This most miserable of God's creatures was found by one of the Infirmary Surgeons a few days ago (in the middle of January recollect), in a cell in the town gaol naked, the straw on which he lay, or kennelled rather, saturated with filth, and the door of the worse than pig-stye full of chinks and holes through which every wind of heaven sifted … The poor outcast of humanity, of whose condition we speak with pain and, we add, with shame, to think that in 1834 and in a Christian town, such a tale should remain to be told, wears God's image and may inherit God's grace. Even amidst all the burden and down-pressing of those afflictions with which Heaven has afflicted him, the immortal spark still glimmers through, though dimly. He has received the elements of education, and can communicate by writing his wild wants and wishes.' (*Dumfries Times*)

~ JANUARY 30TH ~

1915: On this day, the *Dumfries and Galloway Standard* noted that
'… Mr Edward Compton [eminent actor-manager and father of
Whisky Galore author Compton Mackenzie] is paying a visit to the
Queen of the South after a lapse of six or seven years. For this
dramatic treat we have to thank an enterprising management,
who must have experienced a pleasing satisfaction at the support
which the public have accorded the venture. The value attached
to such an opportunity of witnessing the highest dramatic art
cannot be overestimated. In Mr Compton, we have a worthy
follower of the highest traditions of the British stage, one whose
art is on the highest level, and whose choice of plays favours
the classical rather than the modern, and who for many years
has delighted audiences all over the country. It is to be regretted
that Dumfries has not had a larger share of him, but one likes to
think that another seven years will not be allowed to elapse before
Mr Compton returns to us.

The piece staged on Thursday night was Lord Lytton's
conspiracy play, *Richelieu*, in the title role of which Mr Compton
was seen for the first time in Dumfries.'

~ January 31st ~

1838: On this day, the following 'Lonely Hearts' notice appeared in the *Dumfries and Galloway Courier*: 'A Wife Wanted – a Gentleman of Middle Age, and residing not 100 miles from Dumfries … takes this method of expressing his wishes to the fair ladies of Dumfries and its vicinity. He possesses a good Fortune – his face and figure are unexceptionable. Letters addressed J.F., Post Office, Dumfries, will meet with immediate attention. Strict secrecy will be observed. N.B. None need apply who do not possess a good temper, face and figure. Fortune no object. Letters to be post paid.'

He certainly received at least one application for the vacant post. It was couched in humorous verse and appeared in the same newspaper a few weeks later. Here is a flavour of it:

'Tis said that my temper is equable, fine,
Some people indeed have termed it divine …
My figure is handsome, proportioned and neat,
But my gowns must be worn right down to my feet,
For what a misfortune, but no fault of mine,
Both a club and a crook in my left foot combine …
Now your quality third, a beautiful face,
I must say that my own a Countess might grace.

(Mackie, Charles, (Ed.), *Dumfries and Galloway Notes and Queries* (1913))

~ February 1st ~

1841: On this day, the *Dumfries Times* reported that: '... Mr. Daniel O'Connell [the Irish political leader] was to pass through this town, and change horses at the "King's Arms Inn". Between one and two o'clock he arrived in a carriage and four; in a few minutes, upwards of a hundred persons were around the carriage, all anxious to steal a sight of that great man. In a minute or two, Mr. Rankine, wine merchant, came up and ... looked in, and taking off his hat, said that he had a strong desire to have the honour of shaking the hand of the greatest man living, whereupon ... Mr. O'Connell being next to the door, began to take off his glove and said, "Sir, you shall have that honour with much pleasure". Mr. Rankine replied, "God Bless You Sir, and spare you long for your oppressed country's good; you are fighting for her just rights as our immortal Wallace did for us centuries ago." On this the crowd cheered heartily, and a general wish amongst the persons present took place to obtain a shake of his hand, and on starting the crowd gave him three hearty cheers.'

— FEBRUARY 2ND —

1808: On this day, a notice was issued about the 'Preservation of Game' in the area: 'At a Meeting of the Association held in Dumfries on 16th December, in consequence of public advertisement, it was unanimously resolved, that of late the destruction of the Game has been carried to so great an extent, as to require the most active exertions to be used for putting a stop thereto. For this purpose, the Meeting have directed that the utmost rigour shall be used in prosecuting all poachers, unqualified persons, and in particular Carriers, Coach Owners, Innkeepers and others buying, selling, or otherways unlawfully possessed of Game.

The Meeting have already subscribed a considerable sum, have appointed a Committee of their number to direct and assist in enforcing the necessary measures; and for the better detecting of these illegal practices, a reward of TWO GUINEAS will be paid for each information which shall lead to conviction of the offender, by William Thomson, writer in Dumfries, Procurator Fiscal to the Sheriffdom, appointed agent for the Association, who has been directed to bring actions before the Sheriff against all offenders without delay.' (*Dumfries Weekly Journal*)

⚊ February 3rd ⚊

1824: On this day, the following report appeared: 'At a meeting of the Commissioners for executing the Act for Improving the Harbour of Dumfries … the Provost stated that he had called the meeting in consequence of various complaints which had reached him of the want of the proper Measure of Coals being delivered to the Inhabitants, which, having been considered by the Meeting, the following Bye-Laws should be carried into effect from 5th February:

- That a Coal Meter, or a person appointed by him … shall attend at the discharge of every vessel with coal for sale at this port …
- That he shall take particular care that the Coal Measure is fairly filled;
- That no Carter shall receive Coals into his cart in the absence of a Meter; nor shall he deliver them without a Ticket, specifying the vessel's name, and true port of loading, with the number of measures, and signed by the Meter … which Ticket the Carter shall deliver to the Purchasers of the Coals;
- That the Carter, as well as the Meter, shall keep a tally of the number of measures emptied into his cart; and if found one or more measures short, they shall be liable to a Penalty of 10/-.' (*Dumfries and Galloway Courier*)

~ February 4th ~

1812: On this day, extracts from the Dumfries Police Act were printed in the *Dumfries Weekly Journal*, and included the following:

- That no gunpowder shall be sold within the town by candlelight, or before sun-rising or after sunsetting.
- That no merchant or shopkeeper shall keep within his house, shop, or cellar, within the town, more than 20 pounds weight of gunpowder.
- That no wheelbarrows, sedan chairs, carts, carriages, barrels, hogsheads, or casks, be run, drawn, or carried, on any part of the foot pavements, except directly across the same on necessary occasions.
- That lanes, closes, and thoroughfares, shall be cleansed by the occupiers thereof, at least twice in a week.
- That all persons laying down dung for the purpose of transporting it to the adjacent grounds, shall take away the same before two o'clock of the day on which it was laid down, in the months of November to March, and before twelve o'clock noon in the months of April to October.
- That persons plying the streets with water carts shall, on being required in cases of fire, instantly repair to the spot, and supply the engines with water.

~ February 5th ~

1840: The following notice appeared in the *Dumfries Times*: 'Sabbath Breaking – Whereas it having been represented by the Reverend and Presbytery of Lochmaben to the Honourable Her Majesty's Justices of the Peace for the County of Dumfries, in Quarter Sessions this day assembled, that, of late, open and flagrant violaters of the laws, and particularly those Acts of Parliament passed for the better Observance of the Sabbath, prevailed to a lamentable extent in various districts of this County, and, more especially, of the desecration of that sacred day by the driving of cattle and sheep along the public roads, to the grievous annoyance of the lieges going to and returning from public worship, the drivers being in many instances in a state of intoxication, and shocking the feelings of the pious and devout by profane swearing and intemperate and irritating language. The said Justices in Quarter Sessions RESOLVED to interpose their authority, and to put into execution the existing Laws against the Desecration of the Sabbath ... and intimation of such resolution is hereby given to the Public, in order that none, and more especially Cattle Dealers and Drivers of Cattle, may hereafter pretend ignorance of the same.'

― FEBRUARY 6TH ―

1829: On this day, the serial killer William Hare stayed in Dumfries en route from Edinburgh to Portpatrick, thereby sparking one of the largest disturbances in the town's history.

William Burke and William Hare sold the bodies of their victims to a doctor for dissection by his anatomy students. They murdered seventeen people before eventually being caught by police. However, with insufficient evidence to convict the pair, Hare testified against Burke in return for his own immunity from prosecution. Burke was hanged, but Hare was set free by the police, who planned to send him back to his native Ireland. William McDowall wrote: 'A vast crowd, estimated at eight thousand people, collected on the streets – the greatest concourse being in the vicinity of the "King's Arms Hotel", where Hare was located awaiting the departure of the "Galloway Mail".' Hare stayed put in his top-floor room but had he ventured out into the street, McDowall concluded, 'all the nameless rabble of the town, from the Moat-brae to the Cat's Strand would have torn him to pieces without mercy.' In the event, Hare was smuggled safely out of Dumfries the following day. (McDowall, William, *History of Dumfries* (2nd Edn., 1873))

— February 7th —

1792: On this day, it was announced that 'for some winters past, the Ordinary Dumfries Assemblies have been so ill attended, as to induce the Directors to think that no farther attempts need be made to continue them. But as it has been suggested, that the late hour of the Company's meeting, and of leaving the Rooms, is probably the principal cause of their being so ill attended, they have determined to make ONE farther attempt to continue them; such hours of meeting and dismissing being fixed, as may be most convenient for the greatest number of Subscribers. Agreeably to the Resolution, it is hereby intimated to the Subscribers, and others who attend the Assemblies, that there will be an Assembly on Thursday next – the doors to be opened at six o'clock; the dancing tickets to be given out precisely at seven; the music to be dismissed at eleven; and the Rooms to be cleared in half an hour after.

The Directors flatter themselves, that all those who wish to countenance a meeting ... will now, by their attendance, show their inclination to do so, during the remainder of the winter; otherwise, it is highly probable, or rather quite certain, that the Dumfries Winter Assemblies must be discontinued.' (*Dumfries Weekly Journal*)

─ February 8th ─

1913: On this day, the *Dumfries and Galloway Standard* published the findings of a report on crime in Dumfries for the year ending December 31st 1912. 'Proceedings were taken against 565 persons, as compared with 662 in 1911, and 387 were convicted. This is the lowest number recorded for thirty years. There was an almost entire absence of serious crime during the year. There were 530 cases made known to the police, as compared with 662 in 1911. There is a regrettable increase in the number of juvenile offenders dealt with, 94 young persons being brought before the Juvenile Court, as against 60 in the previous year. Regarding the places of residence of offenders, 338 lived in Dumfries, 53 in Maxwelltown, 155 had fixed addresses beyond that area and 112 had no fixed address. Twenty per cent were tramps and vagrants, as against thirty-one per cent in 1911. Of the offenders, sixty-one per cent were … under the influence of liquor when the offences were committed. (There are fifty-eight licensed premises in the burgh, giving an average of one license to 277 inhabitants.) There has been a considerable abatement of the tramp nuisance during the year, and the number of offenders dealt with has fallen to 16.'

– February 9th –

1869: On this day, it was noted that 'the Siamese Twins –
... [natives of Siam, now Thailand] visited Dumfries on
Friday last, and gave afternoon and evening receptions in
the Mechanics' Hall, which were pretty well attended, but
we are glad to say the public manifested no great eagerness to
patronize an exhibition which, though remarkable, partakes of
the repulsive. The brothers Chang and Eng ... have reached
the age of 57, and time has left his mark upon them ... but
they are both wonderfully intelligent, and answer questions
readily and frankly, speaking English with fluency. The fleshy
ligament growing out of their sides by which they are strangely
and strongly attached, was an object of much interest and was
freely exhibited, but no one was allowed to touch it. The twins
are said to be on their way to Paris, to have the connecting
ligament severed. It is to be hoped that they may not lengthen
the list of martyrs to science.' N.B. It was reputedly from Chang
and Eng, who died of natural causes in 1874, that the old term
'Siamese twins' – meaning conjoined twins – first came into use.
(*Dumfries and Galloway Courier*)

~ FEBRUARY 10TH ~

1306: On this day, Robert the Bruce, prior to becoming King of Scotland in March 1306, slew his rival the Red Comyn at Greyfriars Kirk: 'Angry words fall from both the barons ere they enter by the southern gate into the sanctuary of the Grey Friars; and it is Comyn ... who initiates their walk in that direction, from the belief that the rising rage of Bruce would be calmed down by the sacredness of the place. Instead of this being so, it waxes higher and higher. Bruce by-and-by charges Comyn with having tried to compass his death, and with having, to promote his own selfish ends, sacrificed his country. Comyn prevaricates; and, as the accusations are emphatically repeated, meets them with a broad denial: the words "It is a lie!" break from his lips; and the next moment the dagger of Bruce is at his heart. Comyn falls – never, alas, so "red" before, now that the crimson tide of life is flowing over his prostrate frame. Under the influence of overmastering passion, Bruce had thus perpetrated the fatal deed; and his demeanour and speech betray regret – remorse, as he hurries out of the sacred edifice.' (McDowall, William, *History of Dumfries* (2nd Edn., 1873))

~ February 11th ~

1817: On this day, the *Dumfries Weekly Journal* published the following loyal address in response to an attack on the Prince Regent in St James's Park: 'We, the Ministers and Elders of the Presbytery of Dumfries, warmly attached to the happy Constitution of our Country, and to the illustrious House of Brunswick, under whose mild Government we have long enjoyed the most distinguished blessings, feel ourselves called upon, on the present occasion, to express to your Royal Highness our sentiments of dutiful respect and affection.

The daring and atrocious attack made upon your Royal Highness has filled us with astonishment and indignation. We could not have conceived that such outrageous depravity could have been found in any subjects of this realm; and we cannot but ascribe it to the instigation of certain wicked and desperate demagogues, who, by the wilful misrepresentation of the causes of the present temporary distress, and by the wildest and most delusive theories of Government, have misled and inflamed the minds of the ignorant multitude.

We are happy to assure your Royal Highness of the steady attachment and loyalty of the inhabitants of that district of the Kingdom which is under our immediate protection.'

— February 12th —

1851: On this day, the *Dumfries and Galloway Standard* printed the following disturbing report: 'Three individuals belonging to this locality have, at different times within ten days, suddenly disappeared, and not been seen since, or any trace of them. Mr. Maxwell Hyslop, farmer from Buittle, disappeared on the evening of the 28th; on Monday the 3rd, a young man named Thomas Duff, who had been working for some months in the foundry of Messrs. Affleck & Co. at Maxwelltown, was missed from his lodgings in the same inexplicable manner. He had been drinking, it is said, and went out in the evening, and it is surmised that he had fallen into the Nith and been swept away.

On Friday evening last, William Doyle, a founder, also disappeared. About half-past eleven he parted with his son and nephew in Bank Street, but instead of proceeding home, as was supposed, he had gone back to a house in the vicinity of the George Ballroom. About one o'clock in the morning he was seen again in Bank Street, but he never reached home, however, and it is feared that he, too, has fallen into the Nith, which for many weeks past has been greatly flooded.'

─ FEBRUARY 13TH ─

1926: On this day, 'Lady Leslie Mackenzie performed the opening ceremony at a successful cake sale, held in St. George's Hall on Wednesday, by the Dumfries and Maxwelltown Women Citizen's Association, on behalf of the industrial colony for the permanent care of the feeble-minded. There was a large attendance at the opening.

Lady Mackenzie emphasised … that the colony scheme had nothing to do with foreign colonies, and she had the greatest pleasure in helping the Dumfries Women Citizen's Association, because it had done so splendidly already in spreading information and in propaganda work. In these colonies, mentally deficient boys and girls and young men and women could be made practically self-supporting. Colonies like these existed in England, though not in Scotland to any great extent, and they were really worked by the inmates of the colonies, under constant supervision. These children could do nothing almost if they were left alone, but under supervision it was wonderful what they could be trained to do. The Women Citizens in Scotland had now raised their first £10,000 on behalf of the Colony fund, and of that sum the Dumfries Association had donated £175, which they were very grateful for.' (*Dumfries and Galloway Courier and Herald*)

⇀ February 14th ⇀

1797: On this day, 'at a meeting of the Dumfries and Galloway Farming Society, it was proposed and agreed to that, in the event of an invasion in any part of Great Britain or Ireland, the Members will be ready to provide the number of HORSES and CARTS annexed to their respective subscriptions, for the purpose of transporting TROOPS and BAGGAGE for at least two stages from Dumfries, whenever they shall be required by the Commander-in-Chief, and that free of any charge or expense. They hope that the other Members of the Society, and the farmers in the counties of Dumfries and Kirkcudbright, in general, will concur with the same, so that such Troops as may have occasion to pass through these counties, may be conveyed expeditiously, and without expense to Government … A subscription is left in the hands of Mr. William Thomson, writer in Dumfries, the Secretary of this Society, and this Minute the Meeting direct to be inserted for at least two weeks in the *Dumfries Weekly Journal*, so that every person approving of the Measure may know where they will have the opportunity of subscribing.' N.B. A small French invasion force landed near Fishguard on February 22nd, but surrendered within two days. (*Dumfries Weekly Journal*)

⟶ February 15th ⟵

1860: On this day, the *Dumfries and Galloway Standard* reported that 'the Bill for the formation of the Dumfries, Lochmaben, and Lockerbie Railway has been read for a first time in the House of Lords, and the second reading there is fixed for tomorrow. Hitherto, its Parliamentary progress has been smooth, all the requirements known as "standing orders" having been carefully complied with. But a powerful enemy has suddenly sprung up, resolved on stopping its course if possible, and of preventing the people of Dumfries and Annandale from obtaining those benefits which the line in question can alone supply. The Glasgow and South-Western Company, apprehensive, we suppose, of losing a portion of their traffic, mean to object to the Bill; and will, if we are rightly informed, base their opposition chiefly on the alleged discrepancy between the estimates and the anticipated cost of the undertaking. We sincerely hope that they will signally fail in their efforts. The leading promoters of the scheme had a meeting at Lockerbie on Monday, to make arrangements for giving it due support by oral as well as documentary evidence, and in other respects aid the promotion of the Bill.'

~ February 16th ~

1778: On this day, the following notice appeared in the *Dumfries Weekly Journal*: 'Deserted from Lieutenant Heron's Recruiting Party of Edinburgh Volunteers, at the Red Lion near bridge of Tarff, on the road to Dumfries, on the night of the fifteenth of February current, James McClellan ... born in the parish of Buittle or Kelton, in the stewartry of Kirkcudbright, aged about twenty-nine years, five feet six inches high, long nose a little flat on the top, long black hair, grey eyes, swarthy complexion, with a scar upon one of his cheeks; had on when he went away, a coarse cocked hat, a half worn blue upper coat, with white buttons, a turned scarlet waistcoat and whitish corduroy breeches, plated buckles in his shoes, a silver watch in his pocket; and carried off with him a neat Holster Pistol about fifteen inches long, marked on the barrel and lock, J. Sharp, Stanford.

Whoever apprehends the said Deserter, and delivers him to any of Lieutenant Heron's Recruiting Parties at Dumfries, Creebridge or Wigtown, shall have Twenty Shillings as a Reward, to be paid by Mr. Heron of Heron at Creebridge, Provost Clarke or Provost Maxwell at Dumfries, over and above what is allowed by Act of Parliament.'

~ February 17th ~

1909: On this day, it was reported that a new craze had reached the town: 'The great popularity which the new pastime of roller-skating has attained, makes it a matter of congratulation to the inhabitants of Dumfries that a well-equipped and up-to-date rink has this week been established in the Drill Hall. The vogue it has enjoyed during the past twelve months is but a revival of that of fifteen or twenty years ago; but a revival, it should be mentioned, under more approved and suitable conditions. Fomerly, the rinks were furnished cheaply with ashphalt flooring, and plain bearing skates were used. Nowadays, those who wish to "roller-skate" are catered for in more luxurious style. The principal adjuncts of a well-appointed rink are a surface of Canadian hardwood maple and steel ball-bearing skates. In this case, the management have found that the surface of the Drill Hall is even more suitable for the purpose than Canadian maple, and that when treated with chemicals it makes a first class rink.

New attractions will be constantly added, and these will include the formation of a hockey club, if a sufficient number of skaters join once they have become proficient.' (*Dumfries and Galloway Standard*)

⚊ February 18th ⚊

1778: On this day, the *Dumfries Weekly Journal* reported that, on this day, 'being Candlemas Fair, by desire of several Gentlemen from the country, Mr. Dinwiddie will give a Lecture on Electricity [in the Assembly Hall]. Upwards of thirty different experiments will be performed on an excellent Electrical Apparatus – Electric attraction and repulsion will be shown, by ringing of bells, dancing of figures, spider, fly, star &c. The nature of charging explained, glass plates, phials, or jars charged both negatively and positively – a hole struck through several cards; glass tubes burst; spirits and gunpowder fired; metals melted into glass; by explosions from the Electrical Battery. Lightning and Electricity proved to be the same – Method of drawing lightning from the clouds, and of securing buildings from being struck ... Experiments in a Dark Room, Aurora Borealis &c. – To conclude with the description of an excellent Wind Gun, in which the condensed air has a spring capable of discharging twenty bullets, one after another, with one charge. This gun will be discharged several times through a board.

Doors to be opened at half-past six. Tickets: two shillings each, to be had of Mr. Dinwiddie, or at the shops of Messrs. Wilson & Boyd, Booksellers.'

~ February 19th ~

1868: On this day, the following reader's letter, regarding the Nith ferry, was printed in the *Dumfries and Galloway Standard*: 'You deserve the thanks of the public, and especially of the parents and of the young people themselves, who have to cross the Nith six times daily to their work at Troqueer Mills, for the notice of the danger that attends their crossing. It is most alarming to see so many young and thoughtless people pushing into the boat till its edge is only a few inches above the rushing water. I heard a fearful screaming one morning, and when I enquired of Mr. Pringle, the boatman, what was the matter, he said they were such an unruly set – pushing and hauling and screaming – they deserved a dip. But if the boat was swamped, the consequences would be very grievous, and the Town Council would be reflected on for not giving instructions regarding the number allowed to be taken over at one time. I thank most heartily Mr. Carruthers, for again introducing the subject to the Council; and I am very glad to observe that the proposal for a footbridge received so much general support.'

⸺ February 20th ⸺

1839: On this day, the following article appeared in the *Dumfries Times*: 'Sheep Stealing having taken place last winter in the parishes adjoining Maxwelltown and Dumfries … and it already having commenced this winter in the same neighbourhood, a Reward of FIFTEEN GUINEAS is hereby offered to any Sheriff's Officer, Constable, or other Person who shall first apprehend, or give such information as will lead to the apprehension and conviction of offenders guilty of said crime within ten miles of Dumfries or Maxwelltown …'

⸺

1901: 'A case of poisoning from sucking impure ice occurred in Maxwelltown last Tuesday, and has unfortunately ended fatally. It appears that two children in Glasgow Street, a boy and a girl, were found to have been sucking impure ice near a cesspool at the back of their house, and serious consequences followed. They were attended by a doctor, and the girl, who is eleven years of age, is happily recovering, but her younger brother, only three-and-a-half years old, died on Sunday morning.' (*Dumfries and Galloway Courier and Herald*)

~ February 21st ~

1797: On this day, the following blunt notice appeared in the *Dumfries Weekly Journal*: 'The Magistrates and Town Council of Dumfries having observed ... that great numbers of Strangers have resorted to and taken up residence within the borough and jurisdiction thereof, without having any right to do so – to remedy which in future, and that all Strangers and their families may be prevented from becoming a burden on the Town and Community, it has been resolved and enacted by the Council, that all proprietors and possessors of houses within the Royalty, who shall in future let houses or rooms to Strangers who have not sufficient testimonies of their character and circumstances, or who cannot give satisfying security that they and their families will not become burdensome to the public, will be prosecuted with the utmost rigour of law, and punished according thereto ... and Mr. John Armstrong, writer in Dumfries, interim Procurator Fiscal of the borough (to whom all information may be given), has been instructed to initiate action against defaulters, and to prosecute them to conviction.

All persons found begging within the Royalty, and who do not belong to the Town and Parish, or who have not badges, will be apprehended and dealt with as vagrants.'

— FEBRUARY 22ND —

1918: On this day, the following notice appeared in the *Dumfries and Galloway Standard*: 'The Communal Kitchen will be open for the service of the community on the forenoon of Tuesday next. The food will be cooked in the well-equipped kitchens of Dumfries Academy. The meals will be distributed from the following two Distributing Shops: 80 Friars' Vennel and 65 St. Michael Street.

As necessity arises, other shops will be opened. Those obtaining meals … will require to bring their own utensils for carrying away the food. There will be no delivery to houses.

A daily menu will be exhibited in the windows of the Distributing Shops next week, and thereafter at other places in the burgh. The Distributing Shops will meantime be open from 11.45 forenoon to 2 o'clock afternoon. Food supplied will consist of soups, meat, vegetables and puddings.

This Kitchen is being opened to meet the present difficulty which individuals have in obtaining supplies, and to assist in economising foodstuffs. Every effort will be made to have food of the best quality and prepared by a skilled cook. The organisation is to be conducted with a view to its being available and satisfactory to every class in the community. – Town Clerk's Office, Dumfries.'

‒ February 23rd ‒

1916: 'The lighting restrictions, imposed as a safeguard against possible visitation by aircraft, do not come into operation until Friday first; but the authorities have already given the public some idea of the new order of things by only lighting the principal and corner lamps, and these are shaded in a manner to prevent the light being discernible from above. The result is that after the shop lights have been turned out, the streets are plunged in darkness, and pedestrians have to exert the greatest alertness of both ear and eye to avoid collision. During the past few days, there has been a phenomenal rush to shops which provide dark-coloured blinds, and nearly in every case the stocks have been cleared out. The proprietors of large buildings have been puzzling how to comply with the new order without incurring unnecessarily heavy expenditure. The Dumfries municipal authorities, giving an object lesson in thoroughness, are even discontinuing the ringing of the town bells after dusk, in case a German Zeppelin should be flying overhead and the occupants thereof should be able to locate the town by the clanging of the Midsteeple bells.' (*Dumfries and Galloway Standard*)

— February 24th —

1778: On this day, the following notice appeared: 'John Bushby, Sheriff-Clerk of Dumfries, is desired to provide a few soldiers for the honourable Captain Thomas Maitland's Company in Lord Seaforth's Regiment, and a few sailors for the Berwick Man-of-War commanded by the honourable Captain Keith Stewart. It is but a few he can engage, but such as incline to enter either as a soldier or a sailor with Mr. Bushby, may depend upon receiving encouragement to their wishes … Those who incline to enlist as soldiers may have a chance to become Officers by their good behaviour and valour in America, and, for their security and satisfaction, if in three years their promotion is not to their utmost wish, they shall be at liberty to be free. All sailors will be encouraged according to their merit … The Berwick Man-of-War is reckoned one of the finest ships that ever was in England, and it is generally believed she will be sent on such a service as will make the fortune of every Officer and sailor that is on board the ship … Every one entering into Mr. Stewart's service in Dumfries will receive Four Guineas of additional Bounty to encourage soldiers and sailors to enter into His Majesty's service.' (*Dumfries Weekly Journal*)

~ February 25th ~

1795: On this day, it was advertised that 'on Wednesday next, a main of cocks will be fought in the New Room, at the "George Inn" here, between some gentlemen of the Town and County, for Two Guineas the Battle and One Hundred Guineas the Main. To begin fighting at eleven o'clock. Admittance 2*s* 6*d* each.' (*Dumfries Weekly Journal*)

1880: Also on this day, it was noted that 'the horse machine for sweeping the streets, recently ordered by the Dumfries Police Commissioners, was tried for the first time yesterday. It may be described as a large brush roller, formed of split cane and placed diagonally, turning as the wheels move, by pinion wheels on the axle. The machine sweeps a breadth of 6 feet, gathering the dust or thin mud into a line alongside, and by passing again the same way the debris is swept nearer the side of the street, when it is swept into small heaps by the scavengers. Yesterday the machine performed most satisfactorily, and the novelty of a horse-sweeping machine passing along the streets attracted crowds of onlookers. There can be only one opinion: that the machine will be a great improvement in the sweeping of Dumfries streets.' (*Dumfries and Galloway Standard*)

~ February 26th ~

1834: On this day, the town's skin market was in progress, as the *Dumfries Times* reported: 'Dumfries, it is well known, is a great entrepot, where the hare, the rabbit and foulmart skins of nearly the entire middle and southern districts of Scotland, are collected previous to their being disposed of to the manufacturers of hats and others, both in Scotland and in England. The number of skins which are collected … amount, in the course of the year, to millions, and such is the amazing number which yearly come to our provincial market. In respect to price, the sales have this year been more satisfactory than last year, but the market as a whole has hitherto been a very dull one, and what is altogether without precedent, there has not been a single dealer from England present at it. The general price for hare skins has been about 13*s*, the average being a shade lower at 12*s* 6*d* per dozen; for rabbit skins 5*s*, and foulmart or fitch, 12*s*, also per dozen. The other skins fetched 8*s* each. These are low prices compared with former markets, though – as we have said – somewhat better than last.'

⏤ February 27th ⏤

1827: On this day, the public were informed that 'a General Meeting of the Committee for the Suppression of Public Begging was held in the Council Chamber ... when a statement of the accounts was laid before the meeting, with which they were perfectly satisfied, as well as with the accuracy and care with which the books had been kept by Mr. Robertson, the Collector, and by Mr. Garmony of the Hospital, on payment of the weekly allowances to the poor at the Hospital. They expressed at the same time, however, very general dissatisfaction with the manner in which the police officers had lately discharged their duty in looking after vagrants; and resolved that the allowance in whole to them should be only 30s, and that a person should hereafter be appointed, at a fixed weekly salary, to attend to this business, and upon the sub-committee and Collector alone; and the Magistrates, who were present, agreed to arm him with all the powers they could grant, by making him a constable.' (*Dumfries Weekly Journal*)

⏤

1850: Also on this day, the following advertisement appeared: 'There will be sold ... at the Police Manure Depot, at the corner of the Railway Bridge near St. Mary's Church, upon Wednesday next, SIX LARGE DUNGHILLS, each containing on average, sixty square yards of excellent dung, collected by the Public Scavengers.' (*Dumfries and Galloway Standard*)

February 28th

1835: On this day, 'the "Manfred" was wrecked somewhere in the German Ocean, and a number of puncheons [of Brackla whisky] set afloat, most of which found their way to the shore, and were secured for the interest of the underwriters. The whisky was on account of Messrs. Scott and Allan, Leith, and a stray puncheon, while piloting its way to "bonnie Dundee" was noticed by the captain of a Dutch Galliot ... and taken on board as "de bonne prise". The Custom House officers, however, interfered and lodged the precious Brackla [granted a Royal Warrant in 1835, and known as the 'King's Own Whisky'] in a bonded cellar, from which depot it in the end found its way to the cellars of Scott and Allan. Our townsman, Mr. Dickson ... was fortunate in securing a portion of this most superior article, and Mr. Wilson ... purchased a gallon of it as a treat to the Dumfries Burns Club [whose members eventually enjoyed a particularly fine punch laced with the Brackla whisky, at their dinner in 1840].' (Mackie, Charles, (Ed.), *Dumfries and Galloway Notes and Queries* (1913))

~ February 29th ~

1820: On this day it was reported that 'Mr. Tulloch's scholars gave, yesterday, a public exhibition of their proficiency in the elegant art of dancing, in the Assembly Rooms here, to the high gratification of a brilliant assemblage of spectators, consisting of most of the principal families of this town and neighbourhood. We also refer our readers to an entertainment this evening of Scotch and Highland Music. From the great satisfaction that Mr. Grant universally gives, we are sure our musical friends will enjoy a high treat; and, we would recommend to them not to omit the present opportunity of witnessing this young man's astonishing performances.' (*Dumfries and Galloway Courier*)

1820: Also on this day, it was revealed that 'during the last three or four evenings, Mr. Hinchsliffe, jeweller, has been closely besieged by a crowd of anxious spectators, collected to view the splendid gas apparatus which he has lately got introduced. The light produced is of the most chaste and brilliant description, and infinitely superior to any we ever before witnessed. We hope this example will be "luminously" imitated.' (*Dumfries Weekly Journal*)

— March 1st —

1905: On this day, the Cairn Valley Light Railway came into service, and the *Dumfries and Galloway Standard* printed the following report: 'Yesterday witnessed the completion of a project which has been the subject of intermittent agitation for forty years. The line of railway connecting Dumfries with Moniaive and traversing practically the whole length of the Cairn Valley, was officially opened by a train making several journeys over it carrying a large party of invited guests; [but] today the ordinary service is being inaugurated. Keen interest was naturally excited by the crowning event of an enterprise certain to affect to a material extent the fortunes of the district; and while there was nothing of the nature of an organised public demonstration, this feeling manifested itself in various ways, notably by the display of flags at various points in and around Moniaive and at houses on the route, and by the congregation at the various stopping places and at spots where roads are crossed, of groups of old and young who waved a kindly greeting to the streamer-decked iron horse and the passengers. The new railway is of a total length of eighteen miles, for the first two of which north of Dumfries the main line is utilized.'

— March 2nd —

1910: On this day, the *Dumfries and Galloway Standard* reported that flooding at Whitesands caused havoc at the day's livestock market: 'Early in the morning the rising water invaded the Hoddom Castle Inn, and before mid-day it was within a few yards of the footpath along the Whitesands. Consigners of stock to the marts had no little difficulty in getting their animals forward, and the only approach was by way of Bank Street. Drovers had an anxious and uncomfortable forenoon, having to wade to a depth of some feet to get the animals turned into the marts. The supplies of stock, owing to the stormy morning, were lighter than usual, but it was half-past one before the sales were concluded. By that time the water had risen considerably and, having invaded the entrances to the marts, farmers found egress cut off by several feet of water. Some were driven in a trap which plied between the foot of Bank Street and the marts for some time, and others used carts and cabs to make their escape. Some few cattle were driven through the water, and a small number of sheep were got out in floats; but the bulk of the stock remained overnight in the marts.'

~ MARCH 3RD ~

1900: On this day, the *Dumfries and Galloway Standard* reported the Relief of Ladysmith in the Boer War, and the celebrations that ensued in the town on hearing of this momentous event: 'As soon as General Buller's despatch announcing Lord Dundonald's entry into Ladysmith was posted at the "Standard" office on Thursday at a quarter to eleven, the Scottish standard was hoisted at the Midsteeple and the town bells were rung. Flags were also speedily displayed at the Town Hall, the Maxwelltown Town Hall, and many places of business. Lines of streamers crossed Castle Street at the premises of Messrs. Lennox and Provost Glover; Buccleuch Street at Messrs. Dunbar and Son, and Pattie's; and Friars' Vennel at several points. All the schools in the two burghs were dismissed for the day, and bands of juveniles paraded through the town with flags and sticks, and an encounter between the armies of Dumfries and "the Brig-en" occurred on the Old Bridge. The meeting of the Town Council was made the occasion of special rejoicings. In the evening, the Town Band marched through the streets, and some fireworks were set off in the Academy playground.'

‒ March 4th ‒

1788: On this day, the following notice appeared in the *Dumfries Weekly Journal*: 'Eloped from her Friends – a young lady, disordered in her mind, about fifteen years of age, of a thin habit, with dark eyes and chestnut-coloured hair; and having on her left arm the marks of an old fracture. She is dressed in a dark striped callico gown, white cotton petticoat, black silk cloak and bonnet, black and white shawl, cotton stockings and black stuff shoes. There is reason to think that she comes from Dumfries, or from some place in that quarter … Since Friday forenoon, she has been staying with John Carruthers [who] will endeavour to keep the Lady, and take proper care of her, until she is claimed by her friends.'

1882: Also on this day, the *Dumfries and Galloway Standard* announced that Professor Moores, phrenologist, physiologist, and physiognomist, was in the process of conducting a series of lectures at the Mechanics' Hall. 'Last night, Mr. Moores displayed a considerable knowledge of physiology in his comprehensive treatment of "Our Secret Vices", (for gentlemen only!) This lecture was followed by a mesmeric entertainment.'

～ March 5th ～

1834: On this day, the *Dumfries Times* recorded this 'curious incident of a beard in the night-time': 'The Police Court on Friday was just about breaking up, when an old and somewhat importunate personage came pushing in. "The Court's up, man", exclaimed the Sergeant. "Up? They maun sit down again then till I make my complaint," came the reply, and to the bar he went. "Well?" asked the magistrate. "What is your complaint?" "Can you no see?" said the man. "I see nothing," rejoined the Judge. "Aye, aye, you see nothing on this side, but do you see nothing on that?" turning up the two sides of his face alternately. The magistrate now saw that one half of the old man's face had been newly mown, while the other exhibited a six days' growth at least. "Do you ca' that nothing?" continued the complainant. He then explained that during the course of his slumbers the previous night, some rogue, without the fear of the courts before his eyes, had shaved the one half of his beard and whiskers, and left the other in all its rudeness and grandeur. Unluckily, the culprit was not forthcoming, and the case was, in consequence, dismissed.'

~ MARCH 6TH ~

1797: On this day, it was announced that 'John Corrie, Merchant in Dumfries, begs leave to acquaint the Public, that he has got to hand a Cargo of fine Salt Herrings, from the Fishery at the Firth of Forth, in barrells and half-barrells, which he can venture to say will keep for any length of time, as they are all re-salted on purpose for keeping.

J. Corrie has also a few Hogsheads of real Dutch Linseed coming … likewise all kinds of Spirits and Groceries of the very best sorts, and which will be sold at the lowest prices of any in this town.' (*Dumfries Weekly Journal*)

1827: Also on this day, an advertisement for sedan chairs appeared in Dumfries: 'The Subscription for purchasing two new Sedan Chairs in this place will remain open ten days or a fortnight longer, after which period it will close; and as the use of the chairs will be confined wholly and exclusively to subscribers and their families, it is requested that if any ladies, either in town or country, still wish to subscribe, they may send their name to the chairmen without delay.' (Mackie, Charles, (Ed.), *Dumfries and Galloway Notes and Queries* (1913))

— March 7th —

1953: On this day, 'the Duchess of Gloucester visited Dumfries and, as Colonel-in-Chief of the King's Own Scottish Borderers, accepted on behalf of the Regiment, the Freedom of the Burgh conferred by the Provost, Magistrates and Councillors, in recognition of the distinguished achievements of the Regiment since its formation, and of the long association which the Borderers have had with Dumfries.' Along with the Freedom of the Burgh there was accorded to the Regiment the privilege of 'entry into the Royal Burgh on ceremonial occasions with bayonets fixed, drums beating, and colours flying! Immediately after the ceremony, carried out in brilliant spring weather on the Whitesands, the Borderers exercised their newly-acquired right in a march through the streets of the town … for the first time in their 264 years' history. The parade on the Whitesands and the ceremonial march made a stirring and colourful spectacle for the thousands of citizens of the burgh and visitors who assembled to witness the Freedom ceremony, and who lined the streets during the march. Following the ceremony, Her Royal Highness was conducted to the Municipal Chambers, where a considerable number of municipal dignitaries and others were presented to her.' (*Dumfries and Galloway Standard*)

– MARCH 8TH –

1881: On this day, the *Dumfries and Galloway Courier* reported that a great snowstorm in and around Dumfries had brought chaos to local rail services: 'On Friday, the Pullman from London, due at 5a.m., did not arrive till 5p.m. No train from Stranraer reached Dumfries until six in the evening, an obstruction having occurred near remote Loch Skerrow. On the same line, between Castle Douglas and Dumfries, a train got fixed in a drift near Kirkgunzeon Station. On Saturday morning about one o'clock, a luggage train from Dumfries to Castle Douglas went off the line between Kirkgunzeon and Southwick, and in consequence the mail that usually leaves at five in the morning did not get away until eleven in the forenoon. The train due from Glasgow at 10.52a.m. encountered a drift at Carronbridge, and did not arrive until nearly three o'clock. The Edinburgh train was still later, and there was no train from Castle Douglas until four in the afternoon. The drifts on the turnpikes about Dumfries practically closed all the roads to wheeled traffic, and, as a consequence, of the many country carriers that usually come into town on Saturdays, there were not more than one or two.'

~ MARCH 9TH ~

1872: On this day, the following report appeared in the *Dumfries and Galloway Standard*: 'A grand Ball, in connection with the Dumfries No1 Company of Volunteers came off in the Assembly Ballroom yesterday evening ... There was a large attendance; and besides members of the Dumfries Company, there were also representatives of several local corps present. Music was supplied by Mr. Brydoe's quadrille band, and dancing was begun and carried on with great spirit till an advanced hour in the morning.'

———

1872: Also on this day, the same paper carried the following article: 'Harry Liston's "Merry Moments" – A capital singer, a graceful dancer, a rare comedian, a rich delineator of character, a tolerably fair ventriloquist, and a marvellous mimic; of Mr. Harry Liston all this may be truly said. And when he brings all his versatile powers into play, as he did in the Mechanics' Hall here, on Thursday night, he makes the moments pass merrily and pleasantly away. He appeared in upwards of a dozen personations, including a Lancashire yokel, a Hibernian boy, a languid swell of the Lord Dundreary type, a languishing young lady singing, as such, in fine soprano, and a moody young gentleman, Mr. Dismal Doleful.'

— March 10th —

1937: On this day, the following report appeared in the *Dumfries and Galloway Standard*: 'House hunters in Dumfries were out in force last night ... storming the Municipal Chambers in response to the invitation of Mr. E. Fyfe, the Convener of the House Letting Committee of the Town Council, to meet him and state their position, and their claims for preferment in the allocation of council houses.

Mr. Fyfe had the support of several members of his committee, but they did not bargain for the rush which overwhelmed them, and for the hour-and-a-half which had been allotted for hearing the applicants, the Chambers were besieged by a continuous stream of anxious house-seekers, eager to state their woes and advocate their cases for improved housing conditions.

Upwards of a hundred people formed in queues on the stairways and corridors of the building, waiting for their turn for an interview. The committee did their best, and succeeded in interviewing about forty applicants. Over two hundred in all must have responded to the Convener's invitation.

The disappointed ones were evidently loth to leave the building, and even after it had been announced that no more interviews would be given, they stood in groups exchanging confidences about their housing conditions.'

~ March 11th ~

1794: On this day, the following item appeared in the *Dumfries Weekly Journal*: 'Remarkable instance of sagacity in a dog. – The Benevolent Society of this place convenes upon the first Thursday of every month; the deceased Mr. Wilson was one of the institutors, and had been a regular attender. At the meeting on Thursday last, Mr. Wilson's dog, which had long followed him, came of his own accord to the Society, at the ordinary hour of meeting, and took his place at the foot of the seat his master had usually occupied – a circumstance which, in no small degree, affected the members assembled.'

1828: Also on this day, readers were informed that 'the owners of the "Queenberry" and "Lord Nelson", constant traders betwixt Liverpool and Dumfries, beg leave to warn the Shippers of Goods of the danger in clandestinely sending Whisky in packages said to contain other Goods, as the Officers of the Customs at Liverpool repack every Hogshead, Barrel, Bale and Box. Besides forfeiting the Goods, the person sending the Whisky incurs a penalty of £50 for each gallon.

For the accommodation of the public, these vessels shall after 1st April next sail every 14 days from the respective ports.'

— March 12th —

1816: On this day, following a renewal of the Property Tax, after the end of the Napoleonic Wars, the Seven Incorporations of Dumfries unanimously agreed on presenting a Petition to the House of Commons: 'That when the late arduous struggle, happily terminated, rendered extraordinary supplies necessary, the Petitioners, along with their fellow-subjects, cheerfully submitted ... to the Taxes on Income and Property, which go under the general term of Property Tax, though of all others the most odious in its nature, inquisitorial in its operation, and oppressive in its consequences; and they did so the more readily as it was declared to be only a War Tax, and promised to be only co-existent with the imperious necessity that imposed it. But the Petitioners, with astonishment see, when the cause is annihilated, the effect is continued; that all pledges and promises are disregarded, and, with pain they say it, good faith is set at nought.

Bankruptcies, to an unprecedented number, are daily taking place; agriculturists are, in general, ruined; a great part of the labouring class is entirely out of employ, and those that work cannot obtain payment. Therefore, the Petitioners most humbly entreat the protection of your Honourable House, against a continuance of the Property Tax, in any shape, or under any modification whatever.' (*Dumfries Weekly Journal*)

― March 13th ―

1920: On this day, the *Dumfries and Galloway Standard* reported that 'the Provosts and Magistrates of Dumfries and Maxwelltown yesterday afternoon met a deputation of unemployed ex-servicemen and civilians in the two burghs, with regard to the increase in unemployment. Mr. Gray, in introducing the deputation, said that many of the men on behalf of whom he was speaking, were married men with children dependent upon them, which was the saddest aspect of it all, and there were a great number of ex-servicemen. He did not wish to draw any distinguishing line between the ex-servicemen and the civilians. They were all alike. He quoted extracts from speeches made in Dumfries during the war, as to what would be done for the men when they came home. He knew that the Provosts and Magistrates were anxious to relieve the sufferings of their fellow citizens. He wished to impress upon them that a number of men were undoubtedly suffering, and their wives and children also … There was a sum of at least £250 per day less being spent in the town than a fortnight ago. Businessmen, grocers, were telling him that they were feeling the effects badly.'

~ MARCH 14TH ~

1796: A lack of food had driven some sections of the town's populace to riot, when the high price of oatmeal following several poor harvests had led to hunger among the poorer inhabitants. On this day 'the Council met with the Sheriff-Substitute of the county, and several justices, to devise means for allaying the present excitement, and to prevent further breaches of the peace ... They issued a printed notice: "Disturbances of a very serious nature having taken place within this burgh and the neighbourhood about the want of meal, the Sheriff-Substitute of this shire, sundry justices of the peace for the county, and also the Stewartry of Kirkcudbrightshire, and the magistrates and Town Council of Dumfries, think it necessary to give this public intimation, that a very large quantity of meal is now purchased by the town for the supply of the inhabitants until a new crop comes in, and that it will be sold out as the necessities of the community require. Notice is also given, that if, after this intimation, the tumults which have already taken place are persevered in, the civil power will think it incumbent on it to call out the assistance of the military to repel such outrages..."
(McDowall, William, *History of Dumfries* (2nd Edn., 1873))

~ March 15th ~

1825: On this day, the Dumfries and Maxwelltown Mechanics' Institute was founded: '… at a meeting held for the purpose in the Trades' Hall, presided over by Provost Thomson; and in the course of the following year it was in full working order … At first the annual subscription was 8*s* per annum; for children of members, and apprentices, 4*s* … Fully twenty years ago [in the mid-1840s], when the Institute was in a somewhat sickly condition, Mr. Cristopher Harkness, afterwards provost of the burgh, became its secretary … It is now, and has been for a lengthened period, one of the most prosperous societies of the kind in the United Kingdom. There are connected with it an excellent reading-room, a well-selected library of nearly 8,000 volumes, a course of lectures during the winter, and classes for young lads whose early education has been neglected. The terms are only 4*s* a year for adult males, 3*s* for females, and 2*s* for apprentices. Usually the membership numbers between 600 and 700. A very elegant and commodious hall, built for the Institute from a design by Mr. Alexander Fraser, architect, was opened about the close of 1861.' (McDowall, William, *History of Dumfries* (2nd Edn., 1873))

— MARCH 16TH —

1836: On this day, the following notice appeared in the *Dumfries Times*: 'To be disposed of for Two Guineas: A pair of handsome Ponies, well matched and broke to harness, one six, the other seven years old, black, without a white spot, will be SHOT for, within half a mile of Dumfries, on Thursday 17th March. Pigeons from trap – five birds to each subscriber. The birds will be provided, but each Gentleman pays for them. Distance from trap, 21 yards. No Subscriber to shoot more than twice; he may shoot once for himself and once as proxy. No shot to exceed one ounce and a half of lead. The birds must fall within a hundred yards of the trap. No Gentleman to raise his gun to his shoulder till the birds are fairly on the wing. It is requested that those intending to Shoot will come forward by Wednesday evening, so that a sufficiency of birds may be provided.

Twenty Subscribers at Two Guineas each. Tickets to be had of Ambrose Clarke, George Inn. If more than Twenty Subscribers, the second best shot will receive the overplus money. Subscribers to meet at the George Inn at 10 o'clock.'

~ March 17th ~

1812: On this day, the *Dumfries Weekly Journal* announced that a reward of twenty guineas was to be offered in exchange for information leading to the conviction of the culprit in a case of supposed murder, after the mutilated body of a woman was found near Buccleuch Street on the day after the town's Candlemas Fair. 'The body was carried to the guard room where it was exposed, and the drum was sent through the town, requesting the inhabitants to come and examine it, in order to be claimed. It was, after some time discovered that she was a washerwoman from Kirkcudbright, the mother of Margaret Hannay (wife of James Pagan), in Kirkgate of Dumfries. And a violent suspicion having arisen against William Towalls, an Irishman, at present a weaver in this place, he was immediately secured and imprisoned. A precognition was commenced by the Magistrates and Procurator Fiscal and is still going on. In the course of the investigation, it appeared that the deceased and Towalls had been in company together, in various public houses in the town, in the course of the evening, and were both seen seemingly much intoxicated on the street, between the hours of ten and eleven o'clock at night.'

~ March 18th ~

1857: On this day, the *Dumfries and Galloway Standard* carried the following article: 'Unless certain publicans in Dumfries are grossly belied, they are systematically carrying on an illicit traffic in liquor, and thus putting the authorities at defiance. The Superintendent of the burgh police avers that this is the case, and complains that he has been prohibited by his employers from taking effectual means for detecting and punishing the delinquents. The police, he states, are trammelled and powerless in the matter; and the Excise officials, it appears, have not thought it their duty to interfere. Supposing that the unlicensed sale of spirits is carried on to the extent described, and that the offenders, as is affirmed, are encouraged in their lawlessness by the apathy of the Police Commissioners and the Excise, then affairs have come to a pretty pass in our burgh. Only conceive of five or six unlicensed places in Dumfries being perpetually the scenes of nocturnal boozing, and the prolific nurseries of crime, just as if there were no such thing as public-house certificates, as if the police constables were imaginary beings, the police rates illusory, and the Excise a myth. It is high time, we say, that means were tried to punish the unlicensed traffickers and protect the community.'

– MARCH 19TH –

1904: On this day, the *Dumfries and Galloway Courier and Herald* reported on a major event in the town: 'The walking craze, which took a hold of the public some time ago, does not seem to have wholly died out, and the latest person to occupy the public mind in this respect is Dr. Deighton, the well-known English athlete, who is engaged on a walk from Land's End to John O'Groats. The doctor, who trains on Bovril, started from Land's End on February 29th, and intends to complete the walk in the remarkably short space of 24 days.

A large crowd of people met him at the outskirts of Dumfries on Wednesday, and escorted him to the King's Arms Hotel, where he was to put up for the night … The doctor addressed the crowd from the hotel window, thanking them for the cordial welcome they had given him, recommending to all athletes an abstemious life, and to everybody the use of Bovril. He stayed in Dumfries overnight and left on Thursday morning, at six o'clock, on the further stages of his journey. On his arrival in Dumfries, he had completed 560 miles.'

— March 20th —

1844: On this day, the *Dumfries and Galloway Standard* reported a curious incident that occurred while a sheep was being driven to the town's slaughterhouse. It bolted into the river en route, then 'entered the aperture of a common sewer ... and entirely disappeared. One or two of the flags covering the sewer, a few yards from the entrance, were lifted, in order to intercept the subterraneous adventurer, but it had got the start of its pursuers. A young man and a boy offered to follow the animal on its voyage of discovery, and procured a lantern for the purpose. By this time, the owner of the sheep had been apprised of the circumstance, and warned them of the danger to which they were exposing themselves. Being, however, determined on continuing the pursuit, they soon came within sight of the animal, which, not exactly relishing their company, proceeded before them at a moderate pace, till it reached the further extremity of the sewer, where it was secured ... Neither the pursuers nor the pursued were anything the worse for their excursion underground. And what is more singular still, the candle continued to burn in their lantern until they returned to the place where they had entered the sewer.'

~ MARCH 21ST ~

1871: On this day, it was reported that 'the shocks of an earthquake were felt in the North of England and South of Scotland on Friday night, and were experienced in Dumfries. The first shock occurred about 7p.m.; this was slight and was noticed by few … However, the principal shock occurred in Dumfries about 11.15p.m., and was distinctly felt in several houses in various parts of the town. It lasted only for a few seconds, but the tremor and upheaval of an earthquake were unmistakeable. Walls were heard to shake and windows to rattle … cage birds fell off their perches and, in one case we have heard of, two Australian love-birds were found lying at the bottom of their cage almost insensible. At Mabie, the shock was very distinctly felt in a ploughman's house, where an umbrella and a bundle of sticks were thrown down, and the man graphically described the shock "as if he had been on a horse which was shaking itself."

The shock of Friday night was extensively felt in Cumberland, Northumberland, Durham, Lancashire and Yorkshire.' (*Dumfries and Galloway Courier*)

— March 22nd —

1911: On this day, the Chief Scout and founder of the movement, Lieutenant-General Sir Robert Baden-Powell, visited the town to review the Boy Scouts of the Dumfries Division. About eighty scouts – drawn from the troops belonging to St Michael's Church, Dumfries Academy, St John's Church and Cargen – mustered at Palmerston Park on a fine but chilly afternoon. 'As they filed into their separate stations in their picturesque garments, displaying the variegated neckcloths by which the different troops may be identified, they presented a fine appearance of fitness and vigour. The scoutmasters were then presented to their distinguished chief, who extended to them his left hand, scout fashion. The programme included fire drill, tent pitching, ambulance work and field telegraphy. It was a matter of great surprise to the uninitiated to find what a wonderful store of useful articles could be produced at short notice from knapsacks and trouser pockets, and to what excellent use the innocent-looking "staff" could be put.

The boys gave three hearty cheers for General Baden-Powell when the proceedings terminated. He was afterwards entertained in the Royal Restaurant by Provost Lennox and the magistrates of the town.' (*Dumfries and Galloway Standard*)

~ MARCH 23RD ~

1812: 'At a meeting of the Council ... the important subject of the moss lands belonging to the burgh was introduced by Provost Staig. He stated that a few days ago, he and the other magistrates had visited certain of these mosses situated within the royalty, over which sundry individuals had enjoyed the liberty of casting turf; and that as their servitudes had expired, or would soon cease, the property might now be fenced or otherwise disposed of as might seem best. They had also, he said, gone to Whinnyhill, where a considerable number of feus had been taken and several houses built, by which the locality had been greatly improved, and the revenue of the town increased. As Mr. Joseph Gass had originated the village, and done much to foster its growth, he proposed that it should be called Gasstown, in compliment to its founder. Provost Staig's propositions were cordially approved of.' (McDowall, William, *History of Dumfries* (2nd Edn., 1873))

1912: 'The Scottish Prison Commissioners have purchased from Mr. Brown, the Hermitage, the whole of the field adjoining Dumfries Prison, immediately to the west. Dumfries has been selected as the site of the Borstal establishment for young women prisoners from all parts of Scotland, whom it is wished to protect from association with ordinary criminals, and seek to reclaim by a prolonged period of occupation and supervision.' (*Dumfries and Galloway Standard*)

— March 24th —

1837: On this day, the following notice appeared in the *Dumfriesshire and Galloway Herald and Advertiser*: 'Mrs. Johnston, formerly of the Grapes Inn, begs leave to intimate to the inhabitants of Dumfries and Maxwelltown, and surrounding country, that she has been induced by the recommendation of friends to discontinue the sale of all Intoxicating Liquors, and to open her Establishment on Wednesday next upon the Tee-Total principle, for the sale of Coffee (plain, or mulled with eggs), tea, soups, sandwiches and other refreshments. The House will be open in the morning, so as workmen and others may have Tea or Coffee. By strict attention to the comfort of her customers, she hopes to obtain a share of the patronage and support of the Friends of Temperance.'

1829: 'The Dumfries Presbytery's [Anti-Catholic] Petition to the House of Lords was returned from London, because it was not written on parchment, and because, from the manner in which it was attested, it would have been received as the petition of the moderator and clerk only. The transcriber had not been instructed to insert the usual clause, bearing that it was signed by those officers "in name and by appointment to the court." The petition from the Presbytery of Dumfries was, without delay, written out anew, and in a very beautiful style, by one of the clergy, on vellum, and attested with due attention to form.' (*Dumfries and Galloway Courier*)

~ March 25th ~

1800: On this day, the following notice appeared in the *Dumfries Weekly Journal*: 'The Head Distributor of His Majesty's Stamp Duties in North Britain, hereby gives notice to every Person using or wearing Hair Powder, that they will receive Certificates for the ensuing year from the Head Office at Edinburgh and at all other Stamp Offices in Scotland.

To prevent mistakes, the Public are hereby apprised that a duty of One Pound One Shilling only is to be paid for each Certificate; and that no more is to be demanded of any person upon taking out a Certificate, except when there are more than two unmarried daughters in a family; in which case a double Certificate stamped with two stamps of One Pound One Shilling each is required to be taken out. Exemptions from the tax: Clergymen not possessed of an annual income of £100; Subalterns or Non Commissioned Officers, or Private Men, belonging to any regiment in the Army, Artillery, Division of Marines, Corps Of Engineers, or Fencible Corps; Officers in his Majesty's Navy under the rank of Commander; Officers or Privates in any Corps of Yeomanry or Volunteers, either Cavalry or Infantry.'

~ March 26th ~

1834: On this day, Robert Burns's widow, Jean Armour, died. The following week's issue of the *Dumfries Times* printed a fulsome tribute. 'Mrs. Burns expired on Wednesday night at about half-past eleven o'clock. She had a paralytic stroke about eighteen months ago, and in the course of last summer a second, from which it was not expected that she would recover. She sank under the third visitation of the same fatal malady. Mrs. Burns's name is so intimately interwoven with the immortal verse of her highly gifted husband that the announcement of her decease, though in good old age [she was sixty-nine], will hardly be listened to without interest by even the least thoughtful of his admirers … She never forgot the name that she bore, nor could the least charitable point to an action of her life that was unworthy of it … Accustomed to see all descriptions of company, her manners were distinguished for their ease, and, but for the obscure street, the humble roof, and the little parlour, she might have been readily mistaken for a specimen of that now almost forgotten class, a genuine old Scottish woman of quality.'

~ March 27th ~

1845: On this day, the following report appeared in the *Dumfriesshire and Galloway Herald and Register*: 'Yesterday, a meeting, called by public advertisement, assembled in the showroom of Mr. Aitchison, cabinet-maker, and formed themselves into an Association for taking under religious tuition, and training to habits of industry, those neglected little girls who infest our streets as beggars, and have no prospect but vice and misery as its accompaniment, unless rescued by the benevolent. Dr. Duncan read a most interesting communication regarding the formation and success of an association having the same object in Perth, with the most encouraging promises of happy results.'

1875: 'The Dumfries Mounted Volunteers: This gallant corps of Borderers assembled on Wednesday, under the command of Captain Johnstone Douglas of Lockerbie, at the Militia Barracks yard, Dumfries, to undergo drill and sword exercise. Under the directions of Sergeant Spenser, the Volunteers were drilled for about an hour, principally in the sword exercise. Considering the corps has been so recently formed, and that the occasion was only the fourth drill, the Volunteers acquitted themselves in a manner very satisfactory to all competent to judge of the movements. By their martial bearing they showed that they were no degenerate descendants of their moss-trooping sires of the 16th century.' (*Dumfries and Galloway Standard*)

~ March 28th ~

1799: On this day, several men of the Oxfordshire Light Dragoons (at that time camped in Dumfries) were imprisoned, after stealing some meat from the town's Flesh Market. Subsequently, the following handbill was discovered pinned to a wall near the King's Arms: 'Intimation to the Magistracy and others who were the cause of imprisoning and turning our Men over to the Civil Law, for committing a small depredation when drunk. We do consent and promise to destroy your houses, and yourselves shall share as bad a fate, first opportunity, if not liberated in 48 hours. We are etc., the Oxfordshire Dragoons and others.'

The Commanding Officer of the Regiment immediately refuted these sentiments. 'The whole Regiment to a Man,' he thundered in print, 'write in declaring that they will not only support the Magistracy, but every part of His Majesty's Civil Government to the last drop of their blood; and that they further offer the reward of a whole week's Pay, amounting to One Hundred Guineas, to any person who shall discover the Author or Adviser of the said Bill, so that he or they may be convicted of the same. In the name of the Oxfordshire Light Dragoons, C. Auriol, Lieut.Colonel.' (Mackie, Charles, (Ed.), *Dumfries and Galloway Notes and Queries* (1913))

∽ March 29th ∽

1843: On this day, Dumfries held its annual hiring fair: 'The High Street, from Friars' Vennel to Bank Street, was one dense crowd, and presented a very animated appearance – which was not a little enhanced by the numerous attendance of wandering minstrels, Cheap Johns, sweetie and toy stands, as well as a beautiful exhibition of superb moving wax figures at the foot of Bank Street.

Everything seemed to pass off harmoniously till six o'clock, when a country smith, who had got more whisky than sense in his head, was sitting with some friends in Mr. Swann's Coffee-house, High Street. He commenced bantering with them about the qualities of a gun, loaded with small-shot, which he had in his possession. He then went downstairs and fired it off into the street, which was very crowded at the time; and we are sorry to add, wounded two young men, and a little girl who was playing the tambourine. One of the lads was rather severely injured; but the other lad and the girl were, we are happy to hear, only slightly so. With this exception, all passed off in the most harmonious manner, although there were a great many intoxicated.' (*Dumfries and Galloway Courier*)

⌁ March 30th ⌁

1866: On this day, the *Dumfriesshire and Galloway Herald and Register* reported on the 'impressive but in Dumfries somewhat rare spectacle of a military funeral ... The deceased, Mr. Frederick Mens, surgeon-dentist in the town, was an efficient and respected member of No.1 (Dumfries) Company of Rifle Volunteers, and on Saturday last his remains were interred in St. Michael's churchyard, with military honours ... The funeral procession started from the residence of the deceased in Queensberry Square and, besides the Volunteers, was joined by several of the relatives, and a large number of the friends of the deceased gentleman, and by 24 brethren of the Thistle Lodge of Freemasons, Dumfries, of which the deceased was a member. To the mournful music of "The Dead March in Saul", played by the fine band of No.1 Company – the firing party preceding the coffin with reversed arms, and the coffin itself borne on the shoulders of four stalwart Volunteers, who were relieved in turns – the procession passed slowly down High Street and St. Michael Street, followed by a large crowd. In St. Michael's churchyard, the coffin having been lowered into its resting-place, three volleys were fired over the grave ...'

⁓ March 31st ⁓

1875: On this day, it was reported that 'Messrs. Strange and Wilson's Aetherscopic entertainment opened in the Mechanics' Hall on Monday evening. The apparatus is very extensive, occupying a considerable portion of the hall. The first part of the entertainment consisted of an adaptation of Schiller's poem, "The Storm of Thoughts", presented in 30 beautiful tableaux. In this piece there were some marvellous illusions, produced by means of the aetherscope – mortals, and what are termed "spirits", appearing and disappearing rapidly, generally amid very brilliant light. The second part was an adaptation of Dickens's Christmas story, *A Haunted Man and the Ghost's Bargain*, again with wondrous effects by the aetherscope. Professor Pepper's great illusion, "We are here but not here", was the third part of the entertainment and indeed a wonderful illusion. Persons are seen to walk about in the hall quite close to the audience, then enter a box standing upright which is locked and to all appearance secure; but while inside they disappear. The door having again been unlocked, they mysteriously return. The concluding part, "Man's Metamorphosis", produced some extraordinary effects, such as "one human being changing into another" – to appearance, we mean – the intrusion of a ghost, and the illusion of a "floating head".' (*Dumfriesshire and Galloway Herald and Register*)

— April 1st —

1828: On this day, the following report appeared in the *Dumfries Weekly Journal*: 'A link of communication betwixt Dumfries and Liverpool has been supplied, which will no doubt be of great advantage to Dumfries, and to Kirkcudbright, Wigtown, and the whole surrounding country, as well as to places in more distant quarters. The "St. Andrew" steam-boat, intended as a "feeder" to the "Countess of Lonsdale" steam-packet, betwixt Carlisle and Liverpool, arrived in the Nith from Whitehaven on Saturday last, and sailed again yesterday with a number of passengers, for Whitehaven, Liverpool, London &c. She was visited at Glencaple Quay on Saturday by a great number of persons, all of whom were delighted with the elegant style in which she is fitted up, and the ample accommodation for the passengers. In the afternoon, a number of individuals concerned in the vessel, and their friends, dined on board. On Sunday, the town was almost emptied of its population; and though the tides were not near their height, she came up the river as far as the New Quay, with a vast assemblage on board … The "St. Andrew" is well and favourably known in Glasgow as one of the best boats of her size that ever left the Clyde.'

― APRIL 2ND ―

1659: On this day, 'the Court was opened in Dumfries by the "Commissioners in Criminal Cases to the People of Scotland", [presided over by] Judge Mosley and Judge Lawrence; and ten women, each charged with divers acts of witchcraft, were brought before them for trial. The proceedings appear to have lasted until the 5th. One of the accused, Helen Tait, had a rather narrow escape – the jury, finding by a plurality of voices that the "dittay" in her case was "not clearly proven". Nevertheless, before being dismissed from the bar, she was required to find security to the extent of £50 sterling for her good behaviour, and that she would banish herself from the parish. The nine other unfortunates were all convicted: "The Commissoners adjudge [the nine women] as found guilty of the severall articles of witchcraft mentioned in the dittayes, to be tane upon Wednesday come eight days to the ordinary place of execution for the burghe of Drumfreis, and there, between 2 and 4 in the afternoon, to be strangled at staikes till they be dead, and thereafter their bodies burned to ashes …"' (Maxwell Wood, J., *Witchcraft and Superstitious Record in the South Western District of Scotland*, Norwood Editions, 1911)

~ April 3rd ~

1821: On this day, it was noted that 'within the last few days, different troops of dragoons have passed through this town, some of them on their way to England and others, we believe, to a western county. The first of these divisions (the 7th Dragoons) was commanded by Major Younghusband, who had his headquarters at Mrs. Williamson's Commercial Inn; and on Tuesday last we were a good deal interested on seeing the colours of his regiment hanging from the windows of a house which once had the honour of lodging Prince Charles Edward Stuart, better known by the name of the Pretender. It is only lately, however, that this house has been occupied as an inn; and we presume the colours of Major Younghusband formed the first military banner that has graced its walls since the year 1745, when the Highlanders, headed by the Pretender, then in full retreat from England, sojourned several days in Dumfries, and did the inhabitants the additional honour of levying upon them a pretty heavy contribution. The Commercial Inn being then a private house, was deemed the most convenient place for a royal residence; and where our townsmen now sit for an evening discussing the merits of Mr. Plunkett's Bills, the Pretender gave audiences to fierce and rival chieftains.' (*Dumfries and Galloway Courier*)

~ APRIL 4TH ~

1797: On this day, the following solemn address, from the Presbytery of Dumfries, 'to the People within their Bounds', regarding the French threat, appeared in the *Dumfries Weekly Journal*: 'You have learned, from various quarters, brethren, that the nation, with whom we are engaged in an arduous contest, and whom we have reason to regard as determined enemies, both to the Christian Religion and to the excellent Constitution of this country, are preparing to invade our native land.

You are threatened with the destruction of that Religion, which your fathers justly valued more than their lives; and with the destruction of that Constitution, under which we have so long flourished. You are threatened with the "spoiling of your goods", however small your portion of them may be, and are in danger of becoming the abject slaves of an haughty and rapacious conqueror.

But blessed be God, that, amidst all these apprehensions, we are possessed of such resources, as, if called forth with unanimity and vigour, need leave no room for despondency. If, animated by that spirit of bravery and independence, which hath long distinguished the British nation, we now "acquit ourselves like men", we shall find abundant means of safety and protection.'

— April 5th —

1803: On this day, the *Dumfries Weekly Journal* printed the following caution: 'The Magistrates of Dumfries, having of late observed that a great many young, thriving Oak, Ash, Beech and Fir trees, in the Castle Dykes planting, have been cut, stolen, and carried away; as also that the principal branches of a number of trees on the Dock Braes have been lopped off, in a most unwarrantable manner and to the great hurt of the Town and the beauty and ornament of the place, they therefore offer a Reward of Ten Guineas, to be paid on conviction, to any person who will give information so that the person or persons guilty of such illegal practices may be punished for the same.

And intimation is hereby made to the Public, that if any person trespasses in that way in time coming, they will be prosecuted and punished as severely as the law authorises.'

1837: Also on this day, the *Dumfries Times* announced that: 'Mary Rudd begs respectfully to intimate to the inhabitants of Dumfries and its vicinity that, on 1st May next, she will open a School for instruction in Moravian Work, Flowering, Plain Sewing, and English Reading, at No. 6 Nith Place, where she hopes to merit a share of the public favour. Specimens of the various kinds of work will then be exhibited.'

~ April 6th ~

1882: On this day, the *Dumfries and Galloway Standard* reported the unveiling of the Burns Statue: 'The unveiling of the statue was looked forward to with much interest many months prior to the ceremony, not only by the inhabitants of the town and district, but we may safely say by the admirers of the Poet in whatever land located …

Five streets converge upon the irregular square at the head of the High Street where the statue stands, namely High Street, Friars' Vennel, Castle Street, Church Crescent, St. Andrew's Street … As far as the eye could reach along all the streets converging on the square, there were only human faces to be seen, hemmed in by the houses on each side, the windows of which, and even the roofs of some of them, were filled by spectators. The vast multitude exceeded in numbers anything that we remember ever to have seen in Dumfries …

In the evening there was a brilliant display of fireworks; and the streets were rendered almost impassable by the large crowds of people who had turned out to witness the various illuminations … The chief attractions were at the upper end of the town [where] the large crescent (of which the statue is the central point), was well lighted by the illuminations of the shopkeepers on every side.'

~ April 7th ~

1778: On this day, the *Dumfries Weekly Journal* informed its readers that, 'the Magistrates and Council of Dumfries, having resolved to let the Lighting of the Town (including furnishing the oil and wicks for the lamps, and a man to clean and light the lamps), to one or more persons, jointly for a certain sum for the whole annually, to be paid by the town, as can be agreed upon; they desire any person or persons, who are inclined to contract with the town, for one year after WhitSunday next, to lodge their proposals with one of the town-clerks as soon as convenient.'

1869: Also on this day, the following report appeared: 'A short time ago a pair of rooks took up their abode in the top of a chimney in English Street, but a cat which belonged to the house below, thinking that the birds were intruders, ushered out by a skylight, boldly attacked them and drove them away. The rooks flew off, but returned in a very short time with a powerful reinforcement of their fellow bipeds, numbering nearly a hundred. Such a noise was made by the clamorous brood that the people of the house could not understand at first what was the matter; and as for puss, as soon as the feathered multitude began to light upon the roof, she made off in a perfect panic.' (*Dumfries and Galloway Standard*)

‑ April 8th ‑

1788: On this day, the following announcements appeared in the *Dumfries Weekly Journal*:

'Mrs. Carruthers takes this method of informing her friends and the public, that she still continues to carry on the heckling business, and sells all kinds of lint and tow, at her shop in Bridge Vennel; where she also gives out lint to be spun, and every encouragement for the spinning of it, as usual.'

'On Sunday last his Majesty's Proclamation for the dutiful observance of the Sabbath, and the discouragement of vice and immorality, was read in the pulpits of both churches in this burgh, and suitable exhortations were subjoined. It is to be hoped that the inhabitants will be duly attentive to an object with which the duty of individuals, and the best interests of society, are so intimately connected.'

'To be sold by public roup, within the Custom House here upon Wednesday the 16th current, at midday, the HULL of the cutter "Betty" (to be broken up), with her furniture, apparel, and float boat entire. Also, a Manx boat with her furniture and apparel entire.

Likewise, seven-and-a-half Gallons of Brandy, and seven-and-a-half Gallons of Geneva; for private use only, being below the strength of 1 in 6 under hydrometer proof. And 8 Gallons of British Sweets. The boats and their materials may be viewed at Conheath, by applying to John Stothart, tide-waiter; and the Spirits at the Custom House, any time before the day of the sale.'

~ April 9th ~

1834: On this day, the *Dumfries Times* printed an account of Jean Armour's funeral: 'Mrs. Burns's remains were deposited on Tuesday in the vaults of the Mausoleum. The invitations were very general, and, we believe, with very few exceptions, religiously attended to. The little street in which the mansion of the deceased is situated, the entire length of St. Michael Street, from thence to the churchyard gate, and the churchyard itself, were crammed with men, women and children, and among the women were very many of a rank and appearance that are seldom seen mingling in crowds of any description. The coffin was extremely neat, and without any tawdriness of ornament. The head was supported, of course, by Mr. Robert Burns [son], but there were few persons within reach of the handspokes, on which the coffin was borne, that did not, after an old and affecting Scottish custom, show their respect for the memory of the unconscious inmate, by assisting to carry her remains in their passage to their honoured resting-place. On Monday night, after the vault had been opened, the scull of the poet was taken out of the grave, for the purposes of taking a cast of it for the edification of the craniologists of Edinburgh.'

~ April 10th ~

1940: The following report appeared in the *Dumfries and Galloway Standard*: 'The most intensive air raid precautions test yet carried out in the burgh of Dumfries took place on Sunday. At half-past twelve all the personnel were at "action ready" stations in the burgh, and within a few minutes the report and control centre at the A.R.P. headquarters in Castle Street was a hub of industry. Then followed a test of the efficiency of the communications received and radiating from the report and control centre. There were scenes of intense activity as messages started to flash in from wardens confronted with incidents in eleven different parts of the town. Each incident called for the attention of several services, such as demolition squads and rescue squads, where victims had been trapped by fallen masonry; fire-fighting services, where incendiary bombs had created havoc to property and danger to life; decontamination and gas identification personnel, where gas threatened whole residential areas; and ambulance and first-aid parties for treating injuries.

Some of the incidents were spectacular in the extreme, and one in particular, that in the Coach and Horses Close, the civil defence expert characterised as the best staged and most expertly handled he had yet seen.'

~ April 11th ~

1820: On this day, it was reported that 'yesterday, the journeymen hatters belonging to this town, having lately struck work with the view of obtaining an advance of wages, met at the dockhead, and entered into a discussion upon their alleged grievances. The result of this deliberation was, that a number of these men threw up their employment and left Dumfries. This assemblage of hatters having been seen by several persons, a report immediately went abroad that there had been a meeting of Dumfries Radicals. But this report we are enabled to contradict on the best authority. At the same time we may mention that on Sunday last, a written paper was posted on the walls of the Old Church, calling on the public to come forward and attend a meeting in favour of reform &c. This paper was of course immediately taken down and handed over to the Procurator Fiscal. A respectable merchant of this town, who was a passenger in the London Mail on Saturday last, mentions that there was a man on the top of the coach who continually eulogised the cause of the Radicals. It seems probable therefore that the written paper in question was posted up by this person.' (*Dumfries and Galloway Courier*)

~ APRIL 12TH ~

1808: On this day, the following notice appeared: 'Whereas a MAD DOG is understood to have bit several dogs in the town last week, the Magistrates do order the inhabitants to keep all their dogs in close containment for the space of one month from this date. They have given orders to the Burgh Officers and Constables to destroy all dogs found going at large during this period, within this burgh and liberties thereof.' (*Dumfries Weekly Journal*)

1825: Also on this day, the same newspaper reported on a strange friendship: 'A merchant of Dumfries, a few days ago, discovered a very large well-fed rat at the bottom of a sugar barrel which he had recently emptied and, wishing to make an example of the intruder, he put his cat into the barrel, expecting that a few moments would suffice to number the imprisoned burglar with the dead. On returning a short time afterwards, he found the rat not only alive, but the cat and it lying together at the bottom of the barrel, hugging each other with the most cordial goodwill and with no disposition to quarrel. Thinking, as the cat was young, that it might have been afraid to attack the enemy, he put another strong elderly one into the barrel beside them, believing it would make short work of the rat. On again returning, he found that as good an understanding subsisted between the rat and the TWO cats, as when there was only one.' (*Dumfries Weekly Journal*)

─ April 13th ─

1659: On this day, between 2 p.m. and 4 p.m., nine women were taken to Whitesands and burnt at the stake for witchcraft: 'Nine women given to the flames in one day! The scene at the execution must have been so inexpressibly shocking that we dare not examine it too closely. The planting of the stakes, and building up about them vast heaps of peats, straw and other combustibles; the executioners with their ropes and torches; the venerable victims, frail with age, trembling with terror or palsy ... whom the horrid functionaries bind till they shake no more; the attendant ministers striving to benefit their souls before their bodies are charred into blackened clay; the curious onlookers, who would be pitiful, perhaps, were their hearts not annealed by the belief that the miserable women, being witches, are alike beyond the pale of sympathy or forgiveness ... the awful close of all, when, as the clock strikes four, the crowd, which had "supped full of horrors", can see nothing where the nine poor martyrs to superstition stood, save a morsel of blackened bones and a heap of bloody dust, while the grimy hangmen, like so many scavengers of death, are sweeping up and preparing to carry out of sight.' (McDowall, William, *History of Dumfries* (2nd Edn., 1873))

~ April 14th ~

1912: On this day, the White Star liner, *Titanic*, struck an iceberg just before midnight. 'The latest triumph in shipbuilding and the largest steamship in the world has met with swift and appalling disaster,' reported the *Dumfries and Galloway Standard* a few days later. 'News came to hand on Monday morning that the floating leviathan had run into an iceberg and sustained irreparable injury. Early telegrams represented that all the passengers had been taken off by half-past three in the morning by other vessels which hurried to the spot in answer to urgent messages shot athwart the sea by means of wireless telegraphy; but unhappily later information leaves the fate of great part of the passengers and crew in doubt, and gives ground for the terrible fear that sixteen hundred souls have perished.

Amongst those on board the "Titanic" was Mr. John Hume, son of Mr. Andrew Hume, music teacher, George Street, Dumfries. Mr. Hume, who is twenty-one years of age, was bandmaster on the "Titanic", having been transferred from the "Carmania", which arrived home a fortnight ago after a Mediterranean trip. No news has been received from the White Star agency at Liverpool as to whether he is amongst the survivors.'

~ April 15th ~

1662: On this day, 'in a Town Council minute, the Treasurer was ordered by the Magistrates to provide a silver bell four ounces in weight as a prize to be run for every second Tuesday in May [horse-racing having long been popular in the town], by the work-horses of the burgh, "according to the auncient custome"; the regulations being that whenever the bell was borne away by one rider and one horse three consecutive years, it was "to appertain unto the wooner thereof for evir."'(McDowall, William, *History of Dumfries* (2nd Edn., 1873))

1696: Also on this day, it was recorded that 'at the Dumfries Synod, the question of gowns in the Scottish pulpit, and whether the wearing of the gown was consistent with the simplicity of Presbyterian worship, was discussed. The Synod came to this decision: "Hearing that it is a thing very decent and suitable so it hath been the practice of ministers of this kirk formerly to wear black gowns in the pulpit, and for the ordinary to make use of bands; do, therefore, by their act, recommend it to their brothers within their bounds to keep up that laudable custome and to study gravity in their apparel and deportment every manner of way."' (Mackie, Charles, (Ed.), *Dumfries and Galloway Notes and Queries* (1913))

← APRIL 16TH →

1845: On this day, the following report appeared in the *Dumfries and Galloway Standard*: 'On Friday morning last, about ten o'clock, a fire broke out in a cottage in College Street, Maxwelltown, originated, it is said, by a boy bringing a lighted candle into contact with the roof, when removing kittens from a loft or attic, and spread with such fearful rapidity to the adjoining houses, that in a very short time not fewer than five of the thatched cottages were enveloped in flames. As the wind was blowing a strong breeze from the north-east, sparks were carried to a great distance, and no little alarm was created for the safety of other contiguous buildings, and many of their inmates commenced carrying out their furniture to places of security from the possible approach of the flames ... A poor man, while endeavouring to rescue some part of his goods from the burning ruins of his domicile, had thrown off his coat without taking care to leave it in safe-keeping, and when he wished to resume it, found to his utter dismay, that not only his house containing his little all was consuming to ashes before his eyes, but that his very coat had, in the meantime, been stolen from his back ...'

ᕁ APRIL 17TH ᕁ

1827: On this day, the following notice appeared: 'It having been found advantageous to the inhabitants of many of the principal towns in Scotland to institute Societies for Baking Wheaten Bread, for some time past there seems to have been a general wish to have a Company of a similar nature in Dumfries, and a Committee from the Seven Incorporated Trades was appointed lately to correspond with the Societies in Glasgow and Perth … Accordingly, copies of the rules and regulations of the societies in these places, with statements of the advantages derived therefrom, have been received, by which it appears that a very considerable reduction on the price of bread has accrued to the subscribers. Meetings of the Incorporations were held here last week; and one hundred and fifty shares were subscribed·from the funds for behoof of the Freemen, their Journeymen and Apprentices, and the Widows of Freemen. As the Incorporation are desirous that the benefits of the Institution should be extended to the whole Inhabitants of Dumfries and its vicinity, subscription papers, with copies of the regulations before mentioned, have been left in the hands of Convener Howat. The price of each share has been fixed at one guinea, and it is proposed that no individual shall be entitled to hold more than ten shares.' (*Dumfries Weekly Journal*)

— April 18th —

1838: On this day, a report of the following crime appeared in the *Dumfries Times*: 'One day last week a woman, to appearance betwixt 35 and 40 years of age, full-faced and of a dark complexion, and who stated that her husband had been killed in a foreign land, succeeded in levying blackmail from several girls in Maxwelltown by inducing them to purchase rings and other "bijouterie" which, according to her representations, were made of pure gold, but which, after examination, were found to consist merely of brass … She [then] went into the shops of several grocers and bakers, bought in each of them some article of trifling value for which she gave sixpence and got back "the change"; she afterwards left the shops but immediately returned, and declared that she had given the sellers a shilling and not a sixpence, and, of course, claimed the change out of the shilling. The confident and imperious terms in which she expressed herself caused her false and impudent statements to be believed, and induced the grocers and bakers to accede to her demand. Subsequently, she was apprehended and taken before the magistrates. It turned out that she was the wife of a bell-hanger who is travelling through the country.'

~ April 19th ~

1899: On this day, it was reported that 'early yesterday morning an alarming accident took place at Dumfries Gasworks, in the bursting of a large elevated open water tank with such violence as to give the impression that an explosion had taken place amongst the works. The tank ... stands at the head of the yard on strong iron pillars fully ten feet high, and was fed by engine power from an artesian well of considerable depth, the tank thereafter being drawn upon by the works and the Tanneries. The accident occurred about two o'clock in the morning, when there was about 50 tons of water in the tank, and it is supposed that the pressure had been too much, as one of the sides was forced completely out, and the whole volume of water burst with a crash into the yard. One of the men passed the spot a minute or two before, and it was fortunate the accident happened in the night, as otherwise, the yard being much in use, it might have been attended with loss of life, some of the pieces of plating broken off in the fall weighing about 15 cwts.' (*Dumfries and Galloway Courier and Herald*)

~ April 20th ~

1779: On this day, the following advertisement appeared: 'James Sharp, late miner and engineer at Leadhills, is possessed of an effectual cure for that desperate disease, the bite of a mad dog in man or beast, which he has applied with success for many years, as he can evidence by Certificates, which he will produce if required, from great numbers of respectable people within the Synod of Dumfries and elsewhere; some of whom were cured that were not infected till six or eight months after they were bit. His price for beasts is half-a-crown a head, and where there are a great number he is more moderate, as also when any of the human kind are bit or infected.

As his residence is not certain at present, any person who wants his assistance will get notice of him by enquiring at Andrew Black, innkeeper, at the Spread Eagle, near the New Church, Dumfries. Several gentlemen, ministers and others, have been soliciting him to publish his secret; and as he is now up in years, and has no relation to whom he can leave it, he is willing to comply with their request in making it public for the good of mankind upon a reasonable recompense to himself.' (*Dumfries Weekly Journal*)

— April 21st —

1900: On this day came the announcement that 'there is at present on view … in this town, one of the splendid vehicles of the Motor Manufacturing Company Ltd., 47 Holborn Viaduct, London, E.C. Mr. John Lowe … the firm's representative in Scotland, is in charge of the motor, and has touched at Dumfries in the course of an extensive tour throughout Scotland. The car, which looks extremely serviceable, accomplished the journey from Ayr to Dumfries on Thursday in five-and-a-half hours, and is capable of maintaining an average speed of 10 to 12 miles per hour. We understand that Mr. Lowe intends staying in Dumfries for a few days longer.' (*Dumfries and Galloway Courier and Herald*)

1923: Also on this day, the paper noted that 'a new industry has been started in Dumfries, and though it is unlikely to relieve unemployment much, it will be a considerable boon to devotees of tennis. The new venture is tennis-racket making, and thanks to the enterprise of Messrs. G. Young and Son … the best of rackets can now be had home-made, or an old racket can be restrung in a couple of days. Formerly this latter process often took as many months.' (*Dumfries and Galloway Courier and Herald*)

~ April 22nd ~

1647: On this day, the news was revealed that 'the Synod of Dumfries [had] ordered intimation to be made from all the pulpits within the bounds, that a sentence of excommunication had been passed upon John, Lord Herries, Dame Elizabeth Beaumont, Countess of Nithsdale, Dame Elizabeth Maxwell, Lady Herries, Dame Elizabeth Maxwell, elder of Kirkonnell, and about thirty other persons of a humbler degree. What this sentence implied we can scarcely say, though it was not, certainly, of such a serious nature as its name used to import, when Popery was predominant. All persons were forbidden "to reset or resort to" those mentioned under ban, "without licence of Presbytery or the kirk judicatories, upon evidence asked and given, under peril of ecclesiastical censures", but we do not suppose that this decree of isolation would tell very terribly upon the parties concerned. A week after it was fulminated, we read that the Session gave liberty to two individuals "to speak with Lord Herries, notwithstanding he be excommunicat, in respect that both of them have sundry business of good concernment with his lordship."' (McDowall, William, *History of Dumfries* (2nd Edn., 1873))

~ April 23rd ~

1884: On this day, the following report appeared in the *Dumfries and Galloway Courier and Herald*: 'Saturday was Primrose Day. It is marvellous with what unanimity the idea of wearing primroses on the anniversary of the death of the Earl of Beaconsfield has been taken up by all classes. [This was the title conferred on Benjamin Disraeli; the primrose being his favourite flower.] Even the little children in our courts and alleys, in imitative mood, procured the pretty flower to adorn their tattered garments. Both peer and peasant seemed proud to wear a bunch of the golden bloom; and our gracious Queen sent a floral tribute to the great statesman's tomb.

The flower was everywhere conspicuous on the streets of Dumfries and Maxwelltown. Outside the rooms of the Dumfries and Maxwelltown Junior Conservative Association, and in a most commanding position, was a beautiful earl's coronet above a scroll upon which was the now almost national motto, *Imperium et Libertas* … Throughout the day, this striking emblem, happily conceived and artistically formed, attracted general attention. Within the rooms, the portraits of the late Earl, which adorn the walls, were wreathed with primroses.'

— APRIL 24TH —

1689: The Town Council had made an order at a meeting held in early January that, on this day, William, Prince of Orange 'should be proclaimed King, at the Market Cross. A minute of the preceding day states that the Council had fixed "the morrow, betwixt thrie and four o'clock in the afternoon, for proclaiming King William and Queen Mary, King and Queen of Scotland, with all solemnities used in such caises, conforme and in obedience to the meiting of the Estates, their proclomatione published there anent; and appoints intimatione to be made throu the towne be touk of drum to the effect the inhabitants may appear in the Sandbeds at the bating of the drum, in their best arms." The treasurer's accounts show that "10 pound 6 unce of powder", value £8 6s Scots, was burnt on the joyous occasion; that whilst the cannons fired salutes, a bonfire made of "9 gritt loads of peitts", costing £1 16s, sent forth a ruddy blaze; and that the health of the new sovereigns was toasted at the Cross in "six pynts of ale", ordered by Bailie Irving; indoors, doubtless, the same toast would be honoured in more patrician liquor.' (McDowall, William, *History of Dumfries* (2nd Edn., 1873))

~ April 25th ~

1797: On this day, the following stern warning, from the Procurator Fiscal, appeared in the *Dumfries Weekly Journal*: 'The Fishings in the River Nith having for some years past been much injured by the killing of Salmon, Grilse, Salmon-trouts, Sea-trouts and Hirlings, and by the fishing the Spawn and Fry thereof, the proprietors have come to the determined resolution of preventing this injury in time coming; and have therefore directed me to give this public notice, that if any person or persons shall be found fishing for, taking or killing Salmon, Grilse, Salmon-trout, Sea-trout or Hirling, not fully qualified by law, or of fishing for, taking, or killing, or having in their possession, any Spawn, Fry, or young brood of such fish, they shall be prosecuted, fined and punished in terms of the Act of Parliament passed in the year 1792, for regulating and improving the Fishings of the said river. And it is hoped that parents and masters will be at due pains to prevent their children and servants contravening this Act, otherwise they will be prosecuted as being art and part of such contravention. A suitable Reward is hereby offered for the effectual discovery of all offenders.'

~ April 26th ~

1881: On this day, a report of a serious cart accident in the town appeared: 'On Wednesday, a cart of skins, belonging to Mr. Craig, farmer, of Airdrie, Kirkbean, was being unloaded at the Glasgow and South-Western goods station, Dumfries, when the horse bolted, and ran along English Street at a furious rate. Some children were playing near the barracks, and a little boy, five years old, son of Mr. Douglas, hay-dealer, was knocked over before he could get out of the way, and the wheel of the cart passed over his head, inflicting serious injury. A little further on the shaft of the cart struck Mr. John Houston, Senior, of Brownrigg, a gentleman of eighty-six years, and the wheel passed over his shoulder and face. He was removed to the residence of his son, Mr. James Houston of Marchfield, where he lies in a precarious condition, and the little boy is also in considerable danger. The cart afterwards came in contact with a lamp-post near Messrs. McGeorge and Sons' hosiery manufactory, breaking it in three places, but the horse was brought to a standstill at the head of Queen Street.' (*Dumfries and Galloway Courier*)

~ April 27th ~

1802: On this day, the *Dumfries Weekly Journal* reported that 'the foundation stone of the new Academy was laid here with great solemnity, in the presence of a vast concourse of people. At two o'clock, the Magistrates, and Committee for managing the affairs of the Schools, met near the Council Chamber, and from thence walked in solemn procession to the site of the new building … When they had reached the ground, the foundation stone was laid by David Staig Esq., who, having thrice struck the stone according to the rules of masonry, addressed the Gentlemen and Clergy present in an appropriate and excellent speech; and concluded with saying "May the great architect of the Universe prosper the undertaking. Under His auspices may it be soon and happily completed. May it ever enjoy His protection, and remain a seminary of useful learning …" After the address was finished, a general huzza was thrice repeated, and the procession returned in the same order as it came. The town bells rang during the procession, and the Dumfries Volunteers kept off the crowd.'

– April 28th –

1395: On this day, the town's earliest charter still in existence was granted by King Robert III of Scotland: 'Know ye that we have granted to the Provost, Bailies, Burgesses, and Community of our Burgh of Dumfries, our said Burgh, to be held by them and their successors, of us and our heirs, in fee and heritage for ever; With all and every the liberties and privileges, easements, and just pertinents whatsoever, appertaining to the said burgh, or which may afterwards in any way rightly belong to it; Together with our fermes and annual rents in the said burgh, with its customs, tolls, courts and issues of courts, revenues, and the desmense lands of the said burgh; As also the mills and multures, and their pertinents; Together with the fishings in the Water of Nith belonging to us, excepting only the fishing granted by our royal predecessors for the love of God to the Minorite Friars of the same place; and with all other privileges both without and within the said burgh which our said Burgesses and Communities have at any time formerly held or possessed in our reign or that of our royal ancestors in Scotland ...' In return, the royal exchequer required an annual sum of £20, to be paid at Whitsunday and Martinmas. (Translation given in McDowall, William, *History of Dumfries* (2nd Edn., 1873))

~ April 29th ~

1802: On this day, the Royal Dumfries Volunteers were 'stood down': 'In consequence of a letter, dated April 26th, from the Right Hon. The Earl of Dalkeith, Lord Lieutenant of the County of Dumfries, to the Officer commanding the Royal Dumfries Volunteers, enclosing a circular letter, dated Downing Street April 19th, from the Right Hon. Lord Hobart, one of His Majesty's Principal Secretaries of State, to the Lords Lieutenants of several counties in Scotland, which communicated His Majesty's pleasure upon the disembodying of the Volunteer Infantry Corps &c., Colonel DePeyster, Major Commandant, assembled, for the last time, the Royal Dumfries Volunteers on Thursday 29th …'

The Volunteers' chaplain, the Revd Dr Burnside, told the men in his parting address that 'a few years only have elapsed since the country was endangered by the hostilities and violence of an ancient and powerful foe … But we were in danger also from a seditious and revolutionary spirit, which threatened to dissolve all the bonds of society, and to destroy a Constitution which had been the work of ages and the envy of the world … You and your fellow Volunteers throughout the country, can now lay down your arms with honour, since the end for which they were assumed hath been so completely obtained.' (*Dumfries Weekly Journal*)

~ April 30th ~

1836: On this day, 'an important case, springing from a difference of opinion regarding the extent of the Nith, was brought before Lord Moncrieff and a jury at Dumfries. Mr. R.A. Oswald, and other owners of shore-lands far down the estuary, erected stake-nets upon them; which Mr. James McWhir, owner of the Nith fishings, held to be within the boundary of the river, and therefore illegal. Mr. Maitland, for the defenders, maintained that the nets were in the Solway and therefore could not be in the Nith; but Dean of Faculty Hope convinced the jury that a charter of 1395, and sundry statistics which he quoted, gave a range to the river beyond the sandbanks where the nets were planted. A verdict was therefore returned in favour of Mr. McWhir, and the engines were removed forthwith.' (McDowall, William, *History of Dumfries* (2nd Edn., 1873))

1862: On this day, the *Dumfries and Galloway Standard* reported the death of Mary Timney, who had been hanged outside Dumfries Prison the previous morning, and was the last woman to be publicly executed in Scotland. 'The body, a hideous spectacle in the calm, blue, sunny April morning, hung fully thirty minutes, exposed to the gaze of the vulgar crowds on the streets, from whom solitary cries of pain and distress arose at intervals.'

- May 1st -

1827: On this day, the following report appeared in the *Dumfries and Galloway Courier*: 'One of our bakers sold a loaf last week which was supposed by the purchaser to be deficient in weight. This led to a magisterial investigation; when it was found that the loaf complained of was what was called pan or fancy bread, and which when rasped down must be, of necessity, under the regular standard. All the ordinary loaves tried were found to be of sufficient weight. Since the plan of baking standard bread has been tried, many complaints have been made, and we are informed by the magistrates that the bakers are quite willing to recur to the old system of baking both fine and coarse loaves. We are glad of this, but regret much to learn that they will not consent to make what are called "swine" of the coarser kind of flour. We profess to be ignorant of the mysteries of the art, but "swine", as baked formerly, were a boon to the poor, and we would wish to see the boon continued.'

─ MAY 2ND ─

1826: On this day, the *Dumfries and Galloway Courier* reported that James Hensey, having been found guilty of assault, 'was publicly whipped "at the cart-tail" through the streets of Dumfries … [The cart] went along Irish Street to St. Michael Street and, halting at the end of Burns Street, the coat and shirt of the criminal, which had been loosely thrown over his shoulders, were turned up, and the executioner – a strong-boned carter wrapt in a coarse grey greatcoat, with his face monstrously blackened, a red stripe of paint down his nose, and an old torn hat drawn over his brows for concealment – planted himself in the proper attitude, and with a whip of knotted cords inflicted the first 20 lashes of the punishment. The poor creature's back was a good deal marked by this infliction, and his contortions, whining and tears, induced several to call out to the fellow to lash more leniently. The cart then proceeded along High Street, and stopped respectively opposite to Mr. Rankine's, the King's Arms, the Fish Cross, and Friars' Vennel, at each of which places ten lashes were given, making in all sixty, after which it proceeded to the jail, where the prisoner was unloosed and immediately attended by a surgeon.'

~ MAY 3RD ~

1709: On this day, Elspeth Rule was tried in Dumfries for witchcraft: 'No special act of witchcraft was charged against her; the indictment was of a very general nature, that the prisoner was [by] habit and repute a witch; and that she had used threatening expressions against persons at enmity with her, who were afterwards visited with the loss of cattle, or the death of friends, and one of whom ran mad. The jury, by a majority of voices, found these articles proved, and the Judge ordained the prisoner to be burned on the cheek, and to be banished [from] Scotland for life.' (Arnot, Hugo, *Celebrated Criminal Trials in Scotland, 1536–1784*, 1812 Edn.)

1848: Also on this day, the following update appeared: 'The operations in the neighbourhood of the town, in connection with the Nithsdale Railway, are going on rapidly, and the building of the bridge at Nunholm, abandoned last year on account of the floods, has been again commenced. The station will be proceeded with shortly. The site chosen is a spot of ground on the west side of the English road, a little beyond Pleasance, and adjoining Ladyfield Cottage. The station is to be covered, and to consist of three departments: one for passengers, another for carriages, and a third for engines.' (*Dumfries and Galloway Standard*)

‒ MAY 4TH ‒

1824: On this day, the following report appeared in the *Dumfries Weekly Journal*: 'The King's birthday having, from time immemorial, been fixed upon by the Incorporated Trades for shooting for the Silver Gun, presented to them by King James the Sixth, and the usual period of seven years having elapsed since the Royal gift was last contended for, they were roused from their slumbers last Friday by the drums beating the "generale" at 4 o'clock, and again at 6 to warn the members to assemble at the houses of their respective Deacons of Crafts. At 7 precisely, they marched to the Whitesands, the place of general rendezvous. At 8 o'clock the procession began to move, by Friars' Vennel and High Street. As a mark of respect, the venerable Father of the whole Trades, Deacon Johnston, who is now 97 years of age, was placed at the head of the whole body and walked to the Kingholm without any assistance. On reaching the field, the business of the day was begun by the Convener firing the first shot, after which trade succeeded trade, until the whole had shot, when it was declared that the Gun had been won by Alexander Selkirk, a member, and formerly Deacon of the Incorporation of Fleshers.'

~ MAY 5TH ~

1795: On this day, Robert Burns's stirring patriotic ballad, 'Does Haughty Gaul Invasion Threat?' (sometimes called 'The Dumfries Volunteers'), was first published in the *Dumfries Weekly Journal*:

> Does haughty Gaul invasion threat?
> Then let the louns beware, Sir;
> There's WOODEN WALLS upon our seas,
> And VOLUNTEERS on shore, sir:
>
> The Nith shall ran to Corsincon,
> And Criffel sink in Solway,
> Ere we permit a Foreign Foe
> On British ground to rally!
> We'll ne'er permit a Foreign Foe
> On British ground to rally.

There was much more in that vein, and the ballad became instantly popular, swiftly appearing in the *Caledonian Mercury*, the *Scots Magazine* and elsewhere.

—⁃—

1802: Also on this day, the following announcement appeared in the *Dumfries Weekly Journal*: 'New leeches of all sizes are arrived at Inglis's Laboratory [in Dumfries], and selling at the usual prices.'

─ MAY 6TH ─

1826: On this day, the following irate letter appeared in the *Dumfries Weekly Journal*: 'We, the Carters of Dumfries, beg leave to request that you would contradict a statement that appeared in the "Courier", and which we reckon greatly to our discredit, being void of all foundation and a falsehood. It was said that the man who was whipped through the streets last week was whipped by a carter [*see* 2nd May] Now, we consider this a stigma cast on the whole body. The carters are a set of hard working, industrious and useful members of society who, knowing them all in all, have never been known to do anything disgraceful. There is not a carter in Dumfries but would have disdained as much to be a public whipper as the editor of this newspaper would have done. Although it is no doubt absolutely necessary to execute the law, no man can be compelled to be the executioner, and if any one of our number had done such a thing, he would have been disgraced and expelled from the society, nor would any one of us have associated with him after such a disgraceful doing. The man was not a carter at all, nor is there a single carter in Dumfries that knows who he is.'

— May 7th —

1851: On this day, a letter appeared in the *Dumfries and Galloway Standard*: 'Will it be credited that … the right of way is again contested at the Crags, that finest of all our summer resorts? However strange it might appear, it is quite true. When the traveller, after penetrating the mysteries of the Maiden Bower, and surveying the beautiful scenery which stretches from the base of the table rock, seeks to cross into the Bankend road on his way homewards, an ugly paling presents itself in the passage. It does not literally cry out "STOP, TRAVELLER!", but its intentions are as plain as those of a footpad in a pantomime. If he knows his right, and has the courage to maintain it, he will kick down, or at least surmount the barricade, and go on his way; but if he is a stranger, he will probably turn back from the forbidden ground. We were under the impression that the right of way here had been sufficiently made out already, and are really astonished that it should be again denied. Is there no Quintius Curtius amongst us to make a gap in the barricade, and leap through it for the public good?'

━ MAY 8TH ━

1945: On this day, VE Day celebrations in Dumfries were duly reported in the *Dumfries and Galloway Standard*: 'As mid-day approached, the bells of the Midsteeple, silent throughout the war except for a few minutes during a broadcast to the Forces abroad last May, rent the air with a victory peal. This gave atmosphere to the great occasion ... The crowd was impressively large though not particularly demonstrative, and there was an intensity that indicated the spirit of gratitude with which the glad news had been received.

Speaking with quiet deliberation, the Provost said: "It is our privilege as representatives of the County of Dumfries and our ancient and royal burgh to come here on this memorable day to publish the glad news that organized hostilities have now ceased in Europe. Let our first act be in memory of those whose sacrifices have made this day possible." The audience then stood in reverent silence for one minute and then Reveille was sounded by the bugler ...

After the announcement, the Provost's party proceeded from the Midsteeple to St. Michael's Church, where a service of thanksgiving was [held]. At the conclusion of the service, the Town Council returned to the Municipal Chambers and appropriate toasts were drunk.'

— MAY 9TH —

1800: On this day, a meeting of the town's Justices of the Peace was held, at which 'it was represented by Mr. Staig, Provost of the burgh, that, owing to the deficiency of last year's crop, and to other causes, the scarcity of provisions, particularly oatmeal and potatoes, had been severely felt by the inhabitants of the town and neighbourhood who, although willing to pay a price in proportion to such deficiency, were unable to procure a competency for their subsistence.

That the consequences of this want of provisions had, for some time past, manifested themselves in the complaints of the people, and had, upon some occasions, produced tumultuous meetings, riotous assemblies, illegal and unwarrantable proceedings which, upon trials before a Court of Law, must involve the parties in very severe penalties. His object in making this representation was to induce the Meeting to take the situation of the inhabitants into their consideration, and, if possible, to devise some legal means for their relief.

The Meeting having accordingly taken Mr. Staig's Representations into their most serious consideration, they … resolve to use every means in their power for relieving the necessities of the inhabitants, and restoring peace and tranquillity to the town and neighbourhood.' (*Dumfries Weekly Journal*)

~ MAY 10TH ~

1803: On this day, the following notice was published: 'Whereas a letter from Lord Pelham, one of his Majesty's Principal Secretaries of State, transmitted by the Lord Lieutenant of the County (setting forth that considerable Desertion prevailed among the Forces), was laid before the General Meeting of the County, on 30th April last, when it was resolved that Advertisements or Notices should be affixed upon all the Parish Churches and other public places, requiring every person within this County to be aiding and assisting in apprehending such Deserters as are now in the County, or may hereafter be discovered, in order that they may be returned to the several Regiments to which they belong, and offering a Reward of Twenty Shillings to everyone who shall apprehend or inform against any Deserter, so that he may be taken into Custody. All persons are therefore strictly required not to harbour any Deserter, under the penalties prescribed by law, but to use their utmost endeavours for the discovery of suspected persons, and to give notice thereof to the nearest Magistrate or Constable, in order to their being taken up; and the Constables are hereby commanded to exert themselves in putting the law against Desertion into execution.' (*Dumfries Weekly Journal*)

~ MAY 11TH ~

1910: On this day, the *Dumfries and Galloway Standard* carried the following report: 'Soon after the receipt at the "Standard" Office of the message announcing the death of King Edward, Provost Lennox caused the Dumfries town bells to be tolled, and this was continued at intervals throughout the night and during Saturday. Flags were flown at half-mast at the Town Hall, Midsteeple, County Court-house, Maxwelltown Town Hall, and numerous other buildings; and the display of black in drapers' windows, and mourning boards in the windows of these and other establishments, symbolised the all-prevailing feeling of sorrow. A special meeting of Dumfries Town Council was held on Saturday forenoon, amid every manifestation of mourning. The tables in the new Town Hall were draped in black. Provost Lennox, who wore his robes and chain of office presided. Mr. R.A. Grierson, [Town Clerk] then read the following: "The Provost, Magistrates and Councillors of the royal burgh of Dumfries desire, on behalf of the community of the burgh, to join with their fellow citizens throughout the whole Empire in expressing their feelings of profound sorrow in the overwhelming loss which the British people have sustained in the death of our most gracious Sovereign, King Edward the Seventh."'

— MAY 12TH —

1868: On this day, nineteen-year-old Robert Smith was the last person to be publicly executed in Scotland, when he was hanged (for murder) outside Dumfries Prison in Buccleuch Street: 'Askern, the executioner, approached [Smith] and hurriedly drew the white cap over the head of the condemned man. Then a fearful cry issued from the crowd, many of whom turned their backs on the terrible spectacle, and literally ran from the revolting scene. As motionless as a statue the unhappy youth stood upon the fatal drop, while the executioner placed the rope round his neck. And now occurred what was perhaps the most trying part of the horrible business. Askern discovered that the rope had not been fairly adjusted, and he removed it from the convict's neck. In a second or two it was replaced, but what an agony of mind the poor wretch must have suffered in that brief period of suspense. The executioner then shook hands with Smith and, stepping back, drew the bolt, and the criminal was sent to another than an earthly tribunal … At the end of about half-an-hour the body was cut down, and it was then seen that the noose had come in front of the left ear instead of behind, and that the jaw-bone had caught upon the rope – thus occasioning an unusual prolongation of life.' (*Dumfries and Galloway Standard*)

~ MAY 13TH ~

1885: On this day, the *Dumfries and Galloway Standard* reported the arrival of a 'diorama' at the Mechanics' Hall: 'The pictures, which are all on a large scale and artistically got up, embrace views from many lands, and convey a wonderfully vivid impression of the scenes which they represent. Foremost of interest are those associated with the recent military operations in Egypt and the Soudan, and views of the two chief Afghan towns. Several of the more striking incidents of the campaign are portrayed in a very realistic manner. Ingenious mechanical effects are at times introduced with telling results. This is notably the case in the scene representing the entry of General Roberts and his troops into Cabul. This is one of the finest spectacular portions of the entertainment, and the effect is greatly heightened by the appropriate and varied military music supplied by the highly-trained orchestra, the members of which are for the time out of sight. Intervals in the dioramic entertainment are happily filled up with short performances on hand-bells and other musical instruments, a series of clever conjuring tricks, a capital exhibition of ventriloquism, and some light burlesque.'

― MAY 14TH ―

1833: On this day, the following particulars were recounted in the *Dumfries and Galloway Courier*: 'We were shown the other day a chair fashioned according to the taste of the olden time, and said to be the identical one used as a State-chair by the Young Chevalier during the short stay he made in Dumfries, in December 1745, while returning from his romantic but ill-fated expedition into England. Our citizens are sufficiently aware that the Prince occupied that house in High Street, now possessed by Mr. Wilson as the Commercial Inn – then, we believe, the residence of a private gentleman named Lowden, and, in all likelihood, at that period, the most genteel edifice in our gude town. The chair we speak of, which adorned originally the principal room of Mr. Lowden's mansion, was purchased at a considerable period after the rebellion, at a sale of that gentleman's moveables, by a Mrs. Welsh –well-known to our fathers as the hostess of a respectable tavern in Queensberry Street. This old lady gifted it as a precious relic of the Prince to a respectable female, now deceased, and wife of an old citizen still living, from whose recital we detail these particulars.'

— MAY 15TH —

1838: On this day, the *Dumfries Times* reported a shocking occurrence: 'A. Roddan and C. Graham were assisting some persons, who were employed in clipping sheep, the property of Mr. McGill, innkeeper, New Bridge Inn ... While the clippers were at dinner, Roddan took a pair of shears into his hand, and proceeded to try to clip a sheep. Graham then said to him that he was performing the work improperly, but Roddan continued clipping. Graham repeated his former statement, whereupon Roddan became enraged, and, in the paroxysm of wrath, threw the shears at Graham, which penetrated the lower part of the abdomen. We are not aware what attention, or if indeed any, was shown to Graham on his being wounded, but we understand he was not conveyed home till a considerable time afterwards. On being brought home, medical aid was immediately applied, but from the loss of blood, and perhaps other circumstances with which we are unacquainted, it proved unavailing, as the sufferer expired about 5 o'clock in the afternoon. After the decease had taken place, Roddan was apprehended and lodged in Maxwelltown Jail. He is about 18 years of age; the deceased was about 12.'

~ MAY 16TH ~

1900: On this day it was reported that 'a fatal accident of a very distressing kind occurred last night in Leafield Road, to a young man named Robert Grant, who was in attendance on a traction engine belonging to Mr. A. Derby. Grant was what is known as "third man", his duty being to walk beside the engine; but he had temporarily changed places with the second man, and was riding on the engine. When opposite Messrs. Garland and Rogers' saw-mill he stepped off; and in doing so he stumbled, and fell in front of the threshing mill which the engine was drawing. The wheels passed over the right side of his head, crushing it terribly. Information was sent of the occurrence to the burgh police office, and two constables hurried to the place with an ambulance stretcher. On arriving, they found that the unfortunate man was dead. His body was removed to the Infirmary. The house surgeon found on examination that the brain was reduced to a pulp. Deceased was about twenty years of age, and was in lodgings on Whitesands. This is the third fatality that the Messrs. Derby have unfortunately had in connection with their engines in recent years.' (*Dumfries and Galloway Standard*)

~ MAY 17TH ~

1813: On this day, the following notice was printed in the *Dumfries Weekly Journal*: 'At a General Meeting of His Majesty's lieutenancy of the County of Dumfries, held at Dumfries on the seventh day of April last, for putting in execution the Acts of Parliament relating to the Local Militia of the said County, it was agreed that the Nithsdale Regiment should be called out, trained and exercised for the space of fourteen days, exclusive of the days of arrival and departure from the place of exercise; and that the men shall assemble at the military store in English Street (late Lochmabengate) in the town of Dumfries, at ten o'clock forenoon of Tuesday the 1st day of June next, when and where they will receive their billets, &c., which order has been approved by his Royal Highness the Prince Regent. Of all which the persons enrolled to serve in the said regiment are to take notice, and to attend at the time and place above-mentioned, for the purposes specified in the said Acts of Parliament, as they shall answer for the consequences. If any Local Militiaman, not incapacitated by infirmity, shall fail to appear at the time and place mentioned, he will be deemed a deserter, and punished as such.'

⊸ MAY 18TH ⊸

1802: On this day, the following notice appeared in the *Dumfries Weekly Journal*: 'The Justices of the Peace ... notify that by the Acts of the Parliaments of Scotland, ALL PERSONS begging out of their own parish are to be apprehended and committed to the House of Correction, and kept at hard labour for at least one month. And Vagrants, Sturdy Beggars, all who can give no good account of themselves, soldiers and sailors begging who have no regular passes, Jugglers and Players at Unlawful Games, and all who have no fixed residence and employment, or who are idle and disorderly, are to be committed to prison, whipt, and banished from the County.

All Justices of the Peace and Constables are bound, by their Oath of Office, to execute these laws, so far as is in their power; and all worthy Householders ought to be aiding and assisting in apprehending such Vagrants and Beggars, that they and others may be the more able to exercise their benevolence and charity to the poor and distressed of their own parish, whom they are bound by the laws of God and of their country to assist and relieve.'

⏤ May 19th ⏤

1812: On this day, it was reported that 'the Magistrates of Dumfries, having taken into their most serious consideration an alarm, which seems to have been industriously propagated, that there is a scarcity of provisions in the country, which the Magistrates, from all the information they have been able to collect, cannot believe to be the case, and as has unhappily taken place in various parts of the Kingdom, riot and disturbance may be the consequence, in which many innocent individuals may be involved in trouble and distress; to avoid these evils, the Magistrates have resolved to invite, and do hereby solicit, the Gentlemen Farmers, and all others who may have grain and other provisions in their custody, which they can spare from their own families, to send the same to the market of Dumfries weekly, in order to be exposed for sale to the inhabitants, at fair and reasonable prices. And if this solicitation is complied with, the Magistrates will use every means in their power to protect the persons and properties of all Farmers and others, who may bring in provisions for the supply of the town's inhabitants, from injury, insult, or dilapidation.' (*Dumfries Weekly Journal*)

~ May 20th ~

1922: On this day, the *Dumfries and Galloway Courier and Herald* reported that 'Mr. Easterbrook, the forceful speaker of the Reconstruction Society, has held meetings every night during this week, and his addresses have been very refreshing compared with the usual street corner oratory. On Sunday, he competed pretty successfully with the local Communists at the Dockhead. Both parties tried to draw the crowd from the other and, on the whole, Mr. Easterbrook had the stronger pull. A noticeable feature of his meetings when compared with those of his opponents, is the more intelligent class of people who attended them. Last night, another meeting was held in Queensberry Square. The opposition was well represented and by no means silent, and the speaker repeatedly discomfited them to the amusement of the audience, by apt repartee and his clear and quick analysis of their panaceas for the ills of the world. Broadly, he denounced nationalisation and such Socialistic schemes as unworkable, on account of their innate antagonism to human nature. They would destroy the individual by wiping out ambition; all that they would create would be mediocrity. On the other hand, private enterprise stimulated the individual to effort, and this developed him as nothing else would.'

~ MAY 21ST ~

1845: On this day, the following report appeared in the *Dumfries and Galloway Standard*: 'We have heard enough of Metropolitan Golgothas, with their horrid details of exhumed and half-decayed corpses, and the noxious effluvia produced by the putrefaction of the dead, contaminating the atmosphere and affecting the health of the living. Such things may occur in a great city … but we did not suppose that in our own church-yards any such thing could occur as prematurely disturbing the remains of the dead. It appears, however, that St. Michael's burying-ground is much too crowded, and that interments have often to be made in graves not sufficiently ripe. From this cause, a disgraceful and revolting circumstance has occurred within the last few days which has created no little sensation in the town. On Sabbath last, the greater part of a human body, which appeared to be that of a young female, was discovered lying among the tomb-stones in St. Michael's church-yard. It seems that the sexton had removed it from a grave he had opened a day or two previous, but, from culpable neglect, had not reinterred it when the grave was closed.'

~ MAY 22ND ~

1810: On this day, it was announced that 'the Anniversary of the late Right Hon. William Pitt is to be celebrated in the King's Arms Tavern here, on Monday the 28th current, when the Friends of that most illustrious Statesman will have an opportunity of testifying their respect for his memory. Gentlemen are requested to apply for tickets on or before Saturday the 26th instant ... that the number may be ascertained, and matters so arranged as to give perfect satisfaction. Colonel Sharpe of Hoddom will be in the Chair. Dinner to be on the table exactly at four o'clock.' (*Dumfries Weekly Journal*)

***

1839: Also on this day, the following notice appeared: 'A Meeting of the Magistrates, Heritors, and Kirk-Session of the Burgh and Parish of Dumfries, will be held in St. Michael's Church, upon Saturday next, at 12 o'clock noon, when the List of the Poor for the said Burgh and Parish will be taken up, and due provision made for the aliment and keeping of the legal paupers thereof, for the year current from the 1st day of June next, till the first day of June 1840 years; and also to consider and resolve upon all necessary and expedient business, relative to the management of the Poor.' (*Dumfries Times*)

~ May 23rd ~

1942: On this day, 'a beautiful model of a Viking ship, which has been presented to the burgh of Dumfries by the Norwegian community in the town, was formally handed over to Provost Dobie at a pleasant little ceremony in the Municipal Chambers yesterday forenoon. The model had been executed by two members of the Norwegian army. The gift was presented on behalf of the Norwegians by Major Myrseth, who emphasised that it was being gifted on the occasion of Warship Week as an expression of the appreciation of the Norwegians to the people of the burgh for the kindliness and friendship which has been shown to them during the two years they had been in the town.

Mr. McKerrow [curator of the Burgh Museum] said that the Norwegians, who had so deeply entrenched themselves in the affections of Dumfries people, were and would be looked upon as citizens of the burgh. He was reminded that the first time a King Haakon of Norway came to Scotland, about 1200, was when the Norsemen landed at Largs, in an endeavour to capture Scotland. Today, the Norwegians had come on a different errand, to join with the Scots in the fight for freedom.' (*Dumfries and Galloway Standard*)

~ MAY 24TH ~

2008: On this day, the town's football team, Queen of the South, travelled from their home ground at Palmerston Park to the internationally famous Hampden Park in Glasgow to play in the 123rd Scottish Cup Final, after having beaten Dundee and Aberdeen in the quarter- and semi-finals along the way. Also travelling to Hampden Park on this day, of course, were thousands of the team's home supporters. It was the first time that the club (founded in 1919) had, in its long history, played in the Scottish Cup Final, while their opponents, Rangers, on the other hand, were making their fiftieth appearance. In the event, the Dumfries side lost the match 2–3. Although 2–0 down at half-time, Queen of the South managed to equalise during the second half, before Rangers scored what proved to be the winning goal with 18 minutes of the match remaining. Nevertheless, the day was one of great celebration in the town, and the occasion was a source of much local pride.

The players made an open-top bus parade through the town on the following day, when thousands of supporters took to the streets of Dumfries to celebrate their local team's great achievement in reaching the final of the Scottish Cup.

~ MAY 25TH ~

1889: On this day, the following article was published: 'Thursday last was the day recommended by the Town Council for the celebration of the Queen's Birthday in Dumfries, but only a limited number of the shopkeepers closed their places of business, and there was no public celebration of any kind. The banks and public offices were as usual closed, as were also the newspaper offices, and the special facilities offered to holiday-makers by the railway companies were therefore taken advantage of to some extent. The bells in the Midsteeple tower were rung at midday, and again at six o'clock in the evening, and several flags were hoisted during the day. The Dumfries Volunteers assembled on Kingholm Merse in the evening, where they practised the new attack. The men then marched to High Street, headed by the band, and the usual volley firing took place in presence of a considerable crowd of spectators. Hearty cheers were given by the Volunteers for Her Majesty, and the National Anthem was played by the band. The Maxwelltown Volunteers marched to the Old Bridge last night, at the conclusion of an adjutant's drill, and fired a feu de joie. The banks of the Nith on either side were lined with spectators for a considerable distance.' (*Dumfries and Galloway Standard*)

— MAY 26TH —

1845: On this day, the *Dumfries and Galloway Standard* reported that 'between five and six o'clock [in the afternoon], a fire broke out in the centre kiln, connected with the corn-mills belonging to the Burgh of Dumfries. The fire originated from a strong gust of wind, which, on opening the door, rushed into the place containing the kiln fire, and carrying it upwards to the corn that was being dried, it became suddenly ignited, and the fire ascending laid hold of the roof, which was soon involved in flames. The wind was blowing a strong breeze from the east, and the flames spread with great rapidity, and there was every appearance of the whole of the range of buildings being speedily reduced to ashes, and the adjoining property placed in the most imminent danger. Fortunately, however, the alarm was immediately given, and Inspector Newall, and the police with the fire engines, were quickly on the spot, and the utmost exertions were used, which were happily successful, in arresting the progress of the devouring element, with the destruction of the kiln in which the fire originated, and about 70 bushels of corn belonging to Mr. Houston, Broomrigg, Holywood.'

~ MAY 27TH ~

1657: 'Extract from the *Dumfries Burgh Treasurer's Book* of this day's date: Detailed items of expenditure incurred at the burning of two women convicted of witchcraft: "For 38 load of peitts to burn the two women, £3 12*s* (Scots). Given to William Edgar for one tar barrell, 12*s*; for one herring barrell, 14*s*. Given to John Shotrick, for carrying the twa barrells to the pledge house, 6s. Given to the four officers that day that the witches was burnt, at the provest and bayillis command, 24*s*. Given to Thomas Anderson for the two stoups and the two steaves (to which the women were tied), 30*s*."' (Maxwell Wood, J., *Witchcraft and Superstitious Record in the South Western District of Scotland*, 1911)

1885: Also on this day, the *Dumfries and Galloway Standard* reported on 'Servants' "Flitting Day"': 'Yesterday was the WhitSunday removal term for servants in this district, and also for tenants in the country. In the afternoon, there were large numbers of servants in the town, doing their shopping, and the officials at the passenger station had their duties increased by the piles of boxes that passed through their hands.'

1885: 'THAUMA: This "mystery" is holding daily receptions in Greyfriars Hall, and receives numerous visitors. What *The Times* calls a "modern miracle" and the *Morning Advertiser* "a marvellous creation of genius", must be well worth a visit.' (*Dumfries and Galloway Standard*)

~ MAY 28TH ~

1845: On this day, the following article was printed: 'The inhabitants of our good town have, during the last few days, been equally delighted and astonished with the exhibition of the stupendous skeleton of a whale, and certainly a more interesting and surprising spectacle cannot well be conceived, or one more calculated to fill the mind with wonder and admiration for the works of the Creator. This "monster of the deep" was found off Plymouth in 1831, when it measured 102 feet in length, 75 in circumference, and weighed 200 tons. The skeleton is in a state of excellent preservation, and its different parts, and the natural history of the animal, are excellently described by the exhibitor. Besides the whale, which is of itself sufficiently attractive, there are in the exhibition several other skeletons and a number of natural curiosities. We were particularly struck with the appearance of two Peruvian mummies, a male and female, supposed to have been impaled in a cave 300 years ago, the victims of Pizarro's cruelty. We have much pleasure in recommending an early visit to this very interesting exhibition, as we understand it remains but a short time in town.' (*Dumfries and Galloway Standard*)

~ May 29th ~

1833: On this day, the following notice appeared in the *Dumfries Times*: 'Mr Boyle, Professor of the Science of Singing (London and Edinburgh), begs to intimate his arrival in Dumfries, where he will remain for a few months only. Italian, English and Scotch Music taught in the present fashionable taste. Mr. B. is a pupil of the late Signor Garcia, Principal Singer at the Italian Opera Houses of London and Paris; and also of Signor Vercellini, Singing-Master to the late Princess Charlotte. He was educated for a Concert Singer, which bespeaks his capability of giving example as well as precept so necessary for the rapid advancement of amateurs. Gentlemen are assured they may learn very difficult songs under Mr. B's tuition, without being in the least way musicians.'

1833: Also on this day, the same paper advertised that 'David Hunter & Co. beg leave to intimate to the Nobility, Gentry and Public of Dumfries that they have commenced business in the Hat line, with a new and splendid assortment of every article connected with the Trade.

D. H. & Co. particularly call the attention of the public to their Short Napped Beaver Hat, price 20*s*, which for colour, lustre, elasticity, shape and durability, excels anything hitherto offered for sale at the money.'

~ May 30th ~

1705: On this day, the foundation stone of the Midsteeple was laid. The building was completed two years later and restored in 1909, with further major renovation work being carried out in 2008. It stands in the middle of the High Street and is one of the town's distinctive features. The Midsteeple has served over the years as a municipal building, courthouse and prison. Traditionally, its precincts have always been a rallying point for the people of the town; a place of ceremony and festival. During the eighteenth century, the cattle drovers of Galloway gathered here when passing through Dumfries, while taking their beasts on the long journey south to market. Following his death, Robert Burns's body was taken from his home and placed in the courtroom of the Midsteeple, where it lay before his funeral. A year earlier, the poet had mentioned the Midsteeple in his patriotic ballad 'Does Haughty Gaul Invasion Threat?'

> Who will not sing God Save the King
> Shall hang as high's the steeple;
> But while we sing God Save the King,
> We'll ne'er forget the people!

─ MAY 31ST ─

1913: On this day, 'a very impressive ceremony, and one which attracted much public attention, took place, when the handsome memorial which has been erected on the Dock Park in honour of John Law Hume, a bandsman, and Thomas Mullin, a steward, natives respectively of Dumfries and Maxwelltown, who perished in the "Titanic" disaster in April of last year, and who were buried in Halifax, Canada, was unveiled by Provost Thomson in the presence of a very large crowd of spectators. The memorial, which has been erected in the centre of the park a little to the north of the bandstand, commands the attention of all passers-by.

Beautiful summer weather favoured the unveiling ceremony, and a great crowd of townspeople assembled on the Dock Park. A large number of excursionists from Coatbridge, who were spending the day in the town, also witnessed the ceremony. During the forenoon the flags of the Midsteeple and the Town Hall hung at half-mast, and before the hour of the ceremony the town bells were tolled.

The proceedings terminated with the singing of the National Anthem, and the band thereafter played lively music, while the bells peeled forth from the Midsteeple.' (*Dumfries and Galloway Standard*)

‒ June 1st ‒

1904: On this day, it was reported that 'A good deal of interest was created in High Street on Saturday, when, in the neighbourhood of the fountain, a couple of policemen fastened upon a man and removed him to the police office. The police had been on the lookout for street betting, which is very quietly done by the initiated going up to a "bookie" – generally a most inoffensive-like person – and passing over their slips of paper recording their fancy, and, of course, the necessary "rhino". The thing is done all "sub rosa", and it is alleged that this form of gambling is very common in the town, and sapping at the root of the morale of the people, and especially of the working classes.

On Monday morning, a coach wheeler of St. Michael Street was charged in the Police Court that "being a person who conducts business in betting, he did, on Saturday last, in the vicinity of the fountain, engage in betting, and did stand and loiter about said street for the purpose of enabling other persons, to the complainer unknown, to engage in betting, contrary to the Burgh Police (Scotland) Act. Having pleaded Not Guilty, the accused was released on bail of £5, and the case was adjourned."' (*Dumfries and Galloway Courier and Herald*)

— June 2nd —

1778: On this day, the following advertisement appeared in the *Dumfries Weekly Journal*: 'David Pagan, merchant in Dumfries, informs the public at large that the business will now be carried on at the shop, south side of the plain-stones, nearly opposite the Coffee House, where are to be sold wholesale or retail, at the lowest prices, a variety of articles in the woollen and linen drapery and millinery way; such as Broadcloths, Plains, Duffields, Hunters, German Serges, Friezes, Velvets, Velverets, Shags, Cordurells, King's Cords, Fustians, Jeans, Lastings, Men's Hats, Shallons, plated or metal Buttons, Twists, Mohair, Sewing Silks, Buckrams, Glazed Linens, Knee Garters, Bombazeens, Crapes, Dorfeteens, Poplins, Printed Cottons, Durants, Callimancoes, Flannels, Demities, Checks, Cotton and Silk Handkerchiefs, Muslins, Plain Lawns, Long Lawns, Cambrics, Satins, Persians, Silk and Thread, Laces and Edgings, Plain and Figured Gauzes, Gloves, Mitts, Ribbons, Worsted Caps … They manufacture and sell wholesale at their workhouse, thread stockings of different kinds. They also frame stockings in the customary way and, as they intend doing it for ready money only, they flatter themselves that they will be able to do the work in such time and in such a manner as will give general satisfaction.'

~ JUNE 3RD ~

1839: On this day, the Crichton Institution for Lunatics was opened (and its first patient was admitted on the following day). 'The great principles upon which this Institution will be conducted,' declared a contemporary advertisement, 'are justice, benevolence, and occupation … The Patients, in so far as is consistent with their condition, will be induced to regard the Asylum as a home, and those to whose care they are confided as friends and companions. The Resident Medical Officer and Matron will associate constantly with the Patients; direct their pursuits and employments; suggest and join in their amusements; conciliating their affections and obtaining their confidence, by treating them on rational and enlightened principles; by undeviating kindness, and by a scrupulous attention to the gratification of all their desires, whenever these are compatible with, or conducive to, health and tranquillity. Great care has been taken in the selection of the attendants, to secure persons of irreproachable character, good education, and of mild but firm disposition. Whenever coercion is unavoidable, solitary confinement, in padded rooms, is resorted to, in preference to any of the other modes of physical restraint, which have been so long in use, as being of a less irritating character, and in no way interfering with the perfect performance of all the bodily functions.'

~ JUNE 4TH ~

1787: On this day, Robert Burns made his first appearance in Dumfries: 'He came, on invitation, to be made an honorary burgess; neither the givers nor the receiver of the privilege dreaming, at that date, that he was destined to become an inhabitant of the town. All honour to the Council that they thus promptly recognised the genius of the poet. Provost William Clark shaking hands with the newly-made burgess, and wishing him joy, when he presented himself in the venerable blue coat and yellow vest that Nasmyth has rendered familiar, would make a good subject for a painter able to realise the characteristics of such a scene.' (McDowall, William, *History of Dumfries* (2nd Edn., 1873))

1793: Also on this day, with the French Revolution in full swing, George III's birthday prompted a demonstration by the people of Dumfries in support of the established order: 'An unusual display of loyalty eminently manifested itself through all ranks of people in this place. It is but justice to notice the ardent loyalty of the rising generation, who, having procured two effigies of Tom Paine [the revolutionary, and author of *Rights of Man* (1791)], paraded with them through the different streets of this burgh; and at six o'clock in the evening consigned them to the bonfires, amid the patriotic applause of the surrounding crowd.' (*Dumfries Weekly Journal*)

~ JUNE 5TH ~

1810: The *Dumfries Weekly Journal*, of this date, announced a forthcoming performance at the town's theatre of 'Mr. Cartwright's Musical Glasses and Philosophical Fireworks; a unique entertainment consisting of a performance on his improved Grand Set of Musical Glasses in three parts. A variety of English, Irish and Scots airs, of which Part One is to conclude with Handel's Concert Minuet; Part Two to conclude with Marshall Saxe's Minuet, with Variations by Cartwright, and Part Three to conclude with the Overture to the Poor Soldier by Shield. The whole to conclude with "God Save the Queen". The perfection of the Harmonics, or Musical Glasses, has been the object of Mr. Cartwright's study for several years; and, he is emboldened to say, that he has been honoured in the performance with the applause of the most scientific performers of Music.

The evening's amusement will close with an elegant display of Philosophical Fireworks by Mr. Cartwright Junior, which are both novel and splendid. They are produced by inflammable air alone, totally free from any obnoxious quality that can offend the sense in the most remote degree, yet they display several thousand Figures, variegated, beautiful, and astonishing.'

— JUNE 6TH —

1829: On this day, the charismatic and somewhat controversial Scottish theologian Edward Irving visited Dumfries, en route from the General Assembly. 'He arrived by the mail coach at six o'clock in the morning, and prepared himself for meeting a company of clergymen at Miss Goldie's, Summerhill. The same evening he preached at St. Michael's Church. "Next day [he noted in his diary], I preached in the Academy grounds, upon the banks of the Nith, to about ten thousand people." Impartial spectators, however, estimated the crowd at six thousand or seven thousand people. The preaching tent was placed midway between the Assembly Rooms and the Academy buildings. The Cameronian Church was not there then, nor the wall around the Academy grounds. The whole space was a mass of people; and on the outskirts of the great multitude there were over a dozen carriages drawn up, the dickies and tops of which were covered with listeners. All the churches in the town were nearly empty. There were only two houses built then near to the Assembly Rooms, and Mr. McGowan, architect, who had acquired most of the building ground there, named the new street Irving Street, in honour of the occasion.' (Mackie, Charles, (Ed.), *Dumfries and Galloway Notes and Queries* (1913))

‒ JUNE 7TH ‒

1952: On this day, the *Dumfries and Galloway Standard* printed the following two reports on an outbreak of foot-and-mouth disease:

'Mr. H. George McKerrow, secretary of Dumfries Cornets' Club … decided to carry through the ceremony of Riding of the Marches this year, although in a restricted itinerary. Mr. McKerrow communicated with the agricultural authorities, explaining that the club had no desire to aggravate the condition created by the outbreak of foot-and-mouth disease, but would like even in a restricted form to maintain the continuity of the ancient custom of Riding the Marches. He was informed that there would be no objection, provided the riders confined themselves to the highways and kept off the fields. The club readily agreed to fall in with this arrangement [abandoning] the itinerary from Maidenbower through the Crichton Farm, Bankend Road, and the gallop over the Kingholm.'

—‒—

'With four outbreaks of foot-and-mouth disease in the county within two days, the directors of the Dumfries Agricultural Society decided on Wednesday to cancel the county show fixed for July 26th. A sports meeting at Crocketford, a young farmers' field day at Lockerbie, a harvesting machinery demonstration at Auldgrith, and a farmers' union outing are also among the events cancelled.'

— June 8th —

1858: On this day, the *Dumfries and Galloway Courier* printed the following item: 'The Russian Gun – This piece of ordnance has now been for a fortnight [positioned where] it ought not to be allowed to remain … [there is] an impression of unmitigated ugliness in the thing itself and entire unsuitability to the prominent position it occupies. Our authorities deserve every credit for the trouble they took in procuring an interesting memorial to the Crimean campaign, but the error committed has been in undue estimation of its value, and want of consideration as to its appearance in so prominent a position as that fixed upon. No one we suppose could have conceived that the effect would be so bad as it is, but now that this has been seen and recognised, the sooner the intended ornament is removed to some less conspicuous position the better. The Dean of Guild should be instructed to deal with this as he would or should with any other nuisance.'

N.B. The Russian Gun is a cannon. After being brought to Dumfries from Crimea, it had been placed in the town's Church Square. It is now housed in the grounds of Dumfries Museum.

─ JUNE 9TH ─

1840: On this day, the *Dumfries Times* reported a 'Trial of Suspected Dogs': 'James Kerr and John Payne, fleshers here, have had for some time a flock of sheep grazing on Priestlands. Early on the morning of the 25th ult., Mr. Murray, farmer, Conhuith, which is divided from Priestlands by the Cargen Pow, discovered sixteen of these sheep in that water. He next found nineteen more, in Conhuith meadow, dead and sadly torn. It having been guessed that this ruinous work was done by vicious dogs, and the dog of a person in Dumfries having been seen coming home from that quarter in a bedraggled state that morning, it was suggested that an emetic be administered to the dog in question, and also to another dog which belongs to a person near the scene of carnage, to see if they should vomit any wool. If they did so, they might immediately be shot as destructive pests. The Dumfries dog could not be made to vomit. The other dog did so but … no wool was discharged. Of course, there was no apparent cause to destroy either of the dogs.'

~ June 10th ~

1667: On this day, 'the [Town] Council resolved to give effect to a permissive law adopted by the Convention of Burghs, in favour of making uniform all the weights and measures used in the town – the weights to be according to the Lanark standard; the firlot [a unit for the measurement of grain], according to the Linlithgow standard; the ell-wand, rule and foot measure to be furnished by the Edinburgh Dean of Guild; and a measure called a guage, or jug, to be made after the Stirling model.' (McDowall, William, *History of Dumfries* (2nd Edn., 1873))

1794: The following notice appeared in the *Dumfries Weekly Journal*: 'Wanted for the Dumfriesshire Light Cavalry, from one hundred to one hundred and twenty horses. Those who are willing to contract for any number of the above, may apply to David Staig Esq., Provost of Dumfries, who will show a pattern horse. The horses are to be from fourteen-and-a-half hands to fifteen hands one inch high. From five years complete to seven years off. Dark Bays, Browns, Blacks or Chestnuts.'

~ JUNE 11TH ~

1795: On this day, the *Dumfries Weekly Journal* reported that 'as there have been different reports of the mutiny which took place here [on this day], among the soldiers of the 1st Fencible Regiment, we have it in our power from authority to give a true state of that transaction.

One of the men having been confined for impropriety in the field when under arms, several of his comrades resolved to release him, for which purpose they … endeavoured to force the guard-room, but they were repelled by the Adjutant and Officer on guard, who made the ringleader a prisoner. The Commanding Officer of the regiment immediately ordered a court martial. When the prisoners were remanded back from the court to the guard-room, their escort was attacked by 50 or 60 of the soldiers, with fixed bayonet. The escort, consisting of a corporal and six men, charged them in return, and would not have parted with their prisoners, but at the interjection of the Sergeant-Major, who thought resistance against such numbers was in vain.' Eventually, the prisoners 'were paraded at the Dock, the mutiny articles read, and a forcible speech made to them by the Lieutenant Colonel. They were then ordered, as a mark of returning duty and allegiance, to face to the right and march under the colours, which was instantly complied with.'

~ June 12th ~

1850: On this day, the *Dumfries and Galloway Standard* reported a disturbance on the streets of the town: 'It appears that last Wednesday night a tryst had been set by two individuals to have a pugilistic encounter on the Green Sands. This got wind, and a crowd collected on the spot, and a party of the police went down to stop the proceedings. However, the combatants did not show face. The crowds dispersed although, it seems, not swiftly enough for the police, who tried to hurry people along. As a result, arrests were made of several individuals, who had complained to the officers of the law about their officious behaviour. This only served to inflame matters further. Those arrested were lodged in the station-house by the Steeple. By this time it was nine o'clock, and a crowd of perhaps four hundred in number occupied the vicinity of the station-house ... though they did not make any actual breach of the peace. Superintendant McNab and some of his men were meanwhile parading in front of the lock-up, and were occasionally hooted. Sometimes, when the challenge was thus given by the crowd, the police pounced, till eventually they had their list of prisoners swelled up to six.'

⚊ June 13th ⚊

1908: On this day, the *Dumfries and Galloway Courier and Herald* reported that 'at Dumfries Sheriff Court on Wednesday, two local men were charged with having, on Sunday 10th May, used the Kingholm Merse for the purpose of playing cards. Constable Hogarth stated that about 3 o'clock in the afternoon, he was on duty at Kingholm Merse along with Constable Begg. They were in plain clothes. Seeing a crowd of men playing cards, they concealed themselves. Among the men were the two accused. They were playing for money, which was in their caps. The constables, after watching for a time went forward, but the accused ran away. Constables Hogarth and Begg later found cards in the possession of both of the accused. This practice of card playing was very frequent on a Sunday, and the townspeople complained of it.

The Sheriff said he had very little doubt about the matter. It appeared that great annoyance had been caused to people by card playing in public places on Sundays, and that the bye-laws in connection with the matter were necessary. This was the first case that had been brought up and, that being so, he thought a small fine would meet the case.'

— JUNE 14TH —

1965: On this day, the fondly remembered 'Paddy' line closed. 'After 100 years of service,' Sheila Mair reported in the *Dumfries and Galloway Standard*, 'there was a perceptible sadness in the air at Dumfries railway station … as passengers boarded the Stranraer train for the last time … The train was crammed with railway enthusiasts, including people who were travelling simply because it was the "last time" … Regular travellers between Dumfries and Stranraer were in short supply, but this was not surprising as it was a Saturday. During the week 20 or so people embark at Dalbeattie and travel to Castle Douglas, but the train, especially in winter, often completes the journey with few passengers.

On its way back to Dumfries the train was greeted everywhere with affection and enthusiasm. Men working on the line stood bareheaded and waved farewell as it thundered past. In response, there came from the engine a series of long, mournful whistles which rose clearly above the steady beat of the engine and the sound of flying wheels … The number of men made redundant by the closure was 150, but of these most had found other employment or accepted the resettlement sum offered by B.R.'

⤙ June 15th ⤚

1838: On this day, the *Dumfriesshire and Galloway Herald and Advertiser* reported some of the findings of a recent enquiry into the condition of handloom weavers in the town: 'It appeared that the number of weavers at present belonging to the town and its vicinity was about 450, and that on account of dullness of trade it was decreasing; but that formerly ... it was about 500, and that upwards of half this number were Irish; that the great portion of the items manufactured were ginghams; that good operatives, after working 12 hours a day, and paying for room rent, winding of "pirns", candles &c., could earn, on an average, only 4*s* each per week, and inferior hands less; and that there were no manufactories in town to which the children could be sent to procure themselves a livelihood, though in certain instances young females could, by flowering and "seaming" stockings, earn 2*s* per week, and thus to a certain extent benefit their parents. It also appeared that no relief had been afforded to the weavers during the stagnation of trade which took place last year; and that they had not received any portion of the funds raised, by voluntary subscription, for the relief of the poor in the town and neighbourhood last winter.'

‒ June 16th ‒

1718: On this day, 'The Tolbooth became ruinous and was ordered to be taken down. Its date is uncertain, but it is mentioned first in 1481. It was set appropriately in the market place, the centre of the town. It was a building with cellars in the basement, four shops on the ground floor, the council chamber being above these. Access to the chamber was by an outside stair at the north end, under which was another shop. It had a bell tower, a room of which was used for a prison. Originally thatched, it was slated in 1532, and had an outside clock as early as 1533, which the burgh officers were instructed to protect from meal-dust by putting a cloth over the face. The key was put to a grim use. The peats taken from peat-stealers were kindled at the Market Cross, the key was heated therein red-hot and laid on the cheeks of the thieves. [The Tolbooth] was subsequently rebuilt, being used for many years as a Council Chamber and Town Clerk's office.' (Shirley, G.W., *The Growth of a Scottish Burgh*, (Thomas Hunter, Watson and Co., 1915))

~ June 17th ~

1794: The following items of news appeared on this day in the *Dumfries Weekly Journal*:

'On Friday last, the Dumfriesshire Loyal Archers had their First Meeting on the Kingholm, in the vicinity of this town, when a number of good shots were made. The centre of the target was hit by one of the archers, at the second round; and a crow having alighted on the green, at the distance of about 200 yards from the archers, they bent their bows, and sent a flight of arrows at it – one of which, viz. the arrow of Mr. H., pinned it to the ground. After enjoying themselves for some time, and well pleased with their first essay, the members adjourned to the King's Arms tavern, where they dined, and spent the evening together, in all the mirth and harmony which always has, and, it is hoped, ever will distinguish the proceedings of the loyal and well affected part of his Majesty's subjects.'

'The signal and glorious victory [over the French navy] by the Grand Fleet under the command of Earl Howe was celebrated here in a very distinguished and loyal manner, on Saturday last. The morning was ushered in by the ringing of bells, which continued almost the whole day. At twelve o'clock noon and six in the evening, the cannon from Mount Loyal, on the opposite side of the river, announced the joyful news to the neighbouring county. In short, we never witnessed more general and real pleasure than was manifested on the occasion.'

~ June 18th ~

1810: On this day, 'a Charter was granted by King George III to Mr. Marmaduke Constable Maxwell of Terregles, as feudal superior, erecting Maxwelltown "into one free and Independent Burgh of Barony, named now and in all time coming the Burgh of Barony of Maxwelltown, with all the powers, privileges, and jurisdictions whatsoever pertaining and belonging ... to any free and independent burgh of barony which was erected in Scotland since the date of the Act of Parliament passed in the twentieth year of the reign of George III. All the male inhabitants within the prescribed territory of the said burgh, of lawful age and having right by feu disposition or a hundred years' tack of a house and garden ground, or land of the annual value of five pounds sterling, shall have the right of a burgess of voting on the day of election, and of being elected to the Corporation or Common Council, but under the following provision: None shall be elected Provost or Bailie who is not a resident burgess. The first day of election shall be on the 11th day of September 1810, and every succeeding election shall be on the 11th September annually.'"
(*Dumfries and Maxwelltown Amalgamation Souvenir Booklet*, 1929)

⚊ JUNE 19TH ⚊

1937: On this day, J.M. Barrie, the author of *Peter Pan*, died in London, and in a lengthy tribute, the *Dumfries and Galloway Courier and Herald* recalled his early years spent in Dumfries. He arrived in 1873, aged thirteen, and became a pupil at the Academy. He lived in Victoria Terrace with his brother, A. Ogilvie Barrie, who was the local HM Inspector of Schools.

'[Barrie] found fun in writing, and it was at Dumfries that he first appeared as an author. The magazine in which he made his literary debut was a manuscript production founded by his friend and schoolfellow, Wellwood Anderson, in May 1875. It was necessarily limited in circulation, and was called "The Clown". It ran to four numbers and to it Barrie contributed four articles.

It was in Dumfries also that Barrie made his first venture in playwriting, in which he afterwards achieved such worldwide renown. This was again with his friend Anderson. They were the leaders in the founding of the Dumfries Amateur Dramatic Club of those days which, after a very short run, had more distinguished patrons than any Dumfries club has had before or since ...' The following year, Barrie left Dumfries to study at Edinburgh University.

~ June 20th ~

1829: On this day, one of the town's longest-serving and more unusual prison inmates died, after spending twenty-six years in jail. James McAdam was a Chelsea Pensioner, who had been wounded in the head while serving in the American War of Independence. After his return to Scotland, he travelled the land, and is alleged to have assaulted a woman at Closeburn in July 1803, when she had refused his offer of a cake that was later found to be laced with poison. Subsequently, he was deemed insane and unfit to be tried.

A local newspaper reported that, in the later years of his confinement, 'he had the privilege of walking in the yard at his pleasure, and humanity must approve of this indulgence. Indeed, we have heard it reported that on more than one occasion he has been ordered about his business, and even put out of the jail door, but that so completely was he at home, and so much did he relish the state of captivity, which had now become a second nature to him, that he would not leave the door until he was readmitted to his old and well-known habitation.' (Mackie, Charles, (Ed.), *Dumfries and Galloway Notes and Queries* (1913))

‒ June 21st ‒

2012: On this day, the Olympic Flame visited Dumfries prior to its arrival at the Olympic Stadium in London seventy days later for the lighting of the Cauldron at the Olympic Games Opening Ceremony. It is estimated that 8,000 torchbearers were given the opportunity to carry the flame on its ten-week journey around the British Isles (during which time, it is thought, the flame came within 10 miles of 95 per cent of the population).

The route taken by the flame through Dumfries began at the town's Burns Statue at 7.50 a.m. From there it was carried down Buccleuch Street and along Whitesands, before being taken up Bank Street and into the High Street. Turning into Great King Street, the torchbearers then went by way of Loreburn Street and English Street into the Annan Road. The flame's progress through Dumfries came to an end at the Brownrigg Loaning junction, just over half-an-hour later. Despite the early start, thousands of people lined the streets to watch this once-in-a-lifetime event, and roads along the route were temporarily closed to traffic. The Olympic Torch subsequently went on to visit Annan, Eastriggs and Gretna.

⁓ June 22nd ⁓

1910: On this day, the *Dumfries and Galloway Courier and Herald* announced that 'a very unusual combination of interests – political and domestic – will be brought together in the "Suffrage Exhibition and Sale of Work", to be held in St. Mary's Hall tomorrow. Dainty embroidering and wood carvings will be on sale – in many cases the work of the versatile Suffragette; in addition, a history of the Suffrage movement will be shown in pictures, and a delightful comedy, "How the Vote was Won", will be presented by friends and sympathisers in Dumfries. The play puts the case for Woman Suffrage in a nutshell, and is at the same time deliciously funny.

The most interesting feature of the exhibits will be the prison cells. Probably few persons realise the difference between the treatment respectively of what are called "political offenders" and the women Suffragists who are sent into the second division, owing to the refusal of the Home Office to have them treated as political offenders. Here it is possible for everyone to realise exactly the extent of these differences, and the effect of the distinction made against these women. The visitor will see two prison cells. The larger cell is occupied by a political offender. The smaller cell is that of a second division prisoner, every detail being represented with the greatest accuracy.'

⁓ JUNE 23RD ⁓

1980: On this day, the actor John Laurie died. He was born in Dumfries in 1897, the son of an employee at one of the town's tweed mills. After attending Dumfries Academy, he trained to become an architect before serving in the First World War. However, Laurie turned to acting when he came back from the Front, and trained at the Central School of Speech and Drama in London. He made his professional stage debut in 1921, thus embarking on a career that would span nearly sixty years. By the outbreak of the Second World War, he had become a leading man both in London and at Stratford-upon-Avon, and had played most of the major Shakespearean roles, including Hamlet and Macbeth.

It was not long before Laurie began to appear in films as well. One of his early roles was as John, the crofter, in Alfred Hitchcock's classic *The 39 Steps* (1935). He went on to make scores of film and television appearances, before securing the part – towards the end of his career – as Private Frazer in BBC TV's Home Guard comedy *Dad's Army*, which ran originally from 1968 to 1977. Laurie's portrayal of the dour and wide-eyed undertaker made him a household name, and instantly recognisable wherever he went.

~ JUNE 24TH ~

1896: On this day, the following statistics were printed by the *Dumfries and Galloway Standard*: 'The half-yearly census of vagrants in the Burgh of Dumfries was made on Sunday night, when it was found that the total number of homeless persons within the burgh was 140. Of these, 129 were accommodated in common lodging-houses, 10 in hospitals and poorhouses, and only one slept out, on the Dock Park. Of adults, there were in all 93 males and 35 females, and the children numbered 12. There were 93 of Scotch nationality, 31 English and 16 Irish. The total of 140 is the largest which has been recorded since these enumerations were first made in 1889. In June of that year, the number of tramps found in the burgh was only 48. The highest number recorded in the intervening period was 130, for June 1894. At the December census, the number is always less than in the summer, in explanation of which it is stated that many betake themselves to England at the Christmas season, in the hope of participating in the good cheer that then prevails. A larger number are also in winter classed as permanent inmates of the workhouse.'

— JUNE 25TH —

1816: The following report was printed in the *Dumfries Weekly Journal*: 'The anniversary of the glorious and ever-memorable Battle of Waterloo – the most distinguished day in the British annals – was commemorated in this town by several private parties, and by a public dinner in the King's Arms, at which the Chair was taken by the Provost, D. Staig Esq., to whom Major Miller acted as a croupier. On the first toast being given, which was the health of our venerable Sovereign, the bells were set a-ringing, and continued during the whole of the evening. The Prince Regent's health was next drunk, amid loud applause. Many cheering and patriotic toasts followed from the Chair, particularly the Hero of the Day, WELLINGTON; Lord Hopetoun and the gallant 921; Captain Wilkie of that corps., who was present in uniform ... The Wooden Walls followed, with three times three; and the healths of Sir Robert Laurie and Captain Charles Johnston, who were present. Mr. Maitland of Eccles proposed the health of our worthy Provost for his conduct in the Chair, and for his active exertions in promoting the Waterloo Subscription.'

— JUNE 26TH —

1798: On this day, the *Dumfries Weekly Journal* printed the following warning to its readers: 'As there is a person who calls himself a Doctor, entitles himself a Physician, imitates my writings and advertises a Medicine and a Publication in a name similar to mine, and also copies my Advertisements, verbatim, from the different newspapers, several of which have been refused insertion by the Printers, as being an exact copy of what they had previously inserted for me: Against this insidious mode of conduct, Dr. Brodum requests the Public ... to pay attention to the following: That on the seal of my Medicines is the name of Dr. Brodum; and in each direction bill is my degree, authenticated by the College of Physicians, as a regular bred man; and observe it is marked with FRHS – And if the Public do not find my arms and degree (as before-mentioned) on the bottles, they may be assured they are not genuine.

Dr. Brodum's valuable Medicines, the Restorative Nervous Cordial and Botanical Syrup, and also that curious and interesting Publication, the Guide to Old Age, are sold by appointment by: Wm. Inglis, Surgeon and Druggist, Dumfries, at whose Laboratory may be had (Gratis) Pamphlets and Bills, showing the recent Cures performed by them and other celebrated Medicines.'

⁓ JUNE 27TH ⁓

1809: On this day, the *Dumfries Weekly Journal* notified its readers of a disturbing occurrence: 'A Boy Lost – Disappeared from his employment on Saturday the 20th of May last, and has not since been seen or heard of: Thomas McMaster, son of Robert McMaster, Carter in Dumfries, and Apprentice to Samuel McClellan, Stockingmaker there. The lad is fourteen years of age, pale complexion, tarnished in the face, with red hair, and blue eyes; about 5 feet 2 inches high, and of a straight and slender make. Had on when he disappeared, a short blue coat, striped blue and yellow waistcoat, blue duffle trowsers, a pair of shoes, but no stockings.

As his unaccountable disappearance has cast his parents into deep distress, any humane person who has noticed such a boy is earnestly requested to examine him narrowly, and to give immediate information to his father, the said Robert McMaster, or to Samuel McClellan, his said master, who will most cheerfully repay any expense that may attend the same.'

⁓

1820: 'Ramsay's Medicated Spice Nuts are the most pleasant, safe, and efficacious medicine for eradicating and destroying intestinal worms of every description, for clearing the bowels of the slimy matter in which they are bred, and for purifying and correcting the habit.' (*Dumfries Weekly Journal*)

— JUNE 28TH —

1838: On this day, Queen Victoria was crowned. 'The day was one of exceeding beauty, and in every respect well adapted to the amusements in which all classes were engaged. At six o'clock the bells rung a merry peal, which was duly responded to by the stentorian voices of two formidable pieces of artillery, which were brought from the grounds of the Observatory to the waterside. The banners of the Seven Trades were displayed from the Trades' Hall, and a number of other buildings, both public and private, exhibited flags and banners, while there was scarcely a private residence which was not decorated with some testimony of the loyalty of the inmates. In front of the Commercial Inn an elegant portico, composed of flowers, branches and evergreens, was erected. In front, it was surmounted by a crown of flowers, and immediately above the door was a representation of the Royal Arms, elegantly cut from a large block of freestone by our ingenious and talented townsman, Mr. Corrie. The Friars' Vennel was not behind in the universal demonstration. Through a triumphal arch were seen countless garlands, flags and banners along the whole length of the street. The Queensberry Monument was embedded in a perfect forest of bays and branches.' (*Dumfries Times*)

~ June 29th ~

1867: On this day, the *Dumfries and Galloway Standard* reported the arrival of the Carlisle otter-hounds in Dumfries. They were to be based in the town while enjoying a few days' sport in the surrounding country. 'They arrived early on Monday morning under the care of the experienced and well-known huntsman, "Sandy", and shortly after 6a.m. proceeded up the Nith accompanied by a considerable number of persons interested in the sport. A couple of otters were raised, one of which, a fine dog otter, weighing 24 pounds, and measuring four feet, was, after a most exciting chase, fairly killed.

On Tuesday morning at four o'clock, the start was made from the Globe Hotel, and shortly afterwards the hounds were cast-off at the Old College ... Up the Cairn in the early morning, Dallawoodie is reached, but not a find is made. Farther on, Clouden Mills are beat about, and the favoured isle adjoining, but disappointment again presents itself; and it is not until Irongray bridge is neared that the drag is taken up, by Old Swimmer and Ben, who follow up their clue in fine style for half-a-mile or so.' N.B. Sadly, the otter in question did not survive the day's hunting.

~ June 30th ~

1845: On this day, the *Dumfries and Galloway Courier* reported that 'a proposal is under consideration for introducing into the Queen of the South a properly graduated set of musical bells, capable of performing a number of tunes, the expense of which could not be great, so well is the art now understood. The whole of our steeple clocks were purchased by subscription; the same means are yet open, and were an apparatus still more scientific than a cathedral chime placed in the belfry, it would form a great additional attraction to the Midsteeple. Even flounder sellers would rejoice in such an acquisition, rehearse the marvel on the coast, and bring their children on gala days to enjoy the treat. Nay, even our Magistrates and such as sit in the Council, would be none the worse for the measured harmony without. It is just possible the daws might object, regarding, as they do, the Steeple as their own particular howff; but after a little time the black rascals will become ashamed, when accustomed to better music than their own. Let the good work, therefore, go forward, and the public drink in by anticipation long drawn out, the pleasing sweetness of "Speed the Plough", "Charlie is my Darling", and "Willie the Young Chevalier" &c.'

~ July 1st ~

1925: On this day, the *Dumfries and Galloway Standard* announced that 'the new Post Office at Dumfries, which is in the course of erection in King Street, and promises to be an attractive addition to the architectural features of the town, was the scene of an interesting ceremony on Saturday, when the foundation stone was laid with Masonic rites by the Right Worshipful Provincial Grand Master Mason of Dumfriesshire, Brother John Bryce Duncan of Newlands. The foundation ceremony has had to be postponed for various reasons on several occasions, and such progress has been made in the construction of the building, that the stone which had to be selected for the observance of the usual ceremonial custom was the corner stone at the south-east. From the point of view of the spectators who crowded the street in front of the building, this had its advantages, because they had the opportunity of having a better view of the proceedings than they would otherwise have had. Two platforms had been erected midway between the first and second storeys, and the official parties gathered on these. Fortunately, the event was favoured with ideal weather conditions, and there was bright sunshine throughout.'

~ July 2nd ~

1818: On this day, the poet John Keats wrote the following letter to his brother Tom, having stayed the night in Dumfries: 'In Devonshire they say, "Well, where be ye going?" Here it is "How is it wi' yoursel'?" A man on the coach said the horses took a hellish heap o' drivin'; the same fellow pointed out Burns's Tomb with a deal of life. "There de ye see it, amang the trees white, wi' a roond tap?" The first well-dressed Scotchman we had any conversation with, to our surprise confessed himself a Deist. The careful manner of delivering his opinions, not before he had received several encouraging hints from us, was very amusing. Yesterday was an immense Horse Fair at Dumfries, so that we met numbers of men and women on the road, the women nearly all barefoot, with their shoes and clean stockings in hand, ready to put on and look smart in the town. There are plenty of wretched cottages whose smoke has no outlet but by the door. We have now begun upon whisky, called here Whuskey, very smart stuff it is. Mixed like our liquors, with sugar and water, 'tis called toddy; very pretty drink, and much praised by Burns.' (Colvin, Sidney, (Ed.), *Letters of John Keats to his Family and Friends*, 1891)

~ July 3rd ~

1833: On this day, 'in the course of exercising some young dogs on the Lochar Moss on Friday last, a couple of sportsmen put up a great many coveys of muirfowl, the whole being of as large a size and as vigorous on the wing as perhaps they had ever witnessed at this day of the year. In putting up the last covey that came in their way, they were witnesses to a species of encounter that, though pretty well acquainted with field sports, had never come under their observation before. The covey, ten in number, flew towards a neighbouring plantation, which they no sooner approached than a magpie of the common breed sprung from a tree and, striking at one of the covey, both the striker and the struck came headlong to the ground. The sportsmen hastened to the spot but, before they could reach it, the ill-omened bird was soaring aloft with the dead muirfowl in its beak. They pursued the plunderer to the tree where its nest was deposited but, not having guns with them, and the tree being a lofty one, mistress Mag was able to deride their endeavours to disturb her.' (*Dumfries Times*)

～ July 4th ～

1842: On this day, the *Dumfries Times* reported on a disturbance: 'We regret to say that, on Saturday night last, unexpected rioting broke out between 10 and 11 o'clock, in consequence of … a recent rise of 2*d* per stone on oatmeal. There is no scarcity of food, but nearly one half of the population being unemployed, wages both scarce and low, there can be no doubt that a rise of nearly 10 per cent on the staple food of our poor and almost destitute population had the tendency, unfortunately … to excite the mere women and boy population of our dingy classes to physical demonstration, which all good men of all classes must denounce in unqualified terms. The result of this infatuated ebullition of a half-starved population was, that in a few hours the windows and doors of six of our most respectable and industrious meal-dealers in Dumfries and Maxwelltown were literally smashed to atoms. Provost Fraser, with some other authorities, congregated in the Council Chamber … [and] were enabled to get the misguided mob dispersed in a few hours, and without any other force being necessary than the healthy check and gentle coercion of our efficient municipal constabulary force.'

─ July 5th ─

1823: On this day, the following report appeared in the *Dumfries Weekly Journal*: 'Thomas Wilson, better known perhaps by the name of "Blind Tam", who has for the last sixty years discharged the duty of bellman for this Burgh, was presented with a silver medal (bearing a suitable inscription), a silver-headed cane, and a complete suit of new clothes, as a trifling mark of the estimation in which the services of this individual are held by the inhabitants at large. As a public servant, he has performed his duty with great fidelity and with nearly as much exactness as the clock beside him itself; and tho' his station in life may be humble, he has always maintained the character of an honest, industrious, and upright man. He is fond of sacred music, remarkably cheerful in his temper, and, to a steadfast loyalty to his king, he joins a most sincere devotion to his God.' N.B. Wilson, who acquired his nickname after going blind when still only a child, went on to ring the town bells for another two years, before suffering a fatal stroke while ringing the evening bell on a Sunday in April 1825.

‒ July 6th ‒

1849: On this day, Dr Burns made the following entry in the Dumfries Burgh Records: 'Bailie Nicholson introduced the Rev. Dr. Duncan of the New Church, and a deputation from the Kirk Session, Dumfries, appointed for the purpose of consulting with the Town Council as to replacing the communion cups sometime ago stolen out of the Church. Dr. Duncan stated that there was a certain sum of £42 or thereby, being an excrescent fund in the hands of the Kirk Session independent of the collections for the poor, which the Session wished the Council to sanction to be appropriated for the purpose of replacing the said Communion Cups. After this subject had been fully considered by the Council, Mr. Dunbar moved, seconded by Mr. Dinwiddie, that the Council agree to the recommendation made by the Session, which motion was unanimously agreed to, and the concurrence of the Council granted accordingly. The Council authorised the Kirk Session to receive up the old silver in the hands of the Procurator-Fiscal, to be appropriated as afterwards may be directed. The Council instruct that the weight of the new Communion Cups be reported to the Council and the same to be entered into the Council book.' (Mackie, Charles, (Ed.), *Dumfries and Galloway Notes and Queries* (1913))

~ July 7th ~

1795: On this day, the *Dumfries Weekly Journal* printed the following report: 'Escaped from Justice: Henry O'Neil, son of John O'Neil at Stoop, in the neighbourhood of Dumfries, about twenty-two years of age, five feet nine or ten inches high, a stout well-made man, with dark hair hanging loose, dark complexion, and a little pitted by the smallpox; had on when he escaped, a blue jacket, striped vest, and white trousers, a small round hat and tied shoes. He is supposed to have gone on the road towards Edinburgh, in order to enlist into some corps, or as a sailor. He was about to be apprehended in consequence of the late Comprehending Act, but fired upon, and severely, if not mortally wounded several of the military, while in the act of apprehending him; whereby he effected his escape. It is therefore requested, that any person of the above description, offering to enlist or otherwise discovered, may be apprehended and lodged in any of his Majesty's Jails, and notice thereof sent to the Magistrates of Dumfries, who will pay to the person so apprehending the said Henry O'Neil, a reward of Five Guineas, besides all expenses.'

~ July 8th ~

1794: On this day, it was reported that 'as almost all the considerable towns in Great Britain and Ireland have entered into Subscriptions for the relief of the destitute widows and families of the gallant seamen and soldiers, who were killed or wounded in the glorious victory obtained over the French fleet by Lord Howe, on the 28th and 29th ult. and 1st current – It is hoped that the Town of Dumfries, which has always been distinguished for its Loyalty, will cheerfully come forward and contribute to this humane and laudable purpose; and, in this expectation, a Subscription Paper is lodged at the Bank Office here, where all persons may have an opportunity of contributing according to their inclinations.' (*Dumfries Weekly Journal*)

1908: Also on this day, 'an Annual Visitor – In Dumfries Police Court yesterday, before Bailie Thompson, Sarah Foster or Kay, vagrant, pleaded guilty to being drunk and incapable in St. David Street on the previous day. The Fiscal (Mr. T. McGowan), stated that the accused turned up in the town every year when the militia assembled. She was fined 21/-, with the option of twenty days' imprisonment.' (*Dumfries and Galloway Standard*)

– JULY 9TH –

1922: On this day, the 'Dumfries War Memorial was unveiled by General Sir Francis Davies, K.C.B., the officer in charge of the Forces in Scotland. The memorial has been erected in Newall Terrace near St. John's Episcopal Church, and the open-air service at the unveiling was attended by a gathering of the townspeople numbering close on six thousand. Crowds thronged Newall Terrace, Lovers' Walk, and the Station Road ... The memorial has been erected at a cost of approximately £1,400. It is of striking and very handsome design and is entirely a Dumfries production, having been designed by a Dumfries sculptor, and fashioned by craftsmen belonging to the town. The figure is that of a soldier of the King's Own Scottish Borderers in service dress, standing with rifle reversed, as if in silent remembrance at the grave of a fallen comrade. The statue itself is unique as a piece of workmanship, by reason of the fact that it is the first time on which an attempt has been made to cut the figure of a soldier standing with rifle reversed out of one solid piece of granite.' (*Dumfries and Galloway Standard*)

~ July 10th ~

1909: On this day, the *Dumfries and Galloway Standard* announced that 'Following the manner of advertisement favoured by the Suffragettes, pavements were chalked in the course of Thursday afternoon, announcing the open-air meeting in Queensberry Square at eight o'clock. An open-air "Votes for Women" meeting being a novelty in Dumfries, groups of curious onlookers were to be observed in the Square shortly before that hour. An empty lorry drawn up on the north side of the railings in the Square seemed to confirm the chalked announcements ... Some speculation was rife as to whether or not Mrs. Pankhurst, Mrs. Billington Greig, or some other Suffragette personality would appear. It was, however, Miss Macaulay and Miss Cottonhaig who arrived at eight o'clock, and on their mounting the lorry a large crowd at once gathered. In a few minutes it had increased to one of at least six hundred persons, while there was also a not inconsiderable number of listeners at open windows in the vicinity. The proceedings were introduced by Miss Cottonhaig, who stated that the meeting was being held under the auspices of the Women's Social and Political Union, the object of which was to obtain votes for women, on the same basis as they were given to men.'

― July 11th ―

1882: On this day, a report under the headline 'Salvationists on Holiday' appeared in the *Dumfries and Galloway Courier*: 'On Tuesday last, three hundred members of the Salvation Army from Carlisle and the surrounding districts, visited Dumfries in order to escape the temptations offered by Carlisle Races. They arrived by special train at about half-past ten, and paraded the principal streets of Dumfries and Maxwelltown, with band and banners, en route to the Mechanics' Hall, where they retired to "feed the hungry". At about three o'clock, the forces were again gathered together and marched to the Sands, where a "great Salvation Fair" was held. A large circle was made, and the usual blasphemous outpourings were indulged in, to print which would be to copy pretty faithfully the wild articles that have appeared in the "War Cry" [the organ of the Salvation Army]. Large crowds were attracted to all their gatherings, and their peculiar antics provided holidaymakers with considerable amusement. A mass meeting was held in the Mechanics' Hall in the evening, and the visitors left the town at half-past nine. A few more such orgies will hasten the much dreaded reaction which is certain to follow.'

~ July 12th ~

1849: On this day, the following cases, heard at the Sheriff's Criminal Court in the town, were reported in the *Dumfriesshire and Galloway Herald and Register*:

'Mary Kerr, or Mullins, Maxwelltown, accused of theft by wearing apparel from a public bleaching ground, aggravated by previous conviction, pleaded guilty, and was sentenced to be imprisoned for 60 days.'

'Robert Brown and Willian Hedley were placed at the bar, charged with the theft of two hens from a byre at Muirend of Closeburn. They pleaded guilty, and were sentenced to be imprisoned for twenty days.'

'William Smith and John McKinley were charged with having stolen three ferrets from a gamekeeper's premises at Kirkbean on 21st May, and of continuing the theft into Dumfries, or of resetting the ferrets in Dumfries, in the knowledge that they had been stolen. They pleaded not guilty, but evidence having been adduced, the Sheriff found Smith guilty of continuing the theft into Dumfries, and McKinley guilty of reset. Smith was sentenced to be imprisoned for forty days, and McKinley for thirty days.'

'Marion Clarke, needlewoman, pleaded guilty of having stolen from a house in English Street, where she lodged, a silk gown, and was sentenced to be imprisoned for ten days.'

– JULY 13TH –

1921: On this day, a meeting was held by Maxwelltown Town Council, at which the subject of aeroplane flying on Sundays and 'its bearing upon the right observance of the Sabbath' was discussed.

'A letter from the Air Ministry was read, stating that the Air Council do not see their way to issue regulations prohibiting Sunday flying, although they disapprove of any flying on that day which would prove an annoyance during the hours of religious services. The Air Navigation Regulations of 1919 contained provisions for prohibiting low flying and trick or exhibition flying over city or town areas and populous districts, and that in the event of a contravention of these provisions, the police were competent to take proceedings against the pilot or owner of the aircraft concerned.

Ex-Provost Nicholson said that however much they disapproved of flying on Sunday, it was clear the Council had no power to prohibit it, but the police had power to take action if there happened to be low flying over a town. The matter was then allowed to drop.' (*Dumfries and Galloway Standard*)

— JULY 14TH —

1801: On this day, the *Dumfries Weekly Journal* printed a guide to what the fashion-conscious young lady should be wearing on her head at the beginning of the nineteenth century: 'A round hat of brown willow, turned up on one side with a bow, and ornamented with an ostrich feather of the same colour; a turban of white crepe or muslin, ornamented with several white ostrich feathers, which are fixed a little on the right side, to hang carelessly over the head; a cap of white muslin, ornamented with wreaths of white ribbon, and a bunch of ivy leaves; a turban of pink crepe, ornamented with bugles of beads, two pink ostrich feathers fixed in front, to fall over the head.'

Advice on walking dresses was also included: 'A round dress of lilac, or other coloured muslin; full sleeves of white muslin or lace; the dress cut low round the bosom, and worn with a white handkerchief; or an open robe of white muslin, with full long sleeves confined to the size of the arm in three places; petticoat of the same, with a narrow flounce at the bottom.'

– July 15th –

1723: On this day, 'the Council, after taking into account a great loss caused by fires, ordained that henceforth all heritors and others, in re-constructing or re-roofing houses joining with or fronting into High Street, should cause the roofs to be made with slates or tiles, and not of straw, heather, broom, breckans or other combustible matter, under the penalty of one hundred pounds Scots.' (McDowall, William, *History of Dumfries* (2nd Edn., 1873))

—

1868: 'The baths at the Mechanics' Institute were opened for the first time on Monday; and the experiment of supplying such a luxury, at a trifling rate, has proved so far encouraging. About thirty persons took advantage of the baths yesterday, and with such sultry weather as we now have, they will hopefully continue to be much resorted to.' (*Dumfries and Galloway Standard*)

—

1896: Also on this day, the *Dumfries and Galloway Standard* announced that 'Mr. Potts [Manager] has arranged to have a highly attractive entertainment at the Theatre next week. The chief novelty is the exhibition of the most recent scientific sensation – the cinemotographe; an apparatus which throws upon the screen a series of photographs of the same objects in motion, men, women, and railway trains etc., in such rapid succession that every movement is reproduced exactly as in life.'

— July 16th —

1858: On this day, the *Dumfriesshire and Galloway Herald and Register* announced the introduction of a novel scheme in the town: 'A project for the convenience of the public, and the special benefit of a neglected class of children, has now been matured by Mr. Gregson. In the town and neighbourhood there are numerous boys from 12 to 16 years of age who have no fixed employment, and are often in great want, and open to all kinds of temptation. Mr. Gregson proposes to take a few of these youths (six or so to begin with) and form them into a light-porter brigade, giving each a coat of corduroy, and a cap with a red band, by way of uniform. The members of this corps will be open for an engagement from anyone to run messages, carry parcels, put in coals, and similar jobs, at the usual rates paid for such pieces of service. The money thus earned will ... be handed over to their parents or guardians as payment for their board, and the surplus, when any, will be lodged in the Savings Bank to the credit of the owners. It is hoped that by this method, the boys may be trained industrially, and be placed in a state of probation fitting them for becoming apprentices to some regular trade.'

⚊ July 17th ⚊

1912: On this day, the *Dumfries and Galloway Standard* reported that 'Mr. Robert Slack, a student of aviation under the International Correspondence Schools, is to visit Dumfries in the course of a circuit flight of Great Britain. Mr. Slack arrived in Carlisle yesterday, and may arrive at Dumfries today, although up till late last night no intimation had been received as to when he would leave the border city. In flying to Dumfries, he will be guided by the Glasgow and South-Western Railway. He will land at Nunholm, the ground of the Dumfries Cricket Club. At each of the towns which he visits, the aviator is giving lectures, accompanied by exhibition flights. His machine is a 1912 model of a Bleriot monoplane, of the single-seated type, and a fifty horse-power Gnome engine, having a seven-rotary cylinder fitted to the aeroplane. The normal speed of the machine is sixty miles an hour. On resuming his journey after his descent at Dumfries, the airman will follow the valley of the Nith to Kilmarnock. The International Correspondence Schools have started a subscription scheme, with a view to buying the machine used by Mr. Slack in his flight for presentation to the nation.'

─ July 18th ─

1848: On this day, the following poignant tale was recounted in the *Dumfries and Galloway Courier*: 'An individual residing in Dumfries got, last winter, a cocker dog, which attached itself in a very marked manner to his son, a young child; remaining beside him as much as he could, and always attending when the boy was drawn out in a little carriage, leaping up and caressing him. Lately, the little boy took ill and died within a few days. During his sickness the dog never left the cradle … and showed the deepest anxiety in various ways. He watched the coffin with the same fidelity, and at the funeral attempted to scrape up the earth thrown into the grave, from which he had to be carried away. When brought home, he ran about the house whining and foaming at the mouth, apparently quite frantic; and has since pined away, so that his master is afraid he will not recover, however anxious he naturally may be to preserve the life of so faithful an animal. The only symptom of activity he has shown was the other day, when the boy's carriage was given away, as being no longer of any use. He attacked the girl who came for it.'

– JULY 19TH –

1893: On this day, it was reported that 'at Dumfries Burgh Court on Monday, George Hudson, engine driver, in the employment of Messrs. Charlton and Wylie, was charged with having – on 10th July – in Irving Street, George Street and Charlotte Street, while in charge of a traction engine, driven the said engine through these streets at a greater speed than two miles per hour, contrary to the by-laws. He pleaded not guilty. Sergeant Adams, who prosecuted, said it was a practice, this fast driving of traction engines … [but] admitted that the accused was only going at the rate of three miles per hour, and that he was not so bad as some of the others. Mr. Charlton asked to make a statement, and said the men employed by his firm were instructed to be very careful in observing the whole of the clauses of the Locomotive Act. This man [Hudson] had told him that he had taken more than twenty-five minutes, without stoppages, to go from the Caledonian station to the end of the New Bridge, and maintained that he was not driving more than two miles an hour.' (*Dumfries and Galloway Standard*)

‒ July 20th ‒

1802: On this day, the *Dumfries Weekly Journal* announced the imminent arrival in the town of 'the PHANTASMAGORIA, or Exhibition of Phantoms. This entertainment has been honoured with more approbation and general applause than any Amusement yet offered to the eye of the Public. The Phantasmagoria has never failed to produce overflowing houses at theatres in London, Dublin, Liverpool, York, Manchester, Edinburgh, and Glasgow, where it is now performing four times a day, so great is the public desire to behold this wonderful and pleasing entertainment. In order to render this Phantomimic Spectrology general in its effects, the total extinction of lights will be necessary.'

1802: Also on this day, 'the Magistrates and Council, having prepared a set of English Standard Measures, and a Scots Mutchkin, for the government of the Traders in this Town, of date 21st June last, ordained that the Spirit Dealers should sell their Spirits agreeable to the said Standards, under the penalties contained in the laws thereanent. Notice is therefore hereby given to all concerned, certifying them, if they do not within the space of one month from this date procure proper measures, and sell agreeable thereto, they will be fined in terms of law.' (*Dumfries Weekly Journal*)

― July 21st ―

1796: On this day, Robert Burns died at home. The poet's decline had begun in Dumfries during the mid-1790s, when the long, hard years of his farming life, coupled with the demands of an ever-expanding family and constant anxiety over money matters, produced the inevitable detrimental effect on his health. At the close of 1795, he became very ill with what was described as a 'most severe rheumatic fever'. As 1796 unfolded, Burns's decline continued, and during the first two weeks of July he took himself off to the hamlet of Brow, near Clarencefield, where he had been sent by his physician to 'take the waters' of the chalybeate spring of Brow Well, and to swim in the Solway Firth. The whole enterprise was almost certainly ill-advised from the beginning, and the weeks that he passed at Brow Well did nothing to restore his health. 'God help my wife and children if I am taken from their head, they will be poor indeed,' Burns wrote to his brother, Gilbert. Burns returned to Dumfries on July 18th, where he died three days later from rheumatic heart disease. (Carroll, David, *Ten Tales from Dumfries & Galloway*, The History Press, 2010)

~ July 22nd ~

1788: The following notices appeared in the *Dumfries Weekly Journal*:

'Broke out of Dumfries Gaol, late on Wednesday night, Henry Riddell, a man of about five feet eight inches high, who appears to be thirty years of age, is well made, and wears his own hair, which is of a light brown colour. He had two coats when he made his escape: the one of a brownish colour, with round yellow buttons; the other is of a blue colour, with broad white metal buttons.

Matthew Rae, about seventeen or eighteen years of age, formerly a drummer in the 27th Regiment of Foot, is about five feet five inches high, rather slender made, has short dark-coloured hair, and had on when he broke the gaol a short blue jacket, corduroy vest, and light coloured breeches. The Magistrates hereby offer a Reward of FIVE GUINEAS to any who will apprehend and secure the above persons; and will likewise defray all necessary expenses that may be incurred in bringing them back.'

'Lost, out of the cart of Mr. John McClure, between Kirkcudbright and Dumfries, a parcel directed to the King's Deputy Remembrancer In Exchequer, Edinburgh, containing papers which can be of no use to no person who has found the same. Whoever will bring the parcel to the Customs Houses of Dumfries or Kirkcudbright, or to John Blacklock, innkeeper in Dumfries, shall be handsomely rewarded, and no questions asked.'

~ July 23rd ~

1715: On this day, it was reported that 'the magistrates of Dumfries having been apprised by letters from London, of the [Old] Pretender's design to land in Scotland, communicated this intention to the Council, and forthwith means were taken to mature the defences of the burgh. It was deemed probable that the debarkation would take place on the shores of Lochryan, or nearer still, at the harbour of Kirkcudbright; and that afterwards an attempt would be made to seize Dumfries, as the chief town of the district ... The various trained bands were drawn out; strong guards were posted at the four ports; and seven companies, corresponding in number to the Incorporated Trades, were formed, composed of sixty effective men each, the provost officiating as commander-in-chief of this municipal force. It was carefully trained almost daily, and [according to local minister, the Revd Peter Rae] "for the more effectual training of the younger sort, a company of bachelors was formed out of the rest, who assumed the title of the Company of Loyal Bachelors."

Stimulated by the example of Dumfries, and the sense of a common danger, many county gentlemen, ministers of the district, and others, made extensive arrangements to protect themselves, and defeat the machinations of the enemy.' (McDowall, William, *History of Dumfries* (2nd Edn., 1873))

— JULY 24TH —

1878: On this day, the *Dumfries and Galloway Standard* reported the visits of two celebrities:

'It will be seen from an announcement elsewhere that Mr. Wyllie, the renowned draughts player, is about to revisit Dumfries in his professional capacity. During his career he has contested about sixty matches, winning forty-six of them, and placed to the credit account of his supporters a sum approaching £1,300. He created quite a sensation when in America, from which he has recently returned; and his arrival here is looked forward to with interest by the draughts players of the town.'

'Mr. Thomas Carlyle arrived in Dumfries on Monday and, with his neice, Miss Mary Aitken, who acts as his secretary, is residing at Park House, on the Troqueer side of the river, and closely adjoining the field in which the Highland and Agricultural Society's Show is about to be held. Mr. Carlyle has, hitherto, when visiting Dumfries, resided at The Hill, the house of his brother-in-law, Mr. Aitken; but in consequence of the illness of Dr. Carlyle, his brother, who is and has been for some time an inmate of The Hill, Park House was retained for Mr. Carlyle on the present occasion.'

— JULY 25TH —

1796: On this day, the funeral of Robert Burns took place. Having served as a private in the Royal Dumfries Volunteers for the last eighteen months or so of his life, it was decided 'at the request of his brother volunteers [that his funeral] should be conducted with military honours. A regiment of the Cinque Ports Cavalry, and the Fencible Infantry of Angusshire, then quartered in Dumfries, offered their assistance on the solemn occasion ... In the presence of an immense crowd of tearful sympathisers, the funeral train moved slowly down to St. Michael's cemetery. A party of the volunteers appointed to perform the requisite military service at the interment were stationed in front, with their arms reversed; the other members of the company supported or surrounded the coffin, on which were placed the hat and sword of their illustrious fellow-soldier ... Arrived at the place of sepulture, the body was committed to the tomb; three volleys of musketry fired over the grave completing the affecting ceremony ... On the forenoon of this sad day, the newly-made widow was seized with the pains of labour, and, just as the grave closed over her husband's dust, gave birth to a son, who died in infancy.' (McDowall, William, *History of Dumfries* (2nd Edn., 1873))

~ July 26th ~

1837: The following reports appeared in the *Dumfries Times* on this day:

'The schooner, "Lord Nelson" of Dumfries, was on her voyage from Waterford, Ireland, to this port, with a cargo of bones, and on Wednesday last, when off Whitehaven, two of her hands set out in a boat to procure medical aid on behalf of William Lowden, the master, who, for some days previously, had been labouring under indisposition. The men having failed to return as soon as he expected, in a fit of frenzy he leapt overboard, and was immediately engulfed in the mighty deep. One man only was in the vessel when these circumstances occurred. As a result, of course, no effort could be made to save him. The deceased sustained the character of a steady and sober man, and gave entire satisfaction to his employers. He was in his twenty-sixth year and unmarried.'

'The Dumfries and Maxwelltown Total Abstinence Society have the pleasure to inform the Friends of Temperance, that the Rev. Mr. Read, Missionary from Southern Africa, has accepted an invitation to a Public Breakfast within the George Street Assembly Rooms on Tuesday next, on which occasion much interesting information connected with the Temperance cause and its progress in Southern Africa will be communicated.'

– July 27th –

1940: On this day, a notice from the town's Provost was printed in the *Dumfries and Galloway Standard*: 'I have been asked to make an especial appeal for recruits for the Local Defence Volunteers, or what is now termed the Home Guard. I realise that the various Voluntary Services have been well recruited in Dumfries and, while tendering to them, on behalf of the Burgh, sincere thanks, I have been informed that the LDV require urgently and immediately 100 recruits.

I would therefore ask all men between the ages of 17 and 65, who are not yet in any of the Defence Services, to enrol at once in the LDV, and I would address myself particularly to those who have shotgun or rifle experience. Time is short, and, while facilities and equipment for training are becoming rapidly available, the man who can use a rifle or a gun now is invaluable.

The Local Defence Volunteers is essentially a Citizen Force, and recruits are confidently expected from every class of people who are now united in the defence of our country, our town, and our freedom. Mr. Somerville and his leaders will welcome recruits at the Drill Hall on Monday, Tuesday, Wednesday and Friday evenings.'

‑ JULY 28TH ‑

1852: On this day, the *Dumfries and Galloway Standard* noted the progress of telegraphic communication between Dumfries and the outside world: 'The Electric Telegraph Company of Ireland have just succeeded in laying their cable across the Irish Channel … The next part of the process will be to lay the wires in the trenches already dug for their reception, from Portpatrick via Newton Stewart to Dumfries. The wires will be carried from this town to Carlisle, and on by the railway lines through Lancashire to London. On the other side of the channel, the wires will extend to Dublin; and thus Dumfries, and other towns in the district, will soon be supplied with telegraphic intelligence from these capital cities, and also from Manchester, Liverpool, Glasgow, and other trading marts. The immense benefit of this we need not pause to point out. Mr. C. Harkness is the agent at Dumfries for the Company, and that gentleman received on Friday last, thirty hampers containing forty miles of telegraphic wire, to become by and by the bearer of countless messages. The wire, which is of the usual thickness, is covered over with gutta percha, and will be immediately laid down between this town and Newton Stewart.'

‒ July 29th ‒

1817: On this day, a stern notice was printed in the *Dumfries Weekly Journal*: 'The Incorporation of Squaremen in Dumfries considering that, for time immemorial their Members have enjoyed the exclusive right of doing all kinds of Mason, Wright, Cabinet, Slater, and Cooper work in the burgh of Dumfries and privileges thereof, and that they obtain the Freedom only by service, marriage, or purchase, and becoming Burgesses; and when any person not a Burgess, and also a Member of the Incorporation, has undertaken any of these descriptions of work, they have been interdicted under authority of a Court of Law. And understanding that James Liddell, Bricklayer, and George Grive, Slater, and some others, are in the practice of engaging in Slater and Mason work, though they are neither Burgesses nor Freemen, the Incorporation hereby intimate to the inhabitants, that they have resolved to prevent such trespass in future, and those employing such men after this notice, will have themselves to blame for any trouble or inconvenience they may be put to in having their works interrupted. ‒ By Order of the Incorporation. Wm. Gordon, Clerk.'

─ July 30th ─

1913: On this day, the *Dumfries and Galloway Standard* reported the opening of the Arrol-Johnston Motor Works: 'The erection of these works marks the opening of an important industrial era for Dumfries, on which great hopes are built. Already they give employment to 250 men; and in the course of a few weeks, it is expected the number will be augmented by the transfer of another 200 skilled workmen from Paisley.

The Dumfries Works have been built on the lands of Heathhall, which the company acquired to the extent of 160 acres. Built of concrete, with a very large proportion of glass in the walls, it presents a striking appearance; and the equipment embraces the most modern appliances which the brains of our own islands and two continents besides have developed.

The Works are in a purely rural district, so that the bulk of the workmen will require to find dwellings in the town. They are very favourably situated close to the line of the Caledonian Railway, and some sixteen houses of a neat type have been erected in line with the Works for occupation by men employed at them. Relays of elegant Arrol-Johnston cars conveyed guests to and from the Works yesterday, and a special train was also run for their convenience.'

— July 31st —

1798: On this day, the *Dumfries Weekly Journal* informed its readers that 'Mr. Ruspini, Surgeon-Dentist to the Prince of Wales, respectfully informs the Ladies and Gentlemen who have done him the honour of consulting him in the line of his profession in Dumfries, if they wish any further assistance, he intends to pass through the town on his return to Edinburgh, and he intends being in Dumfries on Tuesday next. He requests their commands may be left immediately at Mr. Boyd's, Bookseller in Dumfries, of whom may be had Chevalier Ruspini's Medicines, on the same terms as at his house in London.'

—–—

1833: Also on this day, the following advertisement appeared in the *Dumfries Times*: 'Cancer effectually cured – without cutting. Mr. Ward, Surgeon of Newcastle, will remain a week or two longer in Dumfries, at No.16 St. David Street, where he may be consulted in all cases of cancer, tumours and fistula. A great number of individuals afflicted with cancer in Dumfries and its neighbourhood, were cured by his father some years ago, many of whom still remain LIVING PROOFS that this is the safest and most effectual treatment of cancer yet known to the medical world. Their address will be given to any person who may wish to see them; and also, references to above NINE HUNDRED INDIVIDUALS in England, who remain perfectly cured of cancer by Mr. Ward, without either cutting or drawing of blood.' (*Dumfries Times*)

~ August 1st ~

1809: On this day, the *Dumfries Weekly Journal* printed the following announcement: 'To Gentlemen, Farmers, and Breeders of Horses: That famed Stallion throughout the country, called "Pensioner", will be sold at the Repository, Lochmabengate Street, by auction on Wednesday at the usual hour of sale, three o'clock in the afternoon. This excellent horse needs no recommendation, either with regard to size, colour, or performance, he being generally known in this part of the country as a capital Stallion. Having met with such good success this season, as to have served upwards of one hundred Mares at One Guinea and a Crown each, he is, no doubt, a very desirable object to anyone wishing to follow this mode of making money. Henry Grainger [owner of the Repository] would recommend it to anyone that it lies in the way of, not to neglect this favourable opportunity, as he is to be sold without reserve for what he will bring, as the proprietor has not the opportunity now of following up the business as it ought to be. Those wishing for pedigree and performance see the Racing Calendar.'

‑ August 2nd ‑

1841: On this day, the *Dumfries Times* announced that: 'There will be exhibited on Wednesday next, in the Show Room of Bailie Beck, Coach Builder, the Westmorland White Ox, Prince, purchased at the late Royal Agricultural Society of England's Show at Liverpool. He is computed to weigh at least 250 stones, and is by far the largest ox ever shown.'

‑‑‑

1884: Also on this day, the following report appeared in the *Dumfries and Galloway Standard*: 'Mr. J.H. Fergusson, tinsmith and gas-fitter, Dumfries, has just patented an apparatus for the cooling of milk and other liquids. An important end is gained by the rapid cooling of milk when taken from the cow, as this kills the infusoria and enables the liquid to be kept sweet for a much longer time. A number of artificial coolers are already on the market, and are in use in a number of the large dairies in this district; but they are all open to the double objection of being complicated in arrangement and costly. Seldom, if ever, too, do they perform the amount of work represented by the makers and vendors. Mr. Fergusson has set himself to provide an apparatus which will be at once effective and inexpensive, and he seems to have completely succeeded.'

~ AUGUST 3RD ~

1617: On this day, King James VI presented the Siller (Silver) Gun to the Seven Trades of Dumfries, following a dinner given in his honour by the Council and Trades in the Painted Chamber of the Town Clerk's mansion. 'That greater effect might be given to the presentation of the gun, the ceremony was performed on the outside stair or balcony of the hall, in sight of the general community. The crowd below would, we may be sure, include all the journeymen and apprentices specially interested in the proceedings. Alas that the precise words of the royal oration, and those of the eloquent or any other speeches made by the chief of the Trades and the Provost of the burgh in acknowledging the gift, have proved as transitory as the cheers that greeted them. The little "war engine" presented by King James to the Trades was about ten inches in length, and mounted on a wheeled carriage, also of silver. In some unaccountable way the accompaniments of the tube disappeared at a remote period; and about fifty-five years since a butt was added to the tube, which altered the piece from a cannon to a musket.' (McDowall, William, *History of Dumfries* (2nd Edn., 1873))

← AUGUST 4TH ←

1909: On this day, the *Dumfries and Galloway Standard* reported that 'on Wednesday afternoon Miss Helen Fraser, of the National Union of Women's Suffrage Societies, addressed a meeting of ladies in Greyfriars' Upper Hall, as a preliminary step to the proposed formation of a branch of the union in Dumfries. There was a large and interested attendance, mostly of ladies, of whom there were about fifty present. Miss Fraser's address, which was mainly explanatory of the objects of the union, and descriptive of the benefits which the community as a whole would receive, socially, industrially, and morally, from giving women a voice in its government, was listened to with close attention and occasionally applauded. A list of those who were willing to become members of a local branch of the union was taken, and the number of names put down was sixteen. Miss Fraser intimated that she was about to start a propaganda tour between Aberdeen and Perth and through Fifeshire, and that she expected to return to Dumfries in October. A mass meeting will be held in Edinburgh in November, at which Mrs. Fawcett, president of the union, will speak, and it was mentioned that she might possibly visit Dumfries on the same occasion.'

~ August 5th ~

1823: On this day, it was announced that 'at the Theatre, Dumfries (for one night only), Mr. Rogers FSA, and Member of the Philosophical Societies of London and Norwich, has the honour to announce that he proposes, in a few days, to deliver a Lecture on Astronomy, in which he pledges himself to answer and demonstratively refute the objections which Infidels have pretended to draw from that Science, against the truth of Holy Writ. The various phenomena pertaining to the subject will be very familiarly illustrated by new and beautiful TRANSPARENT MACHINERY. At the conclusion of the Lecture, Mr. Rogers will introduce his newly-invented Grand Transparent Microscope, indisputably the largest and most powerful instrument in the world. To those whose highly cultivated minds delight in observing the beauties of Nature, this superb Instrument will open an ample field for wonder and contemplation.' (*Dumfries Weekly Journal*)

1978: Also on this day, the *Dumfries and Galloway Standard* reported that, 'despite gloomy, overcast skies, Dumfries is having its busiest ever summer season, with visitors flocking to the town centre for shopping instead of the usual sunbathing on the beaches. And this year in particular has seen a large increase in the number of foreign tourists, especially those from Scandinavia and the Netherlands. From the beginning of the tourist season, which officially starts in March, 36,276 holidaymakers have visited Dumfries – an increase of 6,000 over the same period last year.'

~ August 6th ~

1811: On this day, the following notice was issued by the Town Clerk: 'The Council having taken into their consideration the state of the Gullet Door, which, there is some reason to believe, is not regularly opened and shut at six o'clock in the mornings and evenings, in terms of the late decision of the Court of Session, in the process with the Heritors of the Fishings in the River Nith; and the Council being most anxious that this should be pointedly and regularly done, not only in compliance with said decision, but for the benefit and advantage of the Proprietors of the Fishings above the Caul, they hereby nominate and appoint Robert Carlyle, Tacksman of the Oat Mill, to superintend the regular opening and shutting of the said Gullet Door, and in case he can discover any person or persons who shall presume to shut the door after six o'clock in the evening, to give information thereof to the Magistrates, in order that such delinquents may be prosecuted. And the Council agree to pay the said Robert Carlyle Ten Pounds for his trouble, for one year from this date.' (*Dumfries Weekly Journal*)

～ August 7th ～

1914: On this day, after Britain had been at war with Germany for three days, the following report appeared in the *Dumfries and Galloway Standard*: 'The extraordinary demand for provisions still continues in Dumfries, and merchants are experiencing considerable difficulty in dealing with the orders which are streaming in. The greatest demand is for flour and sugar, though bacon, tea, and other everyday foodstuffs are also being bought in unusual quantities. It is found impossible by the wholesale firms in Dumfries to carry out all their orders in full, and the grocers are being supplied by them with what they consider a fair share of goods.

In some shops, where there was a large stock on hand which had been purchased previous to the war, the price remained at its normal point, or very little above it; while in other shops, where the stock had run out and fresh supplies had been obtained since the declaration of war, the price had been doubled or even trebled. On account of this state of matters, a movement is on foot to call a conference of provision merchants with a view to having the prices standardised, and a system inaugurated, if possible, whereby grocers with a large stock of any article would supply those whose stock had become depleted.'

～ August 8th ～

1838: On this day, the following report appeared in the *Dumfries Times*: 'On the evening of Tuesday last week, the coach which runs between Dumfries and Kirkcudbright was returning to our town, with a full complement of passengers, and at the foot of the Longwood, about three miles distant from Dumfries, where the road descends rapidly, and turns very quickly, the driver went down to put the drag on one of the wheels. When this operation was about to be performed, the pole, by some means, snapped asunder; the horses then sprang forward, and, despite the exertions of the driver, continued for a short time their career; and ultimately, the coach was overturned. All the passengers sustained light injuries, except for a Miss Grierson from Dalbeattie, who was seriously injured on the spine by a quantity of luggage falling on her, and could only be removed to a house in the neighbourhood. The passengers, with the exception of the female, were afterwards conveyed in an omnibus to town, and such of them as had sustained injuries were put under medical treatment. Provost Fraser and Mr. Spalding, surgeon, visited the female on Wednesday, and though still seriously indisposed, she was conveyed to town that evening.'

~ AUGUST 9TH ~

1902: On this day, the Coronation of Edward VII was marked in the town with due ceremony. The day included a Public Luncheon at the Royal Restaurant, sports competitions on the Kingholm, and fireworks in the evening. The day began, however, with Divine Service on Dock Park, 'immediately after which, an adjournment was made to a spot about 150 yards north of the bandstand, where midway between the boundary wall of the park on one side and the River Nith on the other, an oak tree was planted by Mrs. Houston, wife of the Senior Bailie, in commemoration of the Coronation of King Edward ... The Dumfries Volunteer Band and the pipe band of the Industrial School were in attendance. A handsome coach had been provided for the occasion, the box and sides being very artistically draped in blue, with white cording, and the burgh arms and a crown being emblazoned on each side. The tree was then planted [declared the Town Clerk] in the hope and belief that for long years to come it may be an emblem to the citizens of Dumfries of love of country, of devotion to the defence of our liberties, and of faithful service to the Commonwealth.' (*Dumfries and Galloway Standard*)

⌁ August 10th ⌁

1836: On this day, the *Dumfries Times* printed the following report: 'On the afternoon of Thursday last, a stable-boy belonging to the Commercial Inn of this town, named Alexander Gibson, was on his return from Mr. Wilson's laundry premises, on the Troqueer side of the Nith, with a large quantity of newly-dressed linens in a cart. The horse had always been accustomed to take the ford at the mills, and turned quickly of its own accord in that direction. Before Gibson could get it pulled up or turned, one of the reins broke, and the horse plunged into the river, which was much swollen by the late rains. A servant girl who was also in the vehicle luckily jumped out before it was deep in the water, but the driver was hurried into the stream. The body of the cart was instantly floated off the wheels, and the door having fallen off, the whole of the linens were dispersed. Gibson was for some moments underneath the cart … However, by keeping a firm hold of the horse, he was dragged ashore and, although much exhausted at the time, is not likely to be much the worse for the accident. The greatest part of the clothes have since been fished out of the river, principally at the Castledykes pool.'

1847: On this day, the *Dumfries and Galloway Standard* advertised the sale of a property in the town, which has subsequently become a literary shrine visited by people from all over the world. 'There will be exposed to sale, by Public Roup, within the Commercial Inn, Dumfries, on Wednesday the 8th day of September (if not previously disposed of by Private Bargain), these houses and gardens attached, in Burns Street, which sometime belonged to the late Mr. Maxwell, surgeon in Dumfries, and now to the trustees of the late Mrs. Barker of Langshaw. A portion of the subjects consists of the Dwelling-House where the Poet Burns lived and in which he died, and in which his widow continued to reside until her death. The Property is in immediate proximity to the line of the railway from Dumfries to Kirkcudbright, and possesses many advantages for building. If not sold in one lot, it will be exposed in separate lots.

For further particulars, applications may be made to John Jackson, Writer, Dumfries, or to J. Farish and J. Brand, Writers, Annan, the latter of whom are in possession of the Title Deeds.'

‒ August 12th ‒

1740: On this day, the Old Lodge of Dumfries gathered in the town's Trades' Hall, 'and were honoured with ye company of his Grace the Duke of Queensberry and Dover, and his Lordship the Marquis of Annandale, who all went from said hall in Procession to the Old Church of Dumfries [now St Michael's], and there in regular form did lay ye foundation stone of ye steeple of ye said church, and afterwards in procession to ye said Hall where Severall healths were drunk.' (Smith, James, *History of The Old Lodge of Dumfries*, 1892)

1905: Also on this day, it was reported that 'between Tuesday night and Wednesday morning last, the members of the Dumfries Fire Brigade were summoned to their post of duty by the usual notification – the ringing of the electric bells in the firemen's houses. When the fire engine had been turned out, however, and all the men at their places, it was discovered that it was a false alarm. It appears that the wires of the National Telephone Company had come into contact with the wires leading from the Police Office to the firemen's houses, thus putting the current on to the wires and causing the alarm to be sounded.' (*Dumfries and Galloway Courier and Herald*)

~ August 13th ~

1504: On this day, King James IV of Scotland and his wife, Margaret Tudor, visited the town, and it is recorded that 'there was paid from the royal purse 13*s* to the "pyparis of Dumfrise", presumably as a royal contribution to the costs incurred by the King in employing "local talent" in the musical line as well as his own staff of minstrels ... The young Sovereign [came] for the purpose of holding an "ayre", or criminal court, in accordance with an act passed by his first Parliament ... Though the King came on a grave mission, it was not in the nature of the man to be morose or stern, even at such a period. In his train were harpers and pipers, as well as a dempster and an executioner; and music, feasting and revelry ruled the hours which the serious duties of the court left free. After remaining in the town a day or two, making arrangements for the assize, he passed on a justiciary tour to the Western Border, taking with him an armed escort, and his customary retinue of bards, singers, and bagpipers, including a reverend personage who figures in the books of the treasury as the "cruikit vicar of Dumfries".' (McDowall, William, *History of Dumfries* (2nd Edn., 1873))

~ AUGUST 14TH ~

1832: On this day, the *Dumfries and Galloway Courier* printed an account of the celebrations that followed the passing of the Scottish Reform Bill: 'Friday last was in every respect a "white" day in the history of Dumfries. Trade for once was at a standstill; the shops, with few exceptions, were closed; man, woman and child were abroad, witnessing whatever could be seen … The scene resembled a great annual fair – with this important difference: that buying and selling and marketing in all its various forms were unthought of and unheeded; enthusiasm and hilarity being the order of the day. The bakers may have vended hot rolls, and the gardeners pot herbs in the morning, but these were exceptions to the general rule; on every side, "toil unremitting lent its turn to play". In walking along the streets it was difficult to get quit of the impression that Birnam, or some other woods, had mistaken Dumfries for Dunsinane, and arrived, if not on their own legs and feet, at least in the sense meant by Shakespeare. We have witnessed many anniversaries of Waterloo, but never within our recollection were the gardens and groves laid under contribution to anything like the same extent.'

~ August 15th ~

1836: On this day, the following eye-watering letter, addressed to a medical man in the town by one James Duncan, was printed in the *Dumfries Times*: 'Sir – I cannot omit this opportunity of stating the great benefit I have received from your superior skill and management in bringing forth from me a stone, chiefly by the use of Morison's Medicines. About five years ago I was seized with a pain in my loins and severe sickness. I applied to various Doctors, and took whatever they ordered, but my trouble was no better ... I applied to you, and after you had examined me very closely, and enquired who had been attending me, you said they had been treating me wrong, and ordered me to take Morison's Pills. At length, the medicine succeeded in bringing the stone to the neck of the bladder, and lodged it at the entrance to the uretha. I could make no water. At length, however, you succeeded in bringing the stone carefully away. I passed at that time a large quantity of water, since which I have never had a single pain. I have sent you the stone to make what use of it you think proper.'

~ AUGUST 16TH ~

1871: On this day, the following report appeared in the *Dumfries and Galloway Standard*: 'On Sabbath last, a number of boys and girls – eleven altogether – in the Dumfries and Maxwelltown Industrial School absconded from the institution, by making their way into the yard through a sky-light window in the roof, and thereafter scaling the wall. The first of them made their way out about seven in the morning, and the others near mid-day. The leader appears to have been a Dumfries girl named Mary Jane Leithead, who had only been some six months in the school, and who during the last week had run away three times. The other absconders included William McLade, Margaret Bell, John Holliday and Mary McFarlane. They were all taken back to the school by Sabbath night, with the exception of three of the boys, who were apprehended in Annan on Monday. The girl Leithead and John Holliday were brought before Bailie Scott in the Burgh Court here on Monday, and the former was sentenced to 14 days' imprisonment, and thereafter to four years' detention in the Glasgow Reformatory; and the latter was admonished and sent back to the school.'

⟶ August 17th ⟵

1836: On this day, the *Dumfries Times* noted that 'the pitiful fraud of offering for sale, in our market, butter defective in weight, has prevailed to some extent of late. Thanks to the vigilance of our worthy Dean of Guild and his officers, a check is likely to be given to it, no fewer than about 25 light pounds having been seized last Wednesday, and given to the poor. We understand it to be the Dean's intention, hereafter, to publish the names of all offenders without distinction, and therefore our fair butter sellers had better be on their guard.'

1836: Also on this day, the same paper reported that 'on Tuesday evening last, two pigs were safe in their sty behind a house in Buccleuch Street, but on the next morning one of them was missing. A man was observed not far from the place carrying a pig, and also in Maxwelltown about ten o'clock on Tuesday evening, but as there was no suspicion afloat, he was not looked after. Several gardens and enclosed fields have been entered in the night time, and cabbages, potatoes &c stolen.'

⸺ AUGUST 18TH ⸺

1803: On this day, William and Dorothy Wordsworth and Samuel Taylor Coleridge were in Dumfries at the start of their tour of Scotland. 'Went to the churchyard where Burns is buried. A bookseller accompanied us. He showed us the outside of Burns's house, where he had lived the last three years of his life, and where he died. It has a mean appearance, and is in a bye situation, whitewashed; dirty about the doors, as almost all Scotch houses are; flowering plants in the window.

Went on to visit his grave … When our guide had left us, we turned again to Burns's house … We spoke to the servant-maid at the door, who invited us forward, and we sat down in the parlour. The walls were coloured with a blue wash; on one side of the fire was a mahogany desk, opposite to the window a clock, and over the desk a print from the "Cotter's Saturday Night" …

We were glad to leave Dumfries, which is no agreeable place to them who do not love the bustle of a town that seems to be rising up to wealth. We could think of little else but poor Burns, and his moving about on that unpoetic ground.' (Wordsworth, Dorothy, *Recollections of a Tour Made in Scotland*, 1803)

~ August 19th ~

1905: On this day, it was noted in the *Dumfries and Galloway Courier and Herald* that 'a little credited rumour has been originated that "representative gentlemen" in Maxwelltown are desirous of creating a movement for the amalgamation of the burgh with the sister burgh of Dumfries. We recorded recently in connection with the death of Provost Chicken, Maxwelltown, that of late years an idea of this sort had occasionally "simmered up", but that it was pretty generally recognised that such a movement would be futile in the days of a Provost whose every word and action tended to strengthen independence of spirit among the citizens of the Brig-en' … We also learn on enquiry that in official quarters the subject has not received, and is not likely to receive any serious consideration. The natural outcome of any such movement would, so far as Dumfries is concerned, be a question of further enlargement of its borders; in other words, the annexation and disappearance of Maxwelltown as a separate municipality – a bitter pill which many in the Gallovidian town would not care to swallow.' N.B. The two burghs were amalgamated in 1929.

∼ August 20th ∼

1563: On this day, 'Mary [Queen of Scots] visited Dumfries for the first time. As she was accompanied by her Council, it has been thought that the peace negotiations then going on with England occasioned her journey to the south. But she … was less desirous of securing peace with the English than gaining the favour of the Maxwell family, whose late chief had been lost to her service, but whose present virtual head might still be won over, though he, too, had been holding dangerous dalliance with Protestantism … Before returning to Edinburgh, Mary paid a complimentary visit to the Maxwells, in order, it may be conceived, to secure this object. Secretary Lethington having laid before the Queen certain correspondence between himself and the English Warden on the ostensible business that had drawn her to Dumfries, she broke up the Council and proceeded to Terregles, where she spent the remainder of the day and night, to the high gratification of her hosts, pleased and flattered with having an opportunity to entertain the highest lady in the land, the most accomplished woman of her time – the queen of beauty not less than the Queen of Scots.' (McDowall, William, *History of Dumfries* (2nd Edn., 1873))

~ August 21st ~

1804: On this day, the *Dumfries Weekly Journal* informed its readers that 'by the Statutes of his present Majesty, every person who shall use any Gun, Dog, Net or other Engine for the taking or destruction of Game (not acting as Gamekeeper by deputation duly registered), is required previously to deliver a writing, containing his name and place of abode, to the Sheriff or Stewart Clerk of the Shire or Stewartry where he resides, and to take out a Certificate thereof, stamped with a duty of £3 3s under the penalty of Twenty Pounds. Intimation is hereby made, that offenders will be prosecuted for the statutory penalties. The names of informers will be concealed, and they will be entitled to a suitable reward, on the conviction and recovery of the fines of delinquents.'

1914: Also on this day, the following advertisement appeared: 'Lord Kitchener's Second Army. Wanted at once during Period of War, age 19 to 30 (Ex-Regulars 30–42), For Royal Artillery: Drivers, Gunners, Mechanics, and Men Accustomed to Horses. For Royal Engineers: Sappers, Pioneers, Drivers, Tradesmen, and Men Accustomed to Horses. Apply without delay: Recruiting Officer, Drill Hall, Dumfries.' (*Dumfries and Galloway Standard*)

AUGUST 22ND

1848: On this day, the railway line from Dumfries to Gretna opened for the first time: 'The joy bells of the Midsteeple have announced and ushered in many signal events; but never since they attained their elevation have they heralded such an important circumstance as the inauguration of the lower part of the Nithsdale Railway. The event had long been looked forward to by the people of Dumfries, and now that at length the works were completed – that a fit iron pathway had been prepared for the "steeds of harnessed fire" – eager crowds flocked to the starting place, to see them finally commence their career.

About half-past eleven o'clock the train, which consisted of two locomotives and thirteen carriages, left the station here amid a crowd of deafening cheers, which fairly drowned the snort of the engines and the din of the wheels. The line for some length at first is through a considerable cutting, and on both sides the high ridges were crowded with people … while all along the line cheering salutes of greater or lesser volume announced to the railway passengers that every yard of their progress was watched by sympathising spectators.' (*Dumfries and Galloway Standard*)

— August 23rd —

1899: On this day, the following report appeared in the *Dumfries and Galloway Courier and Herald*: 'A most distressing accident took place on Saturday, when a young boy, three years and nine months old, who lives in the High Street, had his leg torn off above the knee by a passing cab. The accident occurred on the gradient of the High Street opposite Mr. Roddan's butcher shop, near which the boy had been playing. The cab, driven by its owner, Mr. Arthur Dingwall, was proceeding empty at a slow pace down the High Street, and it was not till it had gone half-a-dozen paces past that it was seen that the child had been hurt, the bystanders being horrified to see him lying on the ground, with the right leg completely torn away, and detached from the body. Mrs. Kempsall, Coach and Horses Close, displayed most praiseworthy presence of mind. She took the boy in her arms and got into the cab, and though the child's severed leg was handed in beside her, she kept her head and did all in her power to staunch the bleeding. The boy, although also hurt about the head and hands, is hoped to be able to pull through with care.'

~ AUGUST 24TH ~

1907: The following items appeared in the *Dumfries and Galloway Standard*:

'There is today exhibited in the window of Mr. Reid, Chemist, the first examples of colour photography ever seen in Scotland made by one exposure. The photographs, which are the work of Mr. James E. Goold, Elswick Works, Newcastle, give the full range of all colours, and should be the object of much interest.'

'Among the visitors to the Burns Mausoleum this week, and to the house in which he died, were Mrs. Annie Vincent Burns Hutchinson Scott and her sister, Mrs. Margaret Constance Burns Hutchinson, great-granddaughters of the poet. They were born in Australia, and when their father, Dr. Hutchinson, died, their mother came to England to reside with her own father, Colonel James Glencairn Burns, and her uncle, Colonel William Nichol Burns, at Cheltenham. Mrs. Scott also visited Friars' Carse and Ellisland, and placed a wreath on the tomb of her illustrious ancestor. The ladies were accompanied to the Mausoleum and the house in Burns Street by three members of the Burns Club.'

~ August 25th ~

1837: The *Dumfriesshire and Galloway Herald and Advertiser* contained the following notices on this day:

'Any person or family going from Dumfries to Edinburgh, may have the use of a Gentleman's Carriage, capable of containing 3 inside, and 4 out; but on which no Trunks are to be put. Apply to Mr. Johnstone, Bookseller, Dumfries.'

'Wanted for emigration to New South Wales: Two Blacksmiths, Two Masons, Two Cartwrights, Two Shepherds, One Labourer and a Man who has been accustomed to the Management of a Stallion, to take charge of one on the passage out. Great encouragement will be given to applicants of the above description, not exceeding 30 years of age, provided they are approved of. Certificates of their moral character, and of their being good workmen, will be required. Apply to Mr. Jas. Pagan, Courier Office, Dumfries.'

'Carriages for Sale: A Cab-Phaeton, with glass front and canopy top, which closes in completely – almost new – price £50. Holds four inside and two on the box. Patent Axles and Lamps. Pole and shafts for one or two horses. Also, a very light Two-Wheeled Basket Gig, suited for a pony. Parted with because the owner has no further use for them. Apply to Mr. Inglis, Irish Street.'

∼ AUGUST 26TH ∼

1794: On this day, the *Dumfries Weekly Journal* reported that 'the Contractors for building the New Bridge of Dumfries, having signified that the same is now completed, I am directed to give this public notice that there is to be a General Meeting of the said Committees, and Subscribers to said bridge, on Friday next in the King's Arms Tavern here, at eleven o'clock before noon, for the purpose of inspecting the execution of the work of said Bridge, comparing the same with the Plan and Contracts, and taking it off the hands of the Undertakers, if found sufficiently executed agreeable thereto. – Thos. Goldie, Clerk, Dumfries.'

1817: Also, on this day, the following article appeared in the *Dumfries and Galloway Courier*: 'Yesterday, about noon, as the "Jenny" was on her way from Whitehaven to Dumfries with coals, she sprang a leak nearly opposite to Saturness, and notwithstanding every exertion of Capt. Costin and his crew, in a short time filled with water, and went down. The crew and a female passenger were saved by taking to the boat. Another female passenger, with an infant in her arms, having underrated the danger of her situation, and declined going into the boat, was unfortunately drowned.'

~ AUGUST 27TH ~

1858: On this day, the *Dumfriesshire and Galloway Herald and Register* informed its readers that 'for a considerable period lately, Queensberry Square has been much encumbered by old furniture, fruit stalls, potato carts and other articles of traffic, which have incommoded shopkeepers and others residing in the Square, as well as detracting from the appearance of the Square itself. Mr. James Sloan, merchant, who is a considerable proprietor in the Square, and one of the Commissioners of Police, has for several months past brought the subject under the consideration of the Police Board, but hitherto without succeeding in procuring any abatement in the nuisance. At a recent meeting, he hinted that he was as much entitled to deposit his timber on the Square for sale, as were the brokers, furniture dealers, and others to obstruct it with their articles. Yesterday, with the object of bringing matters to a head, he brought several logs of timber and deposited them near the Monument. On the police interfering, they were given to understand that more timber was forthcoming, upon which the police and Dean of Guild's officer ordered the removal of the potato carts to the New Market, and in a short time the Square was cleared of these; a portion of the timber was shortly afterwards removed, but one large log was left lying across half the width of the Square until after six o'clock in the evening.'

─ August 28th ─

1665: On this day, special instructions were issued to help protect the population of Dumfries from the Great Plague as an important local event drew near. Although couched in the spelling of the seventeenth century, the meaning of the edict is clear: 'The sd day the counsall considering that the pleague incresses in severall places in England, and that the Rood Fair of this burgh is now approaching, to which severall packes of merchandise used to be brought from England, whereby this place may be in danger of infecting if not prevented, they thairfoir prohibite the importing or receiving of any English wair or merchandise within this burgh, or uther goodds whatsoever, efter Wednesday night next. In regaird the sd goods or merchandise are or may be the productioun of the city of Lundon or of some uther infected place in that Kingdome, in wich goods infectioun may lurk and may efter break out. To any of the inhabitantes quho sall receave any such goods, they sall pay the soume of five hundreth merkes and ther houses be closed up and themselves and all family sequestrat without the toun for the space of 40 dayes thereafter.' (Mackie, Charles, (Ed.), *Dumfries and Galloway Notes and Queries* (1913))

— AUGUST 29TH —

1815: On this day, the town's provost wrote to the Committee for the Waterloo Subscription, in London: 'Gentlemen – Some weeks ago, the Magistrates and Council of this Burgh, having taken into consideration the propriety of opening a subscription for the relief of the widows and families of the killed, and of the wounded, at the ever-memorable Battle of Waterloo, I have the happiness to say the proposition was agreed to with perfect unanimity, and most cordially supported and recommended from the pulpit by the clergymen of the two established churches … Commissioners were requested to go through their respective wards, and solicit personally every family and individual, who were thought to fall within the scope of such solicitations. Intimation of the intention, and of the day when the collections were to take place, having been made from the pulpits on the Sabbath preceding, with suitable exhortations, the measure has been attended with the most pleasing success. The amount of the subscription in this small town, where we have few opulent inhabitants, is about Five Hundred and Thirty-Two Pounds, which I have now the pleasure, in the name of the Magistrates and Council, of remitting to the Committee by my draft on Messrs. Coutts &Co.' (*Dumfries Weekly Journal*)

‑ August 30th ‑

1883: On this day, the *Dumfries and Galloway Standard* printed the following letter from an indignant reader, about bathers in the River Nith: 'Whilst fully admitting the benefits to be derived from a practice of the noble art of swimming, I most emphatically protest against the extremely public manner in which that art has recently been indulged by the youth of Dumfries and Maxwelltown. On Sabbath evening last, the climax was reached in that offensive practice by some boys … who actually had the impudence to amuse themselves in their amphibious gambols right to the side of the Suspension Bridge. Over this there were large numbers of ladies passing to church (it being just about six o'clock), and to these at least the occurrence must have been very offensive. Besides this, the spectacle was just between the two most popular walks of Dumfriesians, many of whom had to go out of their way to avoid the sight. A word to the wise is enough. I therefore trust that this will be sufficient to induce the perpetrators of this unseemly practice to bathe at more fitting times and places, or else to induce the police to put a forcible stop to such outrages against public decency.'

~ August 31st ~

1922: On this day, John Hanson (real name John Stanley Watts), the well-known singer and star of musical theatre, was born in Ontario, Canada. However, his parents returned to Britain when he was three years old, and he subsequently became a pupil at Dumfries Academy. After serving in the Royal Air Force during the Second World War, and also qualifying as an engineer, Hanson – a tenor – turned to his first love, singing, and in 1946 embarked upon a professional career in the theatre that would keep him in the public eye for decades. Over the years, Hanson was probably most closely associated with 'The Desert Song', an operetta in which he toured on many occasions during his career, also appearing in a West End production of it during the late 1960s. Other operettas in which Hanson appeared with notable success included 'The Student Prince' and 'The Vagabond King', together with musicals such as 'Lilac Time' and 'The Dancing Years'. He also made more than twenty long-playing records, with his recording of 'The Student Prince' selling over 300,000 copies. He died in December 1998. (Obituary, *The Independent*, December 7th 1998)

~ September 1st ~

1778: On this day, the *Dumfries Weekly Journal* reported a theft: 'Whereas some evil disposed person or persons, on Sunday night last, broke into the garden of the Rev. Mr. Babington, and stole out of his hot-bed frame a large melon, on which he set a very high value … Mr. Babington will give a reward of Two Guineas, to anyone who shall give him information of the person or persons concerned in the said robbery. And as he has reason to believe that said Melon may be exposed to sale, he requests that any person to whom it may be offered will give him information thereof. It will be very easily distinguished, by the singularity both of its size and form; it being remarkably large, of an oblong figure with a singular knob at the smaller end of it.'

1915: Also on this day, it was noted that 'at a sitting of the Dumfries Children's Court on Saturday, four lads living in Irish Street pleaded guilty to have stolen a quantity of apples from a garden in Noblehill. One, on account of his age, was dismissed, and the others were fined half-a-crown each.' (*Dumfries and Galloway Standard*)

~ September 2nd ~

1939: On this day, the *Dumfries and Galloway Standard* reported on the town's preparations for war on the Home Front: 'The immense and admirable work of planning which has been going on during the past few months is now bearing fruit, and Dumfries is ready so far as organization is concerned.

No one can tell what the first impact of war may be. It is expected that the worst aerial attacks would be in the early weeks, and it is then we need the trained men and women.

On Tuesday the Y.M.C.A. in Castle Street was taken over as headquarters, and will be occupied as such shortly. There will be the Chief Warden's office, the store, lecture rooms etc.

The issue of gas masks is almost complete. Over 1,900 were issued on Sunday, and arrangements are being made for the issue of what remains to those persons who have been away from home during the past few weeks. On Sunday persons in Rosevale House, Moorheads' Hospital and other institutions were equipped, as well as many invalids and other persons unable to go for their own.

In Dumfries evacuees will be brought to Dumfries Academy, which will form the central point for distribution.'

~ SEPTEMBER 3RD ~

1793: On this day, the following reminder of the town's horse-racing past appeared: 'Dumfries Races – To be run for, on the course at Tinwald Downs, on Tuesday 1st October, a Purse of One Hundred Guineas to be given by Lieutenants Maule and Oswald, of the West Lowland Fencibles – four mile heats, the runners to carry 12 stones.

On Wednesday 2nd: Fifty Guineas for all ages.

On Thursday 3rd: Fifty Guineas for all ages.

On Friday 4th: Fifty Guineas for three and four year-olds.

On Saturday 5th, or as shall be fixed on the Thursday preceding, Fifty Guineas by the Dumfries and Galloway Hunt, to Real Hunters who hunted last season, with an established pack of hounds, and certified as such by the master of the hounds they hunted with. To carry 12 stones.

The horses to be entered at the George Inn, Dumfries, on Monday the 30th of September, between four and six in the afternoon, when the requisite certificates must be produced. The winner of the Hundred Guineas not to be allowed to start for any of the Fifties without the consent of the stewards. All disputes to be settled by the stewards, or whom they shall appoint.' (*Dumfries Weekly Journal*)

— September 4th —

1827: On this day, the *Dumfries Weekly Journal* reported a shocking discovery: 'Yesterday afternoon, betwixt three and four o'clock, the body of a female infant child was found under the grating which covers the mouth of the common sewer in Bank Street, by one of the scavengers employed in clearing out the sewer. It was wrapt up in a piece of white cloth, tied with knitting, and after being washed it was carried to the Council Chamber, but no discovery has yet been made of the unnatural mother.'

1833: Also on this day, it was stated that 'Mrs. Draffen respectfully begs to announce her arrival in Dumfries, with a large assortment of French and India-Rubber Corsets, of the most fashionable patterns, and also a great variety of Children's Corsets … Mrs. Draffen particularly recommends her Elastic Band, which, for the elegance it imparts to the shape, and the comfort it affords to the wearer, will be found invaluable. Mrs. Draffen will be happy to receive Ladies from 10 till 4 o'clock daily, at No.20 Castle Street until the 15th next, when the urgency of her other engagements will compel her to leave Dumfries.' (*Dumfries Times*)

– September 5th –

1826: On this day, a report celebrating new developments in the town, especially that of gas-lighting, was published: 'For a long period Dumfries was so stationary that it might have been included in the list of what an Irishman calls "finished towns". But a new spirit has gone abroad. If we consider the number of streets in Dumfries and Maxwelltown that have been finished, planned, and partly executed within the last few years, the tenements rebuilt, the houses gutted to make shops of, or in other respects remodelled and repaired – the marvels, in a word, worked by Messrs. Sinclair and Howat, Newall and Inman, Brown, Hair and many others, we are quite sure that the original shooters of the "Siller Gun", were they to rise from their graves at this moment, would scarcely be able to recognise the ancient burgh they lived, died, and earned their bread in. The widening of English Street, and the approach by the Townhead, are both very great improvements; and strangers visiting us from the South and North must now receive favourable impressions of the cleanliness and neatness that characterise Dumfries from the moment they approach the shores of the Nith.' (McDowall, William, *History of Dumfries* (2nd Edn., 1873))

~ September 6th ~

1939: On this day, three days after Prime Minister Neville Chamberlain had announced that Britain was at war with Germany, the following report appeared in the *Dumfries and Galloway Standard*: 'Early on Sunday morning, it became apparent there was a risk that the full quota of evacuees assigned to Dumfries could not be dealt with, and representations were made to the Department of Health on that point. The Department took the view that evacuation must go on, but they sent a representative to Dumfries to try to arrange for as many as possible of the Sunday arrivals being accommodated in the areas of other authorities. Arrangements were made in the burgh for the reception of evacuees in church halls, where provision was made to give the arrivals a meal. Later it was found possible to accommodate all evacuees, the quota being shared between Dumfries and the Stewartry. The Dumfries authorities, working on the assumption that they would have to accommodate the full complement of evacuees, sent a message to the ministers in the town, requesting that appeals should be made from the pulpits for all the accommodation that could be obtained. If the maximum number of evacuees had arrived, it would have meant an additional 2,300, but the transfers to other areas meant that Dumfries had actually only to find accommodation for 340.'

⤙ September 7th ⤚

1819: On this day, the *Dumfries and Galloway Courier* reported that 'last week, Mrs. Cook, the celebrated giantess, made her first appearance in Dumfries, and was pretty generally visited by the inhabitants of this town and neighbourhood. Many persons, however, were disappointed in the expectations they had formed of her extraordinary stature; and it is even asserted that there is an inhabitant of our own good town who might lay claim to the 1,000 guineas which Mr. Cook's partiality as a husband induces him to offer to anyone who can produce an equal to his gigantic spouse. For so large a woman, however, Mrs. Cook is allowed to be uncannily handsome, and as bodies are well known to appear more gigantic from being misshapen, probably this circumstance may account for the disappointment expressed by some of her visitors. In travelling betwixt different towns, we believe the giantess frequently takes the start of her retinue; and among the persons who paid their respects to her on Wednesday last, there happened to be an honest Gallovidian, who had lately overtaken her on the road betwixt Gatehouse and Kirkcudbright. On entering the place of exhibition he was, of course, a good deal surprised at finding his old acquaintance transformed into "a wonderful phenomenon of nature".'

~ September 8th ~

1812: On this day, the *Dumfries Weekly Journal* announced that 'Messrs. Paul Ranson and Jean Pierre Chapelain, two French surgeons, prisoners-of-war on parole in this place, have received from the Honourable the Commissioners of the Transport Board, passports to return immediately to France, in consequence of their active exertions in assisting to extinguish the alarming fire which broke out here on 25th July last. This act of generosity is highly creditable to Government; and while it affords a great relief to the unavoidable calamities of war, it proves that there is no situation, however unfavourable, which may not afford opportunities for worth and merit to distinguish themselves.'

1813: Also on this day, a young William Charles Macready, who would later become the greatest tragedian of his age, made his first of many appearances on the stage of the town's Theatre Royal. The *Dumfries and Galloway Courier* reported that 'Young Mr. Macready has received a liberal education, and the accurate conception of his part [Hamlet], united with the classic grace of his elocution, proves that the labours of his teachers have not been misapplied. His carriage and action were dignified and graceful, and the energy and feeling which animated his delivery, by their instant appeal to the sympathy of his auditors, manifestly evinced that nature was his guide.'

~ September 9th ~

1833: On this day, the following notice appeared: 'At a time when the Members of the Relief Fund Committee were doing everything in their power to mitigate the effects of the direful calamity [a cholera epidemic in the town], it was resolved, among other things, to advance small sums by way of loans to persons who had never received charity, with the view of fostering their independence. In the Minute of Committee, it is expressly stipulated that an obligation for repayment should be taken from each individual. Such obligations were readily granted and, in many instances, by persons most respectable in appearance. Though the Committee may have erred, their object was good; and yet, strange to say, out of fifty pounds expended in this way, only SIX SHILLINGS have been repaid, and these by a single individual. This remarkable and discreditable circumstance was brought under the notice of the last meeting of the Committee, and the Secretary was instructed to say in the newspapers that, unless payment was made to himself, or the Treasurer, within six weeks from the present date, publication would be made of the Names of the Borrowers, in every case wherein a satisfactory reason had not been assigned.' (*Dumfries and Galloway Courier*)

~ September 10th ~

1884: The following ill-tempered letter, published on this day, was signed 'Fair Play': 'May I be permitted, through the medium of your columns, to call the attention of the public to a system of begging that is vigorously carried out in our midst at present. I refer to the Brigade of Nuns, or, as they are sometimes called, "Sisters of Mercy", that are told off in pairs to call at our offices, shops, and dwelling-houses to beg for money for some object connected with their own denomination, and with which those outside that denomination can have no sympathy whatever. Poor, hungry, and naked men and women, who are driven to our doors by sheer necessity, are frequently treated very coldly, and even run the risk of being locked up, but these dressed up dolls are allowed to pursue their calling unmolested, and are, I believe, in the meantime making a good thing of it.

Is this as it should be? I leave the public to judge. If I be allowed to hazard a hint to our Roman Catholic friends in Dumfries, I would say call these "scouts" into "camp", and give strict orders that they are to keep within their own "lines".' (*Dumfries and Galloway Standard*)

— September 11th —

1794: On this day, it was found that the (supposedly) all-male ranks of the Hopetoun Fencibles, stationed in the town since the first week of July, actually contained a woman who, it is believed, had joined the regiment at least eight months earlier. In the eighteenth century, of course, no female was allowed to serve her country as a uniformed soldier (a situation that only changed during the First World War, with the formation of the Women's Army Auxiliary Corps), and disguise was the only option for those wishing to do so.

'She went by the name of John Nicholson (her real one being Jean Clark),' reported the *Dumfries Weekly Journal*, 'and, strange as it may appear, was esteemed a wag among the lasses. It is even said that she caused a lass in the Bridgend of this place to fall deeply in love with her; but who, since this discovery, is perfectly cured. Previous to her assuming the character of a soldier, we are informed, she had accustomed herself to the dress and habits of a man, having been bred to the business of a weaver at Closeburn, and employed as a manservant at Ecclefechan.' (Mackie, Charles, (Ed.), *Dumfries and Galloway Notes and Queries* (1913))

~ September 12th ~

1771: Tobias Smollett's final picaresque novel, *The Expedition of Humphry Clinker*, was published in this year. Composed in an epistolary form it recounts, through a series of letters written by the principal characters, the exploits of the irascible Matthew Bramble and his entourage during a rambling tour they made of the country. The party included his sister, Tabitha and her maid, together with Bramble's nephew and niece, Jery and Lydia Melford. Beginning in Wales, their journey takes them by way of Gloucester, Bath, London and Yorkshire (among other places), before the travellers eventually arrive north of the border. Prior to re-entering England on their return journey, they stop at Dumfries, as Jery Melford informs a friend in a letter dated on this day:

'Having passed the night at the castle of Drumlanrig, by invitation of the Duke himself … we prosecuted our journey to Dumfries, a very elegant trading town near the borders of England, where we found plenty of good provision and excellent wine, at very reasonable prices, and the accommodation as good in all respects as in any part of South Britain. If I was confined to Scotland for life, I would chuse[*sic*] Dumfries as the place of my residence.' (Smollett, Tobias, *The Expedition of Humphry Clinker*, 1771)

~ September 13th ~

1814: On this day, the *Dumfries and Galloway Courier* reported that 'on Thursday last, the anniversary meeting of the Dumfries and Galloway Horticultural Society took place in the Court-house … Over the Judge's bench was placed a large and splendid Crown, composed of a rich variety of flowers, supported by a naval and military column, on which were inscribed … the names of our immortal heroes; on the pedestal of the one was a bust of Nelson, and on the other a bust of Wellington. Behind the bench was a superb transparent painted King's Arms. At each end of the room was placed a fine large arbour, filled with beautiful greenhouse plants, and fruit trees in full bearing, in pots; the whole connected together by festoons of bay leaves and flowers, interspersed with clusters of grapes, which together produced a very fine effect. The paintings were by Mr. Stewart, drawing-master, a very ingenious artist. The large table in the middle of the room was covered with delicious fruit. No sooner were the doors opened, than the house was crowded with the most respectable concourse of the town and surrounding country; and a more brilliant display of youth and beauty never before graced a public assembly in Dumfries.'

~ September 14th ~

1842: On this day, the following announcement appeared in the *Dumfries Times*: 'Mr. Pritchard, late of the Theatre Royal, Edinburgh, the Theatre Royal, Dublin, and the Theatre Royal, Covent Garden, London, respectfully informs the Public at Large that he has taken the Dumfries Theatre for the ensuing season. With a view to meet the wish and gratify the taste of every admirer of Histrionic representation, he will sedulously endeavour to present such entertainments as he hopes will gain general approbation.

Mr. Pritchard has selected a Company of Performers who have maintained their position in the Metropolitan and Provincial Theatres, and they will successively appear in their various grades as rapidly as the opportunity of the cast of characters will permit for their individual advantages. Mr. Pritchard forcibly feels the responsibility of his situation and, being alive to that, both interest as well as inclination must prove his exertions while endeavouring to obtain public favour. He has ever held in view the words of Dr. Johnson, that "He who lives to please, must please to live". Every exertion has been used by Mr. Pritchard to engage a talented and efficient Company, for the representation of our Standard Works of Merit with the most successful pieces of Modern Date, which will be produced in rapid succession.'

~ September 15th ~

1854: On this day, the *Dumfriesshire and Galloway Herald and Register* reported on 'the case of Mr. Thorburn of Ryedale against Mr. Kennedy, the bridge tacksman, for the alleged illegal seizure and detention of his horse and cart at the bridge. Mr. Crichton [acted] for the pursuer, and Mr. Jenkins for the defender. It was alleged by the pursuer that the defender had illegally taken possession of his horse and cart while laden with potatoes, and detained them to the injury of his character and business. He claimed from the defender 4*s*, the sum paid at an inn for keeping and feeding the horse during detention; 3*s* overcharge of customs on potatoes and £1 10*s* legal expenses. Mr. Jenkins denied the seizure, but contended that the tacksman had right to seize parties who refused to pay the dues charged at the bridge. Mr. Crichton said his case did not require him to deny the right to levy dues at the bridge, but he was prepared to prove that the sum asked from his client was too high. The Sheriff said he was aware that constant discussion had been for some time going on at the bridge regarding the right to levy dues, and as this case in some measure involved that question, he would not dispose of it at present, but remit it to the ordinary court roll.'

— September 16th —

1742: On this day, Mary – or Margaret – MacDonald, having been arrested under suspicion of stealing a pair of stockings from a chapman (or peddler) in the town, 'was locked up in the 3rd storey of the pledge house where women were usually imprisoned.

As she was being locked up, she begged for a bit of candle to light her to bed. This the jailer gave her, locked up the prison and went home to bed. He was roused in the night and came and found the place in flames. Only a part of her body had not been consumed with fire. The fire does not seem to have spread.' (Edgar, Robert, (Ed. Reid, R.C.), *An Introduction to the History of Dumfries* (J. Maxwell & Sons, Dumfries, 1915))

1869: Also on this day, the town's infirmary (later the offices for the Health Board) was the focus of a ceremony: 'That the foundation stone might be laid with due pomp and ceremony, "the sons of light" mustered in great force and, with other corporate bodies, made a grand processional march from the Academy grounds to the site … There the first stone of the New Infirmary was laid with mystic rites by the Provincial Grand Master, Mr. Lauderdale Maitland of Eccles.' (McDowall, William, *History of Dumfries* (2nd Edn., 1873))

— September 17th —

1793: On this day, the *Dumfries Weekly Journal* advertised that 'James Creighton, Surgeon and Apothecary, wishes to announce to his friends and the public that he has just now got home from London, with a large and fresh assortment of all kinds of the very best Medicines, which he will sell at his New Laboratory, Plainstones. He prepares an Ointment himself for Corns … superior to anything of the kind yet offered to the public for totally eradicating these tormenting excrecensies. He also prepares an Ointment for the curing of burning, and an Ointment for the Itch, which, upon trial, will be found to be an infallible remedy against that loathsome and troublesome disease … It may be used at all times without any danger of the patient's catching cold, or confining himself to a particular regimen.

At the New Laboratory may also be had materials for Diet Drinks from 7*d* the packet, Worm Cakes, and almost every modern Medicine in vogue in Britain. Also, lastly, all kinds of Horse Drugs, which will be sold on the lowest terms. The poor will be supplied with medicines and advice at all times GRATIS.'

– September 18th –

1839: On this day, the distinguished Circuit Judge, Lord Cockburn, and his entourage arrived at Dumfries: 'I had not been there for several years, and found two or three changes. The old windmill has been converted into what they call an observatory; which means a windmill-looking tower, with a bit of shrubbery round it, ginger-beer in the ground floor, a good telescope in the second storey, and a camera obscura in the third.

I never enter mad-houses, but the new Lunatic Asylum is very striking outside, and stands on a fine site. While asking a little boy on the road some questions about it, he used a word, which it is to be hoped does not truly indicate the character of the internal treatment. He pointed out a man who was walking in a gallery as "the Breaker". "What do you call 'the Breaker'?" "The man that breaks the daft folk." A lad beside us also used the term as one familiar.

I have always liked Dumfries. It stands high in the rank of our Scottish provincial towns and my decision is, that its windows are the cleanest in Scotland.' (Lord Cockburn, *Circuit Journeys*, (2nd Edn., 1889))

— September 19th —

1914: On this day, the *Dumfries and Galloway Standard* reported the unusual death of a horse: 'A cob belonging to Mr. J.G. Kirk, King Street, Dumfries, yesterday met its death under peculiar circumstances. The horse was an Irish five-year-old purchased by Mr. Kirk a fortnight ago. For the past few days, a groom named McGhie had been walking him about the town with a pair of long reins in order to accustom him to motor vehicles. Yesterday afternoon he was proceeding down Leafield Road when, at the entrance to the Glasgow & South-Western Railway Goods Yard, opposite Hoods Loaning, the animal took fright at a passing motor car and, wheeling to the left, dashed across the yard and through the goods shed at the other side on to the rails beyond, dragging McGhie after him. The steam issuing from an engine which was shunting, caused the horse to rear and stand straight up on his hind legs, and he fell back over, striking his head on the rails with great violence. The animal lay perfectly still, and on examination it was found that it had been killed instantaneously.'

~ September 20th ~

1824: On this day, 'there died in Dundee an old gentleman named Sealey, who in his day had been a noted dancing-master. Earlier in the century he had lived at Dumfries, where he was greatly esteemed for his personal qualities. Mr. Sealey had had a remarkable career of nearly ninety years. In his youth, he was an opera dancer at the London theatres; he travelled the Continent and had resided at various Courts. He had performed on the same stage with Garrick, and danced a minuet with the famous Nancy Dawson, in the reign of George the Second. Mr. Sealey maintained a respectable character, was remarkably neat and cleanly in his appearance, and such was his nicety in dress that he changed every article of his out-of-door apparel, including his very shirt, immediately on entering the house.' (Mackie, Charles, (Ed.), *Dumfries and Galloway Notes and Queries* (1913))

1837: Also on this day, the *Dumfries Times* carried the following notice: 'A considerable time ago, we announced to the public that the steam plough of J. Heathcote, Esq., M.P., would, at the request of the Local Committee of the Highland and Agricultural Society of Scotland, work in Locharmoss during part of the week in which the great Cattle Show is to take place at Dumfries. The plough has now arrived at the scene of action, and is being put into working order.'

~ September 21st ~

1853: On this day, the *Dumfries and Galloway Standard* reported that 'a meeting of the joint Committee of the Police Commissioners and Parochial Board was held on Saturday evening, at which it was resolved to take immediate steps for the removal of piggeries and other nuisances …The first, second, and fourth wards were generally in a clean state – the remaining one not quite so satisfactory; but the police and scavengers were actively engaged in cleansing by the application of water with the fire-hose.

The authorities of the sister burgh of Maxwelltown have also been active in cleansing the closes, and whitewashing some of the houses outside, and a few inside. At a meeting of the Police Commissioners held on Monday evening, it was resolved to engage an additional scavenger, and also two men to whitewash and cleanse the houses. Instructions were also given to the Inspector of the Poor to remove all piggeries underneath the floors and windows of inhabited houses; to see that the whitewashing of the houses was properly performed, and that the streets were flushed with water every morning.'

— September 22nd —

1680: On this day, the following report was released: 'Pestered by the children of the Grammar School petitioning for the vacation to begin sooner than usual, the [burghal senate] actually passed a resolution rendering such refractory juveniles, and all who absented themselves from the classes before the 5th of September each year, liable to imprisonment. When they could stoop to such trivialities it is less strange to see them causing habitual drunkards and swearers to sign an obligation enforcing their perpetual banishment from the burgh; or carrying out several stringent Acts of Parliament directed against intemperance and profanity, in accordance with which "persons convicted of drunkenness, and haunting of taverns and ale-houses after ten of the clock at night, or any tyme of the day except the time of travell or for refreshments" were liable to be put in the jugs or jail six hours; and "all persons whatsoever within this burgh or suburbs thereof" were enjoined "not to brew, or to work any other handiework or labour on the Lord's Day, or to be found on the streets standing or walking."' (McDowall, William, *History of Dumfries* (2nd Edn., 1873))

~ September 23rd ~

1939: The *Dumfries and Galloway Standard* reported on local preparations for the National Register. This was an emergency measure enacted at the beginning of the Second World War, to enable the issue of identity cards.

'For the purposes of making the National Register, Dumfries and the surrounding area has been formed into forty-one districts, and an enumerator appointed for each district will start on Monday, with the distribution of the forms. The registration work is in charge of Miss E.A. Brown, the registrar for Dumfries, and the headquarters will be at the Municipal Chambers. The register will be made on Friday 29th September, and the Act requires that those to be included in the schedule are "all persons who spent the night of National Registration Day in this household or establishment, whether as members, visitors, boarders, or servants, or who joined the household or establishment the next morning without having been enumerated anywhere else. No one else may be included." The schedules will be collected on Saturday and Sunday, the two days following on the day of registration. Where necessary, the enumerators will give any help required in the filling up of the forms.'

– September 24th –

1793: On this day, the *Dumfries Weekly Journal* printed the following notice: 'Profile Shades in Miniature: George Bruce proposes to stay a short time in Dumfries, where he will take the Shades of such as are pleased to employ him, at his room at Mr. Brand's, watchmaker, High Street, and humbly solicits all who wish to procure accurate Likenesses of their friends and families to take the earliest opportunity. Time of sitting, Five Minutes.'

1832: Also on this day, the following letter was published in the *Dumfries and Galloway Courier*: 'Sir, I have witnessed with surprise the indecent method adopted here, for transporting patients to the Cholera Hospital. In my opinion, nothing is more calculated to spread the disease, if infectious, or add to the terror already experienced by all classes in Dumfries, than to carry the unfortunate sufferers through the streets upon an open board. I would therefore suggest that, instead of the board now used, there should be substituted a wicker-basket 7 feet long, 3 feet broad, 2 feet deep, and the top (with curtains attached) a foot-and-a-half high. A pole placed on each side will enable two men to carry the patient with ease – Your humble servant &c.'

⁓ September 25th ⁓

1889: On this day, the *Dumfries and Galloway Standard* announced that 'the great autumnal horse market is being held in Dumfries this week, and today also the business of the hiring fair is proceeding in Queensberry Square. There's a large attendance both of employers and servants, and engagements are being pretty freely entered into, at rates which show little change from those of last year. Young ploughmen of experience receive from £9 to £11; "halflins", £7 to £8; boys £5 to £6 10s; dairymaids £7 to £9; byre-women and outworkers, £7 to £8 10s; kichen women £6 to £8 – all for the half-year with board.

The "shows", which form an established feature of the fairs, seem annually to increase in number … Mechanical horses, imitation switchback railways, and other contrivances of the "roundabout" order have for some time been growing favourites, and are represented on this occasion in still greater number and variety. Of shooting galleries there is the usual complement. And in the general medley, the master of the "noble art of self-defence", the conjurors, the exhibitor of monstrosities, and the itinerant photographer, all compete for public patronage.'

— September 26th —

1797: On this day, the following notice appeared in the *Dumfries Weekly Journal*: 'Lost or strayed, on Wednesday, from the Sands of Dumfries, three two-year-old Stots. Two of them are black, and one brawney'd, and one of the black ones a little null'd.

Whoever will give information respecting the above Stots, are requested to do it to David Hay, at Hook, near Lockerby; William McNaight, foot of the Friars' Vennel, or John Coultart, at Townhead, Dumfries, and they will be handsomely rewarded. If they are found in the possession of any person, after this intimation, they will be reckoned as stolen, and prosecuted accordingly.'

1838: Also on this day, the *Dumfries and Galloway Courier* commented on the roaring trade in cattle sent through Dumfries en route to markets in England: 'All the St. Faith's cattle are now on their way, and a weary march it is of some 340 miles. Such of them as were pastured in the Stewartry and shire passed through this town, and formed, we must say, a beautiful sight. Mr. McCubbin had two droves of 400 each, which must have cost somewhere about £10,000, and there were so many smaller ones that from £30,000 to £40,000 will be brought into Galloway by the sales of the approaching market.'

⚊ September 27th ⚊

1837: On this day, the *Dumfries Times* announced a forthcoming procession of the Dumfries Abstinence Society: 'Hitherto, processions of public bodies have been generally followed by dissipation, and have been regarded by drunkards as favourable opportunities for more than usual indulgence.

The Procession of the Abstinence Society is intended to prove that men can be social and happy, and enjoy the recreations of life without the aid of intoxicating liquors. It is likewise designed to afford a manifestation to the public of the happy change produced on some who had acquired an unenviable notoriety, and who, instead of traversing the streets as in former years clothed in rags and degraded below the beasts, will this year walk in the society of the sober and respectable, neat in their clothing, healthy in their bodies, and sound in their minds. It is hoped that this public demonstration of the numbers who abstain from intoxicating liquors and of reformed drunkards, will tend to shame dissipation from our streets, force the lovers of strong drink to retire to darkness, draw forth the approval of all who love the good of men, and encourage many to … join the increasing band that now holds the banner "Abstinence".'

~ September 28th ~

1957: On this day, it was reported that 'the question of providing facilities for old people in Dumfries to enable them to indulge in such hobbies as knitting, carpentry and other handiwork, was considered at the annual general meeting of the Burgh of Dumfries Old People's Welfare Committee, which was held in the Municipal Chambers on Tuesday evening. It was decided that such an innovation would be impracticable until the committee had premises of their own in which an old folks' workshop could be established.

Mrs. Dykes, vice-chairman of the committee, said the suggestion had been made that old folk could help in factory work, and a number of old people were already doing finger glove work in their own homes. They were given certain work to do by factories, which occupied their time and for which they were paid a certain amount. Mr. Aitken, committee secretary, said that the idea behind the proposal was that there should be a workshop which would be open all day. Mrs. Murdoch, committee member, recalled that at one time there was a workshop for the old folk in Queen Street, opposite the Electric Theatre, in which many lovely articles were made.' (*Dumfries and Galloway Standard*)

⁓ September 29th ⁓

1792: On this day, the Theatre Royal opened in Shakespeare Street. The fact that it is still in business today means that it has become Scotland's oldest working theatre (and reputedly the third oldest in Britain). Robert Burns was a member of the Theatre Royal's earliest audiences. There was a suggestion that he might write a play to be performed there but, although that did not come to pass, he did compose several prologues that were spoken on the theatre's stage.

During the nineteenth century this 'pocket edition of a theatre', as the playwright J.M. Barrie described it, where the audience in the dress circle 'could almost shake hands with the man in the pit', attracted some of the finest players in the land, including Edmund Kean, who paid several visits before his untimely death in 1833. William Charles Macready, the greatest tragedian of his age, also performed here.

Barrie, who was educated in Dumfries, paid regular visits to the Theatre Royal during the 1870s. Writing many years later, he recalled the building as 'so tiny that you smile to it as a child when you go in'. Nowadays, the theatre is home to the town's Guild of Players, and also hosts other theatrical and musical events.

∼ September 30th ∼

1939: On this day, the *Dumfries and Galloway Standard* announced that 'The electricity and gas undertakings in Dumfries will shortly be sending out notices to consumers, dealing with the rationing of supplies under the Fuel and Lighting Order, under which there will be control in the national interest of the consumption of coal, gas, and electricity by all domestic consumers, and certain small industrial consumers. All premises will be controlled in this way, with the exception of factories and industrial premises using the equivalent in electricity, gas, and coal of one hundred tons of coal. Munitions factories and industrial plants necessary for the conduct of the war naturally have first claim on fuel supplies. Consequently, the consumption by domestic and other small users will be rationed in order to conserve stocks, and to guard against possible breakdown of communications.

The general principle of the rationing of domestic consumers is that they will only be allowed to use a certain proportion of last year's consumption of electricity, coal, and gas. Actually, in the case of Dumfries, the consumption for the year ended 30th April 1939 will be taken as the basic ration, and the proportion of this which consumers are entitled to use for the present has been fixed by the Secretary for Mines at 75 per cent.'

~ October 1st ~

1828: On this day, the poet and novelist Sir Walter Scott visited Dumfries. He attended a public dinner that was held at the New Assembly Rooms in George Street, at which the Duke of Buccleuch and Queensberry was feted to mark his coming-of-age. Not surprisingly, it was quite a large gathering that contained most of the town's leading lights. Scott, of course, was an immensely celebrated figure at this time, only four years before his death. It was also a period of some turbulence in his private life, as a recent banking crisis in London had led to his financial ruin. However, Scott appeared undaunted by his woes on this occasion. After dinner, he replied to three toasts: the first to 'The Health of Our Great and Illustrious Visitor'; the second to 'The Sheriff of Selkirkshire' (a post to which he had been appointed in 1799); and a third to 'The Literature of the Country'. The *Dumfries Weekly Journal* subsequently reported that 'the worthy baronet touched so playfully on a variety of topics, and excited by his wit so much merriment and good humour, that our reporter, amidst the cheers and laughter which followed, found it totally impossible to discharge his duty.' (Mackie, Charles, (Ed.), *Dumfries and Galloway Notes and Queries* (1913))

～ OCTOBER 2ND ～

1817: Polito's Menagerie had just arrived in town, and on this day, an advertisement in the *Dumfries Weekly Journal* described it as 'indisputably the most grand, rich and complete collection of rare and beautiful living animals ever known to travel in any part of the world, affording an opportunity of viewing, at one glance, every kind of extraordinary, rare and valuable quadruped or bird that ever crossed the ocean.' Among the animals and creatures on display were a boa constrictor, a horned horse, a zebra, an elephant, a camel, three lions, two tigers, several panthers, an ocelot, an African porcupine, a lynx, a wolf, kangaroos, jackalls, a pair of civet cats, a pelican, a great condor, a vulture, silver-headed eagles and more besides. Transporting such a potentially lethal cargo around the country must have been an operation of epic proportions. 'This truly magnificent collection of living animals will be found greatly to excel every other which has yet appeared in any part of the United Kingdom. Indeed, Mr. Polito may, with propriety, challenge the whole world to produce, at one view, so grand an assemblage of the most interesting objects of Natural History, as that which he has now the honour of offering to the Public attention.'

⟵ OCTOBER 3RD ⟶

1929: On this day, the hitherto sister burghs of Maxwelltown and Dumfries were amalgamated: 'The afternoon was a general holiday. Both towns were en fete; all the public buildings and business premises being decorated with flags and bunting; and in the evening illuminated with very effective colour schemes. Delightful weather favoured the outdoor ceremonies, and the bright sunshine added to the general gaiety of the occasion.

St. Michael's Bridge was the scene of the principal ceremony of the day and there, before a crowd of some ten thousand townspeople, the Duke of Buccleuch, Lord-Lieutenant of Dumfriesshire, opened a gateway which had been erected between the two burghs, symbolical of removing all barriers to union. Through the opened gateway the town councillors of Maxwelltown marched, entering into the larger burgh in which their town is now incorporated. At this ceremony, very appropriately, an important part was given to the children, who are the future citizens of Greater Dumfries. As a spirited and enlivening conclusion to a great day in local annals, there was a remarkably fine display of fireworks on the Millgreen.'
(*Dumfries and Galloway Standard*)

~ OCTOBER 4TH ~

1950: On this day, the *Dumfries and Galloway Standard* contained the following report: 'A resolution passed at the annual conference of the Scottish Association of Executive Health Councils, held in Dumfries on Friday, called for meetings to be arranged between executive councils and local authorities "to convert the present lukewarm campaign against tuberculosis into a national crusade." The resolution, which was tabled by the Edinburgh Executive Council, also stated that, as a result of those meetings, there should be made available in Scotland 1350 beds in infectious diseases or general hospitals for the treatment of tuberculosis; that a vigorous campaign should be initiated to attract trained and student nurses to the tuberculosis service; that preventoria should be instituted for the reception of children from homes where open cases of tuberculosis were known to exist; and that a vigorous and sustained campaign of public education regarding the nature and problem of tuberculosis should be opened. The conference was held in the County Hall, Dumfries, and was attended by a hundred delegates from all over Scotland.' (Scotland was the only country in Europe at this time where the annual number of tuberculosis cases had shown no improvement since the Second World War.)

~ October 5th ~

1817: On this day, it was announced that 'the Annual Charity Sermon, for the Dumfries Hospital and Poor-House, will be preached in the New Church by the Rev. James Thomson, Minister of Dundee. The directors of the Hospital are aware of the frequency of calls in favour of one benevolent object or another; yet they are persuaded that the venerable Institution, which now solicits their assistance, whose beneficial effects have been experienced for above half a century, will not be neglected ... The relief of suffering humanity will always have a powerful claim with the truly benevolent. Within the House of Charity, about 60 individuals are supported, besides a number of poor people who receive a weekly supply in their own houses. The young and the old are alike the objects of its care. Some particular circumstances, together with the high price of provisions last season, have involved the Institution in more than usual difficulties. An appeal to the Public has never been made in vain, and at this time it is hoped it will have the desired effect.' (*Dumfries Weekly Journal*)

— OCTOBER 6TH —

1899: On this day, Barnum & Bailey's circus visited the town and erected its great canvas tent at Cresswell. 'The procession, which is the indispensable prelude to a circus performance, was on a scale in keeping with the gigantic character of the Barnum & Bailey concern. It started from the Glebe Road entrance to the show fields and perambulated the town. At the head of the procession was a team of forty beautiful and finely-matched brown horses, controlled by a single driver and drawing the band chariot. Then came groups of tigers, lions, leopards, panthers, hyenas, wolves and bears, all in their separate cages. Most impressive sight of all was the herd of elephants, sixteen in number, and including two of gigantic proportions. One of them, possessing a splendid pair of tusks, weighs five-and-three-quarter tons. In advance of these ponderous but stately children of the East, walked a dozen camels and dromedaries, looking as much at home on the granite causeway of Dumfries as they would in their native deserts of Siberia or Arabia. There were further attractions in the form of an Italian band, and silver trumpets heralding a special tableau depicting the return of Columbus to the Spanish Court after his discovery of America.' (*Dumfries and Galloway Standard*)

━ OCTOBER 7TH ━

1817: On this day, the following letter, signed by 'A Friend to Youth', appeared in the *Dumfries Weekly Journal*: 'After the throng and bustle of the Rood Fair, it may not be improper to advert to that indiscreet scene of noise and confusion, created by the parading of the trades boys on the Thursday and Friday of the fair, by which the peace of the town is very much disturbed, and even the lives and the properties of the inhabitants endangered. I would not have it understood that the innocent enjoyment of youth should be prevented, when kept within reasonable bounds. Recreation is necessary, and makes the young submit to the toils of life with more pleasure. But when amusement degenerates into the excess of drink, noise and tumult, it then proves an injury to the persons themselves, and disgusting to the public. It may be urged that it has long been the practice of the trades boys to parade at that time; even grant this and still allow them the privilege. But they ought to be restricted within the bounds of discretion, and be under due regulations. Limit them to walking soberly through the streets once during the day, and, if so inclined, let them enjoy themselves with a dance in the evening.'

⟶ October 8th ⟵

1919: On this day, the *Dumfries and Galloway Standard* reported that a resolution to a crippling national rail strike had finally been achieved: ' In a remarkably short time there was a large gathering assembled in Greyfriars' Hall. When the announcement was officially made to the meeting, the news was received with the utmost satisfaction, and it was resolved to act upon the advice given by the leaders to resume work at once.

This resolution was loyally carried out by the men, and with so much promptitude that by midnight on Sunday all of them had reported for duty, and everything was ready for the resumption of traffic. The signal lamps were all lit, and the signalmen were out. The first train was started at 4.53 a.m. for Kilmarnock, and within a few hours a full service of trains was provided, with the exception of the through runs to London, but even that was resumed on Monday night at 11.18 p.m. Yesterday, the traffic was working as if there had never been a strike. The principal station officials speak in the highest terms of the behaviour of the men during the strike.'

~ October 9th ~

1960: On this day, 'the largest and most spectacular Civil Defence display ever seen in the south-west of Scotland took place, with Whitesands, Dumfries, as the ultimate assembly point for convoys of rescue, ambulance, communications and emergency feeding vehicles from the town and county as well as from Ayrshire, Lanarkshire, Peeblesshire, Edinburgh and Cumberland.

All this represented a considerable feat of organisation. It also conveyed to the public a vivid impression of the very vital part the Civil Defence agencies can play in emergency conditions. For the purpose of the exercise, it was to be understood that various places in Britain had been under nuclear attack, and that these convoys, complete with refugees, were converging on Dumfries, which had temporarily escaped enemy attentions. Thus the title of the exercise, "Operation Whitesands", and the utilisation of the area between the Suspension and St. Michael's Bridges as an arena for the demonstration of rescue and welfare resources under simulated conditions of mishap. About a thousand townspeople looked on, in company with Civil Defence leaders and invited guests, as the various units moved into action.' (*Dumfries and Galloway Standard*)

‑ October 10th ‑

1789: On this day, the following notice, issued 'By Order of the Solicitor of the Stamp Duties for Scotland', appeared in the *Dumfries Weekly Journal*: 'Information being given, that great abuses and frauds have been committed and practised, in contradiction to the Acts of Parliament respecting hats, gloves and mittens, not only in dealers not taking out licences, but also in their not affixing the tickets to the articles sold, as directed by the said Acts, and even often selling them without licences or tickets at all; Notice is hereby made, that persons contravening the aforesaid Acts of Parliament, will be prosecuted with the utmost rigour for the statutory penalties.'

—‑—

1826: Also on this day, the *Dumfries Weekly Journal* reported the following sad accident: 'On Saturday evening last, a woman by [the] name of Anderson, having gone to Maxwelltown to purchase butcher's meat, on her return mistook, it is supposed, the lamp at the bottom of Bank Street for another lamp upon the street, and having gone too near the edge of the river she fell in. Though people heard her fall in and came to her assistance immediately, yet she was carried down by the strength of the current, and drowned before she could be got out.'

~ October 11th ~

1715: On this day, it was reported that there was an imminent Jacobite attempt to capture Dumfries: 'The town-crier proceeded through the principal streets at eleven o'clock … and in the usual way warned such burgesses and residents as possessed horses to appear mounted and with their best arms at next beat of drum. All that night through great excitement prevailed; few of the inhabitants closed their eyes; the windows looking into the leading thoroughfares were illuminated, for the double purpose of supplying light for the warlike muster, and affording a greater sense of security; and when, about an hour after midnight, the roll of the drum again reverberated through the town, followed by the neighing of steeds, by the ring of their hoofs upon the pavement, as they hastened to the Market Cross … those of the lieges who did not know precisely how matters stood might well be excused for believing that the dreaded enemy, favoured by the darkness, had really stolen a hurried march upon the town: and sure enough, the rebels had moved from Moffat soon after that terrible midnight hour, for the purpose of attacking Dumfries, and would have carried their resolution into effect had not discretion got the better part of their valour.' (McDowall, William, *History of Dumfries* (2nd Edn., 1873))

~ OCTOBER 12TH ~

1715: On this day, the Lord Kenmure 'who figured conspicuously during the rising of [this year], planted the Standard of the Pretender at Lochmaben, encamped at Tinwald and for a time threatened an attack on Dumfries. He desisted, however, and in following the fortunes of the Stuarts in the south, was taken prisoner at Preston on November 13th, impeached before the House of Lords, sentenced and executed at Tower Hill on February 24th 1716.' (Mackie, Charles, (Ed.), *Dumfries and Galloway Notes and Queries* (1913))

1779: Also on this day, the following announcement appeared in the *Dumfries Weekly Journal*: 'Stephenson's Original East India Repository (from London) is now opened in a large and commodious room at James Howat's, Bridge-end, Dumfries, and will continue during this week and no longer. All kinds of Indian Goods (bought and sold by Commission) may be had, Wholesale and Retail, cheaper by Ten Per Cent than ever sold in Scotland before … Seven hundred pieces of India Muslins of all sorts; two hundred pieces of real silk; Grograms and double Taffeties; great variety of Chintz and Shawl handkerchiefs; also a large assortment of ladies' shoes, sprigged and spangled; great variety of Tambor Aprons, Handkerchiefs, Ruffles &c.'

~ October 13th ~

1899: On this day, 'the foundation stone of the [Ewart] Public Library was laid in the afternoon by Miss Mckie … The ceremony was fixed for three o'clock, but it was twenty-five minutes later before it was entered upon. A small platform had been erected, and was approached from Catherine Street by a carpeted gangway. Venetian masts, on which flags were hoisted, and strings of pennons gave a gay appearance to the scene, and the Town Band played during the time of waiting. A large concourse of spectators assembled, and fortunately the weather was brilliant. Members of the two Town Councils and a number of other representative ladies and gentlemen occupied the platform enclosure. Provost Glover led in Mrs. Carnegie, followed by Mr. Carnegie [etc.] …

The proceedings were opened, with the singing of the appropriate hymn, "Let there be light", by a choir organised by Mr. Law Starkey. Mr. Grierson, Town Clerk, deposited in a cavity beneath the stone, a sealed copper box containing all the current coins and various documents and newspapers.' (*Dumfries and Galloway Standard*)

~ October 14th ~

1788: On this day, the founder of Methodism, John Wesley, 'preached in the unfinished meeting-house situated in Queen Street; and again in the evening, when, he says, the congregation was nearly double and, if possible, more attentive: "One or two gentlemen, so called, laughed at first; but they quickly disappeared, and all were still while I explained the worship of God in spirit and in truth …"'

McDowall explains that Wesley had arrived in the town – from Carlisle – on the previous day and that, having made a number of visits to Dumfries since 1780, 'he originated a "society" or congregation in the burgh, which seems at first to have been superintended by a Mr. Dall.' On that previous evening, as Wesley noted in his Journal, 'I preached abroad in a convenient street on one side of the town. Rich and poor attended from every quarter, of whatever denomination; and every one seemed to hear for life. Surely the Scots are the best hearers in Europe.' (McDowall, William, *History of Dumfries* (2nd Edn., 1873))

~ October 15th ~

1834: On this day, the *Dumfries Times* printed a report about a recent curious discovery: 'On Friday, a skeleton was discovered embedded in the mud of the river a little way below Troqueer Moat. It seemed to be the remains of a man of more than ordinary stature and strength. The backbone was long and the ribs of most formidable dimensions. The flesh had been entirely washed from the body, but on the hinder part of the head there was a tuft of hair very thick set and red. Notice of the particulars was duly given to the Kirk Session, which immediately set about the requisite preparations for a decent interment. Previous to ordering the coffin, it was deemed necessary to view the bones that were to fill it, so down went a procession of people to the water's side. The bones and the scalp, with its fiery covering, were gazed at and pondered over. A spectator raised the skeleton and, in the disentanglement of what was deemed a leg, there appeared successively a thigh, an ankle and a cloven foot! It was now plain that the bones were those of "The de'il, or else some outlan' quey", which had been landed at the Moat to alarm the fears and harrow the sympathies of the good folks of Maxwelltown; but which of the two is a point that remains to be decided.'

~ October 16th ~

1804: On this day, the following announcement appeared in the *Dumfries Weekly Journal*: 'To be Let, for such a number of years as can be agreed on, and entered to at Martinmas 1804, the Windmill on Corbelly Hill, with two Kilns and a Granary adjoining thereto … It consists of one pair of best French Stones for grinding wheat; one pair of grays for oats; one pair of shealing stones; and a fourth pair for hard grain; a cylinder and sanners for cleaning wheat; a wire machine of the best kind, for dressing flour; a boulting mill for flour; a set of double sanners, with a dust machine on an improved construction, for oats.

Being in the centre of one of the most fertile districts in the kingdom, within a quarter of a mile of the town of Dumfries, and not above one mile from the ports of Laghall and Kingholm, this Mill is a most eligible object to a manufacturer of grain, whether for exportation, or the ever-ready market at Dumfries. If not set by private bargain, betwixt now and Monday the 29th current, the premises will be exposed to set by public roup, in the Old Coffee-house, Dumfries, on that day, at six o'clock in the evening.' N.B. The former windmill is now home to Dumfries Museum.

⟶ OCTOBER 17TH ⟵

1797: On this day, the *Dumfries Weekly Journal* reported that 'yesterday, in consequence of the brilliant and decisive victory gained over the Dutch Fleet by Admiral Duncan [at the Battle of Camperdown on October 11th], great and unfeigned rejoicings took place here. The morning announced the happy tidings by the ringing of the bells. At one, the Royal Dumfries Volunteers and the 8th Regiment of Foot fired a feu de joye. In the evening, there was an illumination, and though not previously concerted, it soon became universal. The King's Arms and several other houses had the gallant Admiral's name, in large letters, on the windows. Much taste and elegance were displayed by a great many people in illuminating their houses. We have often had occasion to remark the patriotism and loyalty of the inhabitants of this town, but we never recollect to have seen it in a more conspicuous manner. At a period when the insolence of a disorganizing foe was become unbounded, when the season for attempting the invasion of our happy islands was at hand, this disastrous blow to the Dutch cannot fail to be felt by the tyrants of France. May the arm of Providence be outstretched to control their system of havoc, and to shield Europe from their horrible purpose of provoking eternal war.'

— OCTOBER 18TH —

1820: On this day, Edward McGrory was publicly executed in front of the town's prison in Buccleuch Street, having been found guilty of murder. 'After being pinioned, the prisoner ascended to the scaffold, where, together with the Catholic clergyman who attended him, he spent some time in a kneeling posture. At the conclusion of his devotions, the criminal voluntarily and with a firm step ascended the platform, but instead of dropping the fatal signal as had been anticipated, he expressed his intention of addressing the multitude. His language was at first extremely incoherent. With great earnestness the clergyman again entreated him to close his eyes and quietly submit, but McGrory was not to be persuaded … The crowd remained perfectly quiet with the exception of one man, who constantly kept bawling "Give him more rope; give him more rope!" Magistrates were about to interfere, when the minister of the parish, Revd. Dr. Scot, again reminded McGrory of his repeated promises to demean himself differently, and at last he persuaded him to pull the cap over his face, a task he had scarcely performed when the drop fell.' (Mackie, Charles, (Ed.), *Dumfries and Galloway Notes and Queries* (1913))

─ OCTOBER 19TH ─

1846: On this day, the *Dumfries and Galloway Courier* noted that 'universal regret was felt throughout the town on Wednesday morning, when it became known that two vessels belonging to Mr. Robert Thomson, one of our most respected citizens and merchants, had been wrecked in the Mersey, in the gale of Monday night. The two vessels were the "Stuart Menteath" and the "Queensberry"; the captains being brothers to each other. The advices from Liverpool bear that the first-named vessel, whilst coming up the Mersey with a stiff north-east breeze, was caught by the ebb tide and thrown upon the bank ... Soon after striking she began to fill, and before the boat could be got clear she fairly upset, lying on her broadside. In this fearful emergency, the master and crew remained lashed on the broadside clinging to it as their only stay between them and death. The fate of the other vessel, "Queensberry", has been similarly disastrous. She was going up the channel for Liverpool in the same way, when she also struck upon the bank. Fearing every moment that the vessel would capsize, the crew took to their boat. It is gratifying to state that none of the crew in either case has perished.'

~ October 20th ~

1777: On this day, magistrates of Dumfries issued the following order in an attempt to address the problem of swine wandering loose on the streets of the town, which had caused accidents and distress to the local populace: 'All persons who keep swine within this burgh or liberties thereof, shall for the future enclose and lock them up, and keep them within the limits of their respective properties or possessions, and at no time suffer them to wander or stroll abroad, under the penalty of Ten Shillings sterling for each transgression; the one half to be paid to the person who shall give information thereof, and the other half to be applied for the use and behoof of the hospital of this burgh. And that besides confiscation of any swine that may be found loose or without their enclosures … they do command and require the burgh-officers, and authorize and empower all the inhabitants whatsoever, to seize upon any swine or species of them they shall discover wandering loose on any of the streets, or other places within this burgh or liberties thereof, and detain the same till they can give information thereof to one or other of the town's magistrates.' (*Dumfries Weekly Journal*)

~ October 21st ~

1851: On this day, the *Dumfries and Galloway Standard* reported that piped water had been introduced into Dumfries, from Lochrutton Loch: 'At eleven o'clock the Commissioners proceeded from the Council Chamber to the Loch ... Just before reaching the works at Lochfoot, they were received by the men in the employ of the contractor, and the people of the village ... The whole works, from the first pipe downwards, were surveyed, and on arriving at the filters, which are now in a state of great forwardness, Provost Nicholson, assisted by Mr. Gale, formally drew the water from the Loch down the main pipe leading to the town, the band playing the national anthem. The ceremony over, the Provost proposed: "Success to the undertaking this day finished", and expressed a hope that it would henceforth be carried out with as much spirit as hitherto, and that the burghs would never regret coming to Lochrutton parish for water ..." The Commissioners left Lochfoot amid the huzzas of the multitude.

A little after two o'clock, the Water Commissioners and their officers, and the members of the Town Councils, proceeded from the Council Chamber to the fountain at the foot of High Street – the procession being headed by Provosts Nicholson and Maxwell, arm-in-arm.'

~ October 22nd ~

1919: On this day, the following report, concerning the building of much-needed council houses in the town, appeared in the *Dumfries and Galloway Standard*: 'Approval of the Scottish Board of Health having now been received, Dumfries Town Council are in a position to begin immediately the building at Milldamhead of ten blocks of houses of the flatted type ... Houses of the same type are included among those to be built on the Cresswell site.

The activities of the Town Council with reference to housing have extended over a period of eight years, although during four years of that time the work was entirely held up owing to the war, and, since the armistice, prolonged negotiations have been carried on with the Local Government Board in connection with the schemes at Milldamhead and Cresswell. It was during 1911 that the burgh sanitary inspector first brought under the notice of the Public Health Committee the shockingly insanitary and congested condition of the area in Queensberry Square, now known as the King Street improvement scheme ... Eventually, in 1914, the whole area was demolished and a space of over half an acre cleared of slum dwellings.'

~ OCTOBER 23RD ~

1558: On this day, William Harlow, a humble tailor and lay preacher from Edinburgh, spoke in Dumfries where, as Alexander S. Morton memorably phrased it in *Galloway and the Covenanters* (1914), 'he denounced the Mass as rank idolatory, and proclaimed the pure Gospel of Salvation in Christ.' John Knox described Harlow as 'a simple man, whose condition, although it excel not, yet, for his whole and diligent plainness in doctrine, is he to this day worthy of praise.'

McDowall declared Harlow 'the burgh's first Protestant missionary, [who] sounded the knell of Popery in one of its strongest citadels. This took place at early morning watch, "nine houris afore noon", the light of the coming day symbolising, as it were, the dawn of the pure faith which the speaker heralded. Harlow, passing the manor house of Garlies, began his mission there; and then at three o'clock in the morning, "preached in the forehall of Robert Cunninghame, within the burgh of Dunfrese ... What unpardonable audacity for a mere layman; a poor, vulgar maker of material garments; a heretic proscribed and vile, thus to lift up his testimony against 'Holy Mother Church', and speak of her penances, pilgrimages and peculiar dogmas as no better than filthy rags."' (McDowall, William, *History of Dumfries* (2nd Edn., 1873))

— October 24th —

1840: An affecting tale regarding the placing of the 'Old Mortality' Group in the grounds of Dumfries Observatory concerned a raffle to dispose of the sculptures that was held at the town's Commercial Hotel. 'The "draw" took place, and the lucky ticket fell to Mr. John Sinclair, assistant surgeon on the HMS *Excellent*, then in Portsmouth. Mr. Sinclair was a native of Dumfries, and now comes the curious part of the story. On the very day that the winning ticket was drawn on his behalf at Dumfries, Mr. Sinclair met with his tragic death near Southampton [in a road accident]. A Hampshire newspaper commented upon the singular coincidence that Sinclair should have died on the day that he won the "Old Mortality' Group". It further stated: 'Mr. Sinclair had been heard to say that if the prize fell to his share, "Old Mortality and his Pony" should be given to the Dumfries Observatory, and his promise will most likely be fulfilled by his affected friends. It may be said thus to form a monument for himself, and will recall to the memory of his numerous friends, one who was ever a favourite, regarded by all who knew him as a steady, worthy and amiable young man.' (Mackie, Charles, (Ed.), *Dumfries and Galloway Notes and Queries* (1913))

~ OCTOBER 25TH ~

1825: On this day, the *Dumfries Weekly Journal* reported that 'notice is hereby given to all Persons receiving or paying Stipends, Feu-duties, Rents, Tolls, Customs and other demands, in Grain, Malt, Meal, or any other Commodity, that by the Statutes of 5th Geo. IV cap. 74, and 6th Geo. IV cap.12, it is enacted that for the purpose of ascertaining and fixing the payments of the above Stipends &c. ... the Sheriff shall, as soon as conveniently may be, after the 1st of November next, summon and impannel a Jury to enquire and ascertain the amount according to the standards by the said Act established, of all such Stipends ... according to the weights and measures heretofore in use within this county. All persons receiving or paying Stipends, Feu-duties, Tolls, Customs and other demands, in Grain, Malt, Meal or any other Commodity, are hereby required before the 20th day of November next, to lodge with the Sheriff-Clerk a note of all Stipends &c., payable to or paid by them in Grain, Malt &c., and to specify in such note the weights and measures at present used in payment of such Stipends &c, in order that the provisions of said Statutes may be carried into effect. – Sheriff-Clerk's Office, Dumfries.'

~ October 26th ~

1715: The inhabitants of Dumfries had been uneasy for several weeks, as they feared their town might be attacked by Lord Kenmure's Jacobite army. Few among the local population were Jacobite supporters, although at least one Stuart sympathiser attempted to burn down the town, as the events of this night demonstrate:

'A train of gunpowder, nine yards long, was laid at the foot of a close of thatched houses near the centre of the burgh, which, on being ignited, set one of the tenements in a blaze. Fortunately, two of the magistrates were near at hand, by whose assistance the fire was extinguished before much damage or alarm was occasioned. A reward of a hundred merks was offered for the discovery of the guilty parties; and the authorities, fearing that on the approach of the rebels their friends inside would perpetrate similar acts of incendiarism in order to withdraw the loyal inhabitants from their posts, and otherwise create confusion, adopted all possible precautions to prevent or mitigate the threatened evil. The militia of the county was not yet raised, so that Dumfries had to depend for its defence on the volunteer soldiers alone.' (McDowall, William, *History of Dumfries* (2nd Edn., 1873))

~ OCTOBER 27TH ~

1812: On this day, the *Dumfries Weekly Journal* reported that 'Robert Wainskill, alias Wainscott, charged with High Treason, in counterfeiting the lawful SILVER COIN of this realm, escaped from the Constables who had him in charge at Horncastle, in the county of Lincoln, on the night of Wednesday the 26th of August last.

Whoever will apprehend, or give such information to Messrs. Vernon and Franklin, Solicitors to his Majesty's Mint ... or Robert Clitherow, Solicitor at Horncastle, or Mr. Francis Shortt, writer, Dumfries, as may be the means of ... Robert Wainskill ... being apprehended, shall, together with the person or persons apprehending, receive a Reward of FORTY POUNDS, on his ... commitment for trial, for the above offence, on application to the said Solicitors to his Majesty's Mint.

The said Robert Wainskill ... is a Scots pedlar, and is supposed to have lately resided at Dumfries. He is about twenty-five years of age, five feet four inches high, broad face, and pitted with the smallpox, sandy hair, and prominent eyes. Had on when he escaped, a dark loose great coat, black waistcoat, grey fustian trowsers, and shoes; is supposed to have crossed the Humber into Yorkshire, on his way to Scotland.'

~ October 28th ~

1876: On this day, a report concerning one of the town's more prestigious annual social occasions appeared in the *Dumfries and Galloway Standard*: 'The Annual County Ball took place in the Assembly Rooms last night, and as usual was a brilliant assemblage of the gentlemen and ladies of the shire. It was not until nearly ten o'clock that the company commenced to arrive, and the arrivals continued till midnight. The ballroom, the vestibule, and the ante-room were tastefully decorated and fitted up by Mr. Gregan, upholsterer, and Kerr & Fotheringham, nurserymen. An elegant supper, including the choicest dishes, and prepared in a manner that would have tempted the palate of the most fastidious epicure, was purveyed by Oughton & McKinlay, confectioners, Dumfries; supper being spread in the upper room, and refreshments in the room below; and music was supplied by the excellent band of the Scottish Borderers Militia. All the arrangements were attended to by a qualified committee of management (who, by the way, ought in future to make proper provisions for the newspapers being furnished with a complete list of the parties present), and we need hardly say that everything passed off sweetly.'

~ OCTOBER 29TH ~

1834: On this day, the following slightly puzzling notice appeared in the *Dumfries Times*: 'G. Pariss respectfully informs the Nobility, Gentry, and Inhabitants of Dumfries and its vicinity, that his Exhibition of Industrious Fleas is now re-opened at the same apartment at Mrs. Paul's, Assembly Street. G. Pariss hopes to have the honour of receiving the same encouragement and patronage with which he has been favoured since he has been in this respectable town. N.B. Open from 10 o'clock till 5. Admittance 1*s*; children under 10 years, with their guardians, half-price; and from 6 to 9 o'clock for tradesmen; not less than four in a party half-price. The Dumfries Race will be performed by some real Glasgow Fleas, with their riders in full dress.'

1913: Also on this day, the *Dumfries and Galloway Standard* reported that 'the demand for tickets of admission to the Home-Rule meeting to be held tonight in the Lyceum Theatre, at which the principal Speaker will be Mr. T.P. O'Connor, M.P., has proved far in excess of the supply. The local branch of the Irish National League have arranged a torchlight and brass band procession to accompany Mr. O'Connor from the meeting-place to his hotel at the close of the proceedings. A special train will leave Dumfries at 10.30 p.m. for Kirkconnel, and the late express for the south will set down passengers at Annan. Large numbers of people will travel to and from the meeting by motor car.'

~ October 30th ~

1300: On this day, following an invasion led by the English monarch, Edward I, a truce was signed at Dumfries: 'And for this said truce we have given and promise sufferance, both to hold and protect these Scotch people, their persons, their auxiliaries, their allies, their goods, and their property, from us, our auxiliaries, and our allies, until the Day of Pentecost next to come, in the following manner: That each one shall retain what he possesses, and will be able to build, to work, to labour, to sail by the coast, and to do that which he pleases or thinks, during the said truce; and that each one, on the one part and on the other, will be able to go and come and securely trade by sea and by land from the one country to the other, here or there as he pleases, according to the laws and customs of the country … And this truce and this sufferance, in the manner which is before related, we promise both well and faithfully to protect and firmly to hold, by us and by ours, and for us and for ours, both by sea and by land, till the said Day of Pentecost …' (Extract from translation given in McDowall, William, *History of Dumfries* (2nd Edn., 1873))

— October 31st —

1826: On this day, the *Dumfries and Galloway Courier* noted that 'the River Nith is at present so full of salmon that we know one experienced fisher who says that he would cheerfully give £30 or £40 for a single day's fishing of the pool below the Caul [adjacent to Whitesands] alone. The fish, too, are in the very finest condition, a fact which proves what we have always alleged, that the fishing season in the River Nith commences too soon and closes too early. In place of 25th September, close time, as it is called, should not commence until the end of October, and we trust this arrangement will be attended to in the Bill about to be put before Parliament. Our river fishing proved very ill this year, but the tacksmen of the stake nets made a capital thing of it. When long in the sea, the salmon are attacked with a disease called lice. This leads them to ascend the rivers, and they were observed this year creeping along the whole coast of the Solway Firth, searching for what they could not well find, fresh water. For months together, the tacksmen brought ten or twelve baskets twice a week to our market, each containing as many large fish.'

~ NOVEMBER 1ST ~

1854: On this day, the *Dumfries and Galloway Standard* reported the arrival of Mr Colles, with his 'Exhibition of Curious and Amusing Novelties'. Among the 250 or so items on display at No.4 Queensberry Square were magical dancing figures, enthusiastic violoncello players, changeable cards, magical dissolving balls, and mystic telescopes, 'all guaranteed to afford mirth around the winter fireside. High as our anticipations were, they fell far short of the reality. His magical dancing figures are truly astounding. Though seemingly of simple pasteboard, they dance about like tiny figures of flesh and blood, or as the eerie fairy folks are supposed to do on the sward and beneath the moonbeams at this present season of Halloween. These fantastic effigies are about a foot in length; and, on being breathed upon and placed on the floor, commence to caper, with surprising agility and truth, to tunes whistled by Mr. Colles, or any of the company. Then, his experiments with cards, the cap and pea, the intelligent swan, &c. are most effective, and that of the dissolving ball is the most perfect illusion of the kind we ever saw. Mr. Colles's manners are exceedingly polite and agreeable; so that his performances are thereby rendered increasingly attractive.'

← NOVEMBER 2ND →

1838: On this day, the *Dumfriesshire and Galloway Herald and Advertiser* printed the following report: 'On Friday evening last Messrs. Duncan of Edinburgh, Lowrey of Newcastle, and Arthur of Carlisle, peripatetic "Chartists", held forth in our New Markets to a couple of hundred of people or so, a great part of them boys, on the old stock grievances; labouring to prove as usual that we are the most wretched nation on the face of the earth. The saving nostrum, "The People's Charter", was of course amply puffed off, as the only Balm of Gilead. Next evening, Mr. Duncan lectured in the Theatre on Universal Suffrage. We have not been able to learn what sort of audience he had.

Of course, we shall not load our columns with the trash of these trampers, who might be dangerous as firebrands of the fiercest glare, were they not harmless as blockheads of the first water. It is to pestilential itinerants like these, labouring to rouse the populace to open rebellion, that the Magistrates of our Burgh, forsooth, must give our New Markets for their better accommodation in conveying to the people their dirty doses of sedition. And the proprietors of the Theatre, too, must give their places, consecrated to the Muses, to the mean uses of such fellows as these, who scruple not to influence the people from the very stage which was erected to humanise them.'

- November 3rd -

1795: On this day, it was announced that 'the Nobility, Gentlemen and Freeholders of the County of Dumfries, being resolved to have an accurate survey and map of the County ... have appointed a Committee of their number to treat with such persons as are willing to undertake the Survey, and to make such a Map.

As the Map is to be made as generally useful as possible, all the Towns, Villages, Gentlemen's Seats, High Roads, and all objects of any consequence must be laid down upon the Map, and their differences distinctly marked and ascertained.

The Committee meet in the Court House of Dumfries upon this day, Tuesday 3rd November 1795 at twelve o'clock, in order to receive the proposals of any person willing to undertake the Work, and treat with them on the subject.

The proposals must be reduced into writing, and must specify the general plan and arrangement of particulars, which the Surveyor proposes to adopt; and also the time when the Survey will be finished, and the Map ready for delivery; and finally the terms on which the Survey will be undertaken and completed.' (*Dumfries Weekly Journal*)

⏤ NOVEMBER 4TH ⏤

1911: On this day, the *Dumfries and Galloway Standard* announced that 'a Diploma of Merit has been awarded to the Burgh of Dumfries for a banner displayed at the Turin Exhibition. The banner, which is of royal blue silk, measures seven feet long by five feet deep. It was designed and executed by Mr. J.M. Glover, of Messrs. J.J. Glover and Son, decorators, Castle Street. In the centre is a shield form, on which is depicted St. Michael killing the "Great Red Beast". The representation of the saint is the same as carried out in the Town Hall window presented by Provost Lennox; Messrs. Glover being also responsible for the window. In the design, St. Michael is portrayed bearing a silver shield with the red cross of St. George, whilst his right hand is upraised, holding a sword with which he strikes at the dragon. The heavenly bodies are emblazoned on the main shield form, and this again is surrounded by a design of thistles in natural colourings. The lettering, which is in gold, bears the words, "The Royal Burgh of Dumfries", "St. Michael", and "A Loreburn". The whole design is framed in with ornamental corners and lines in vellum colour.'

~ November 5th ~

1793: On this day, the *Dumfries Weekly Journal* reported that 'on Wednesday last, Michael and James Macanallie were whipt through the streets of this town pursuant to the sentence of the last Circuit Court held here. After the executioner had performed the sentence of the law on these men, he was attacked by one of the Breadalbane Fencibles, who were quartered in the town, and was severely beaten. The Magistrates, upon being informed of this circumstance, immediately offered a reward for the discovery of the offender; in consequence of which he was that evening apprehended. Next day he was delivered up to the Military, when he was tried by a Court Martial, and sentenced to receive 100 lashes, which punishment was duly inflicted yesterday'. (*Dumfries Weekly Journal*)

1856: Also on this day, it was reported that, 'a company is in course of formation here for the purpose of running a screw steamer betwixt Dumfries and Liverpool and Glasgow. A vessel capable of making the voyage betwixt the Nith and the Mersey in 12 hours, which would make Glencaple and, in spring tides, Kingholm Quay, can be completed for £3,000, and already, within a week of the plan being mooted, one half of the requisite capital has been subscribed by the Dumfries merchants alone. It is estimated that goods could be brought here at one-third of the rates at present charged by the railway companies."' (*Dumfries and Galloway Standard*)

~ November 6th ~

1832: On this day, William Cobbett, the political agitator and author of *Rural Rides* (1830) visited Dumfries: 'I lectured at the Theatre at half after seven; and, considering that the people have been frightened half to death about the cholera morbus (of which disease great numbers have actually died here), the attendance was wonderfully good. Poor Burns, the poet, died in this town, an exciseman, after having written so well against that species of taxation, and that particular sort of office … I was very happy to hear that his widow, who still lives in this town, is amply provided for; and my intention was to go to her, to tell her my name, and to say, that I came to offer her my respects as a mark of my admiration for the talents of her late husband, one single page of whose writings is worth more than a whole cart load that has been written by Walter Scott.

I was prevented from putting this intention into execution by the necessity under which I was of being at Annan, to breakfast at ten o'clock …' (Cobbett, William, *Cobbett's Tour in Scotland*, 1833)

— November 7th —

1859: On this day, the Castle Douglas and Dumfries Railway opened. 'At half-past six a.m., a train well-filled with passengers started from Castle Douglas for Dumfries, which it reached at twenty-five minutes past seven. The first train from Dumfries Station departed at a quarter-past eight a.m., and had also a fair quota of passengers. Probably because of our familiarity [at Dumfries] with railway communications to more than one point of the compass, the departure of the first train hence on the new line of rail was as quiet and orderly as anyone could desire. There was no bustle except that necessarily occasioned by the traffic ... At Castle Douglas, however, the case was different. Our friends at that end of the newly-opened rail had hitherto no interest in the great railway system which has brought all important districts in the county into convenient and advantageous connection, and the fact of an iron road being brought up to their own doors had something more than the charm of novelty for them. In token of their gratification, therefore, at the inauguration of their railway, the good folks of Castle Douglas assembled in great force at the railway station to welcome the first train into Galloway.' (*Dumfries and Galloway Standard*)

~ NOVEMBER 8TH ~

1861: On this day, the following report appeared in the *Dumfriesshire and Galloway Herald and Register*: 'On Wednesday last, there was more than usual excitement at Stewart's Auction Mart, caused by the sale of nearly three score Shetland bullocks and heifers from Hensol. The Shetland breed of cattle have an elegant and deer-like form; they are very wild, more so than any other native breed, and the Hensol cattle, by the time they reached the Auction Mart, were in a very excited state ... On being driven into the ring, the animals very speedily had it to themselves. One bullock had scarcely entered when he cleared it at a bound, and made for the gate which was closed but not fastened. The bullock made a charge at one side of the gate, breaking two of the rails, and darted through the partially open gateway. It turned up the Sands, charging with its horns everything, man or beast, that came in its way. It passed along the New Bridge, followed by a large crowd, and at last took refuge in a field at Lochfield. All attempts to drive the bullock being fruitless, it was found necessary to shoot it.'

‒ November 9th ‒

1802: On this day, the *Dumfries Weekly Journal* carried the following public notices:

'Mr. Stretton's Ball, for the exhibition of his pupils in Dumfries, will be held at the Theatre on Thursday evening, upon which occasion the stage will be enclosed, the whole forming a spacious and elegant Saloon, brilliantly illuminated.

The dances will consist of those in the highest style of fashion, and most prevalent in London and Bath. Amongst others, the Minuet de la Cour and Gavot, Allemande en Attitude, a variety of Allemandes, Hornpipes &c., particularly a Demi Scots Ballet and Jig, a Scots Chaconne, and Perigrinade with Skipping Ropes. Also, a Pas de Trois, in which Mr. Stretton will exhibit with two of his Pupils, as he also will in other dances during the evening. A Band of Music is provided, consisting of two violins, violoncello, tambourine &c.'

In the same newspaper, Denniston and Kerr of Dumfries announced that they had just received a new stock of muffs and tippets. 'Having established a connection with a first rate fur house, they are enabled to sell their muffs and tippets upon the lowest terms; and as they are to receive regular supplies during the winter season, they hope their assortment will be worthy of attention.'

~ November 10th ~

1866: On this day, the *Dumfries and Galloway Standard* advertised the arrival of 'Blind Tom – the Negro Prodigy'. 'This unique one-sided genius – a negro youth, who is a marvellous adept in music but seems on the verge of idiocy in many other respects – appeared at the Mechanics' Hall on Thursday night … His nervous system seems to be so exquisitely framed, that sounds of all kinds once listened to make a strong and indelible impression on him, and can be reproduced at will, whether these be regular musical compositions, random notes or spoken addresses. There he sits at the instrument, his cranialogical development and facial outline showing that Nature has been niggardly in her gifts to him, but the enchanting melody that he draws from the piano equally demonstrates that she has been exceedingly bountiful in some respects to the blind witless negro boy. To those who have known him for years, Tom is still a perplexing puzzle; but his kind guardian states that he is gradually acquiring glimpses of reasoning intelligence, and that his eyeballs, once impervious to the day, are beginning to experience the difference between light and darkness. At the close, Tom's guardian thanked the audience for their patronage, and poor Tom, with great apparent heartiness, echoed the acknowledgement.'

~ November 11th ~

1918: On this day, the Armistice was signed, bringing an end to the First World War. 'There was an atmosphere of eager expectancy in the streets of Dumfries, and shortly after eleven o'clock quite a crowd gathered in front of the "Standard" office to await the official message. Just about a quarter before midday, the announcement of the cessation of hostilities was put on the office windows. The news was received with rousing cheers, and these were renewed when the Union Jack was hoisted over the building. People without even a nodding acquaintance with each other shook hands enthusiastically, and there were few faces on which for the rest of the day there was not seen a grin. In a remarkably short space of time, an ordinary day became a festival … Flags sprouted from dwelling-houses and shop windows and, at various points on the principal streets, festoons of flags and bunting were suspended arch-like across the thoroughfare. As the news found its way to the public works buzzers and whistles were blown, and the workers downed tools and joined the "peace strike", which soon became fairly general in the town.' (*Dumfries and Galloway Standard*)

NOVEMBER 12TH

1834: On this day, the *Dumfries Times* printed the following notice:
'Hawkers, Pedlars and Chapmen will take notice that, by the Act
for regulating Hawkers and Pedlars in Scotland [they] are bound
ANNUALLY to take out a Licence from the Commissioners named
in the Act, under the penalty of £25, to be recovered by the
immediate imprisonment of any [such person] travelling without
a Licence, until such penalty be paid, or the sum be obtained by
a sale of such goods as the offender may be found possessed of.

The Licence duty is £4 sterling for a person travelling on foot,
and £4 additional for every horse, ass, mule, or any beast of
burden such person may travel with. And before any person can
obtain such Licence, he must produce a Certificate subscribed
by the Minister and two reputable Householders of the parish
or place within which such person has his usual residence. Any
person may seize any Hawker trading without a Licence, or
refusing to produce a Licence after being required to do so, and
may detain him for a reasonable time in order to give notice to
a Constable or any other Peace Officer. From the small number
of Licences taken out for the past year, the Commissioners
have reason to think that the Act must have been in many
instances evaded.'

— NOVEMBER 13TH —

1676: On this day, a local man was brought to book for attempting to sell adulterated meal at the town's market: 'The Council fynes Jon Davidson in Terrachtie in five merks scots money for abusing the meal mercat in mingling his meal with dust, and ordeans the fine to be payit to the treasurer or else ordeans him to be put in prison until payment.' (Quoted in Mackie, Charles, (Ed.), *Dumfries and Galloway Notes and Queries* (1913))

———

1832: The town had been in the grip of a severe cholera epidemic since September 15th, and the disease had claimed hundreds of lives. Forty-four people died on one day alone. However, on this date, the *Dumfries and Galloway Courier* was able to announce that 'the doors of the cholera hospital have been closed, and that its only occasional inmate is a supernumerary nurse, whose instructions are to keep the pest-house ventilated and free from damp … During the past week, from Monday 5th till Monday 12th current, the new cases were reduced to five, and the deaths to two. The recoveries within the same period were seven; and yesterday the patients under treatment were so low as five – most, if not all, of whom are expected to recover.'

⟜ November 14th ⟞

1664: On this day, the Town Council met to discuss 'Janet Burnes, commonly reputed a witche, and quho hath bein banished out of severall other burghis, and put out of this burgh in the month of August last, for cheating the people upon pretence of knowledge of all things done by them in tym past, or that may fall out in tym cuming, with certification to be scurgit if ever she was sein within the burgh thairafter; and being well informed that she was sein within the town on Saturday, they have ordaint that intimation be maid by touk of drum, that none of the inhabitants resset or give meit or drink unto the said Jane Burnes.' (Quoted in McDowall, William, *History of Dumfries* (2nd Edn., 1873))

1878: Also on this day, it was reported that 'at the Burgh Court on Saturday, a tramp was charged with malicious mischief by throwing stones at a window in Dr. Marshall's house, thereby breaking the glass. He pled guilty, but said he was suffering from a swollen neck and Dr. Marshall did not give him what was necessary. Dr. Marshall examined him, and offered linseed meal to poultice his neck, and bandages, but the accused … demanded money. On being refused, he sent two stones through the window.' (*Dumfries and Galloway Courier*)

~ November 15th ~

1856: On this day, the following report appeared in the *Dumfries and Galloway Standard*: 'A petition was read, signed by Charles Hall, master of the Ragged School, and two other householders in Burns Street, complaining of a nuisance in the street arising from a bone depot, and praying the Commissioners to take steps to remove it.

Mr. Blaind said the petition had reference to his bone works in Burns Street; its allegations were utterly false, as the works were kept in such a state as neither to offend sight or smell, or be injurious to health. Even when the boiling of bones was going on, which was only occasionally, ladies had been on the premises, who stated that they saw or felt nothing wrong ... The Commissioners proceeded to Mr. Blaind's bone-works and examined them. The works appeared to be in good order, but Mr. Hall, who was sent for, stated that on particular days the effluvium from the boiling-house was very disagreeable. As the boiler was not in operation, the Commissioners had no opportunity of ascertaining whether or not it created a nuisance.'

～ November 16th ～

1779: On this day, the following announcement appeared in the *Dumfries Weekly Journal*: 'A new Post Coach sets out from the Cross Keys in Wood Street, London, every evening (Saturdays excepted), and arrives at Beck's Coffee-house, Carlisle, in three days. Also sets out from Beck's Coffee-house, Carlisle, on the same evening, and arrives in three days at the Cross Keys, Wood Street, London. To accommodate passengers travelling northward, and to Ireland, a new Post Coach, which connects with the above, sets out from the King's Arms, Carlisle, every Tuesday and Thursday morning at six o'clock, for Dumfries, upon the arrival of which at the George Inn, a Diligence sets out for Glasgow and another for Portpatrick. Also, a Diligence sets out from Mr. Buchanan's, the Saracen's Head, Glasgow, and another from Mr. Campbell's, Portpatrick, every Tuesday and Thursday morning at four o'clock, to join the said Dumfries and Carlisle Post Coach, in which seats will be reserved for those travelling southward. Each inside passenger from Carlisle to Glasgow or Portpatrick, to pay £1 16*s* 6*d*. Children on the lap to pay half-price. Insides from Carlisle to Dumfries to pay 11*s* 8*d*. Outsides 6*s* 8*d*. Passengers taken up on the road to pay 4*d* per mile, in both the Coach and Diligence.'

— November 17th —

1818: On this day, the following letter, signed 'A Constant Reader', was printed in the *Dumfries Weekly Journal*: 'Sir – It is truly distressing to see many young men, such as Clerks and Apprentices, strolling about the streets at late hours, intoxicated, and committing irregularities of various kinds. Between ten and eleven o'clock last Wednesday night, four of these youths knocked or rung the bell at many doors. At one house, they assaulted the maid servant when cleaning the steps, intruded themselves into the lobby and, two laying hold of her in an unbecoming manner, a third abstracted a mat, which he carried off with him, and perhaps threw into the river … They are well known, and I take this mode of checking them, rather than expose their names, in the hopes they will see this and reform their behaviour, and that masters will take a hint to keep a strict watch over the conduct of their servants … Should any of the persons alluded to be guilty of a similar offence, I will consider myself bound to lay delicacy aside, and give full information of the circumstances above-mentioned.'

~ NOVEMBER 18TH ~

1893: On this day, the *Dumfries and Galloway Standard* reported that 'last night the Mechanics' Hall was comfortably filled on the occasion of Mr. George Grossmith's visit. [Grossmith was the joint author, with his brother Weedon, of the immortal *Diary of a Nobody*, published in 1892. At the time of his visit to Dumfries, he was probably Britain's most popular comic performer.] Mr. Grossmith is a humorist, who … presents himself in evening dress, with a white waistcoat, and a pince-nez, which he finds to be both useful and amusing, for when it is not on his nose it is being twiddled by his fingers. Indeed, the fingers have the most of it; and the play, as Mr. Pepys might have observed, is all very pretty.

This twiddling with the eye-glass is typical of much of Mr. Grossmith's entertainment. In the first part, he twiddles over the art of entertaining, in the second part he twiddles over American entertainers, and in the third part he twiddles again. But one does not tire of it, for it is clever, and it tickles …'

NOVEMBER 19TH

1793: On this day, the *Dumfries Weekly Journal* reported that 'on Saturday last, an event took place, which does the highest honour to the 4th, or Breadalbane Fencible regiment, quartered in this town. The whole Officers, non-commissioned Officers, and men present, requested of Col. McDowall that he would accept one day's pay from each, and present it to the fund for furnishing flannel jackets, as a small gratuity towards the comfort of their brother soldiers now in Flanders; and, what is still more meritorious, they would willingly have contributed two or three days' pay, had they been permitted.'

1799: Also on this day, the same newspaper noted that 'there will be sold by public roup, at the King's Arms here, on Wednesday 27th November current, betwixt the hours of twelve and one o'clock, a pair of excellent Carriage Horses, with a neat Post Chaise and harness. The horses are stout, well matched, of a bay colour, and accustomed to the road. The Chaise has only been run for about three years, is quite fashionable, and will answer the needs either of a genteel family, or the Posting line.

For further particulars, application may be made to John Armstrong, writer in Dumfries.'

– November 20th –

1298: On this day, the following document was produced: 'the King [Edward I, 'Hammer of the Scots'] has appointed that in the Castle of Dumfries there should remain twelve men with armed horses, who shall have among them all twenty-four foot soldiers by the appointment of Sir Robert de Clifford [Warden of the Marches]. Also, the twenty cross-bow men who were at Berwick, who were appointed to the said Sir Robert at Durham, and the six cross-bow men whom the said Sir Robert de Clifford shall place there, whom he took from the Castle of Loghmaben[*sic*], and four footmen of his own, whom he shall also provide. Also, a master engineer and four carpenters. Also, one smith and his lad; one engineer and two masons, whereof the amount shall be seventy-six persons …' Provisions were laid in until the end of the following June and, according to the document, these included '3 bushels of wheat; 120 quarters of wheat; of wine 10 tuns; of malt, or of barley to make malt, for beer, 160 quarters; of oats, for provender for the horses, 100 quarters; of oxen 50 carcases; of herrings, 10,000; of dried fish, 500; of salt, 20 quarters; of iron and steel, as much as shall be necessary; of cords and hides for engines …' (Quoted in McDowall, William, *History of Dumfries* (2nd Edn., 1873))

~ November 21st ~

1797: On this day, the following notices appeared in the *Dumfries Weekly Journal*:

'About ten days ago, one Edward Atkinson from Carlisle, who is at times in a state of Lunacy, came to the house of James Graham, at Stocks Fish-house, and took from thence a Gun almost new (a neat Fowling-piece), with the word GRAHAM engraved on the barrel, and also a young brown Greyhound Dog, the property of Mr. Lidderdale, late of Castlemilk. The said Edward Atkinson says he lost the dog in Dumfries, and left the Gun in a house on the road between Dumfries and Annan, but what place, or the names of the persons in said house, he cannot remember. His reason for leaving the Gun, as he says, was, that he did not like to carry it on the Sabbath-day. Any person who will bring said Gun or Dog, or both, to the said James Graham, shall be rewarded, and any person in whose custody they are found shall be prosecuted.'

'Dealers in and Retailers of Foreign and British Spirits and Wines, Manufacturers of and Dealers in Tobacco and Snuff, Common Brewers, Chandlers, Soap-Makers, Tanners, Tawers and Curriers, being required by law to take out or renew their respective Licences for the ensuing year about this time, attendance will be given for granting them at Dumfries on 6th and 7th December.'

~ NOVEMBER 22ND ~

1871: On this day, Manders' Grand National Star Menagerie visited the town: 'The procession took place a little before noon, headed by the renowned Massarti, the great one-armed French lion tamer, riding in the great golden band carriage, followed by the grand dragon carriage, the mother o' pearl barouche, and the Mandernetheca, drawn by elephants, camels, dromedaries and Brahmin bulls, besides fifteen immense caravans, drawn by upwards of sixty powerful draught horses, the finest steeds on the road. Mr. Manders, the proprietor, now has the largest menagerie in the world – more extensive and infinitely superior to all the other menageries in the kingdom put together. Always on the qui vive for novelties, Mr. Manders has just added a baby elephant (thirty-two inches high), the Gun or horned horse, positively the only specimen of that strange animal exhibited; a family of Polar Bears, one of which weighs upwards of half-a-ton, and a group of Indian prairie fiends which have heads like hippopotamus, bodies like bears, claws like tigers, and ears similar to the horse. The antics of the monkeys during the exhibition, and the pelican handicap are said to be the most laughable; and the performance of the giant elephant on the piano and trombone, and the dancing of the hornpipe by the Lilliputian elephants to be the most wonderful.' (*Dumfriesshire and Galloway Herald and Register*)

~ November 23rd ~

1813: On this day, the *Dumfries Weekly Journal* carried the following story: 'The Commissioners of the Nith Navigation observing, with detestation and abhorrence, a late atrocious attempt to injure the shipping in the Harbour, by some evil disposed person or persons who, on the night of Friday 12th inst. thought proper to loosen the ropes, by which the "General Goldie" from Oporto with wine and cork, was moored at the Dockhead of Dumfries, and, in consequence, the Vessel, with her cargo and crew, were in imminent danger of being lost – hereby offer a Reward of ONE HUNDRED GUINEAS, to any person who will give such information as may lead to the conviction of the offenders; and, if required, the informer's name will be kept secret. – By order of the Commissioners, R. Threshie, Clerk.'

1842: Also on this day, the following advertisement appeared in the *Dumfries Times*: 'The Hubbard Profile Gallery, 40 High Street, where an exact likeness in BUST may be procured for one shilling. Seated figures at an additional charge. The superiority of the artists in this Establishment has procured for them the patronage of Royalty and Nobility; the commendation of Artists and Amateurs; the eulogy of most of the Public Prints in most of the towns in Great Britain and Ireland; and they no doubt will receive the additional sanction of all persons of taste and judgement in Dumfries and its vicinity.'

~ November 24th ~

1915: On this day, it was announced that 'the 3/5th King's Own Scottish Borderers, under Colonel Lennox, left Dumfries on Sunday for Ripon, where they are to be encamped along with a number of other Territorial third line units. The men paraded at the Drill Hall at nine o'clock, and were then played to the station by the pipe band, under Corporal Pearson. Large crowds that gathered in Newall Terrace and Lovers' Walk gave the men an enthusiastic send-off. Members of Dumfries and Maxwelltown Town Councils were present at the station platform, and Provost Macaulay said he and his fellow-councillors were present that morning representing the community of Dumfries, to wish the battalion goodbye. He trusted the men would do all they could to maintain the honour of their regiment … and also keep up the good name of Dumfries and other districts they came from. When they went to face the foe, let them remember that they were fighting for their homes, for their mothers, wives and families. On behalf of the Town Council and the people of Dumfries, he wished them all goodbye, and might God be with them until they came back.' (*Dumfries and Galloway Standard*)

~ NOVEMBER 25TH ~

1835: On this day, the *Dumfries Times* announced a 'new communication by steam from Dumfries to Liverpool direct, courtesy of the Dumfries and Liverpool Steam Navigation Company's new and powerful steam vessel, the "Nithsdale". The attention of Travellers betwixt Edinburgh and all the North of Scotland on the one hand, and Liverpool on the other, is especially requested to the medium of communication opened up by the "Nithsdale", which will be found at once the speediest and cheapest for all such travellers. The distance between Edinburgh and Dumfries is only 72 miles, and two coaches run daily betwixt them. Between the two ports of Dumfries and Liverpool, again the average time of passage is only 11 hours. The coaches, also, between Edinburgh and Dumfries, will be found to suit so well the sailing of the "Nithsdale" and the time of her arrival, that in the majority of cases Passengers will be conveyed betwixt Edinburgh and Liverpool without being obliged to stay in Dumfries a night by the way. Under all these circumstances, there can be no doubt that travellers betwixt Liverpool and the greater part of Scotland, will find it in their interest to sail by the "Nithsdale", and still more so when they take into account the cheapness of her fares.'

– November 26th –

1793: On this day, the following notice appeared in the *Dumfries Weekly Journal*: 'Under the Patronage of several Ladies and Gentlemen of Distinction, T. Fraser, late teacher of the Fencible Band of Music, now in this town, begs leave to inform the Ladies and Gentlemen of Dumfries and its vicinity that, on Thursday 5th of December, at the New Assembly Room, he proposes having a Concert of Vocal and Instrumental Music, for his benefit. The Concert will be arranged on a plan, which, he flatters himself, will give general satisfaction. In the Vocal parts, he is to receive the assistance of Mr. Scriven, Mr. Clarke, and Miss Fontenelle, from the Theatre; and in the Instrumental part, he is to be supported by the abilities of Mr. McIntosh, Mr. Westcotte, and Monsieur La Glace from Paris; together with several private Gentlemen, who have honoured Mr. Fraser with offers of their services on this occasion. Upon the whole, Mr. Fraser flatters himself, that from the merit of the different performers, as well as the songs and pieces selected for the entertainment, that it will equal, if not surpass, any musical performance that has hitherto been exhibited in this town.'

~ November 27th ~

1833: On this day, the following announcement appeared in the *Dumfries Times*: 'Notice is hereby given, that application is intended to be made to Parliament, in the ensuing session, for leave to bring in a Bill for the better Paving, Cleansing, Lighting (with Gas or otherwise), and Watching, Improving, Straightening and Widening the Streets, Roads, Lanes, Passages … in and adjacent to the Town of Dumfries, and for regulating the Police thereof, all situated within the parish and County of Dumfries; and for making Common Drains and Sewers in, and for removing Obstructions and Nuisances from, the … places foresaid; as also for supplying the said Town and Burgh with Water; and for erecting a Bridewell or Bridewells, and making regulations for keeping and maintaining the same, and providing labour to offenders committed thereto; and for regulating the Markets within the said Town, and for enabling the Commissioners under the proposed Act to purchase, or take in lease ground, houses, and other parts necessary for the purposes aforesaid; and for Depots of Manure, and for Market Places and Market Steads, and for erecting a Gas Works. Also, for leave to introduce into the said intended Bill, the power to supply the said Town with Water by pipes.'

─ November 28th ─

1906: On this day, the *Dumfries and Galloway Courier and Herald* reported the expulsion from the town of large numbers of German gipsies, who had set up camp on the western outskirts of Dumfries.

'About six o'clock on Monday evening, the Maxwelltown police had them on the march. It had been arranged that a special train should leave the Queen of the South at 1.10 a.m. on Tuesday morning. The Stewartry police, however, naturally had been anxious to get rid of them, and the tribe landed at the loading bank at Dumfries passenger station about half-past seven o'clock. The train was in readiness … The caravans and basket carriages belonging to the tribe were put on the trucks, and the horses also were speedily entrained. A large staff of police was on duty at the loading bank, and, once inside the enclosure, the gipsies were not allowed to get out again. Some of the men wanted to get beer, and, when refused exit, one of them lifted a long wooden pole and declared he could kill fifty 'polis'. A compromise was arranged; the gipsies remained at the station and beer was brought to them. A supply was given out, which men, women, boys and girls, and even infants shared. At 1.10 a.m., the train steamed out of the siding.'

― November 29th ―

1837: On this day, the *Dumfries Times* reported that 'a large party of our tee-totalers, to the number of forty, dined together last Monday, in Mrs. Johnstone's tee-total coffee-house, Bank Street. The chair was occupied by Mr. Broom, and the vice-chair by Mr. Beveredge. To those wondrously conceited supporters of the social custom of a dinner "after the good old way", who think that the abstinence folks cannot dine, and enjoy themselves too, and that "right merrily", a peep into the joyous assembly would have afforded a treat to be envied at. The dinner, substantial and in excellent season, was followed by a dessert of green and dried fruits in great profusion. After dinner, coffee "hot and hot", prepared in Mrs. Johnstone's best style, was served up in four large vases … We have heard it stated by several of the delighted party, formerly used to the "wee drap of barley bree", that, though under some uneasiness lest dulness might prevail, their fears were soon dispelled. The harmonious party was kept up in full glee from four o'clock till near midnight.'

~ November 30th ~

1592: A charter, signed and dated on this day at Holyrood House, and granted to Dumfries by King James VI, related to fairs held in the burgh. It acknowledged that 'there was but one fair yearly, in the midst of harvest, called Rood Day', but allowed the 'Provost, Bailies, Counsell, and Community of the said burgh the previeledges of keeping two other fairs: one upon the first day of February called Candlemas Day, and the other upon the first day of July, in summer, each to continue eight days.' (Mackie, Charles, (Ed.), *Dumfries and Galloway Notes and Queries* (1913))

1901: On this day, it was reported that 'a sale and exhibition of work was held in the Assembly Rooms, in connection with the Edinburgh Royal Repository for the sale of gentlewomen's work. The object of the organization needs little explanation … Ladies, who may unhappily find themselves in straitened circumstances, may be able to find a market for the work of their own hands … Those who assist at the sales, whether at the stalls or by purchases, should have the consciousness that they are aiding the delicately nurtured to overcome their difficulties, and at the same time to avoid the heart burning of dependence.' (*Dumfries and Galloway Courier and Herald*)

~ December 1st ~

1513: Traditionally, shoemaking (and, later, clogmaking) was an important part of the town's economy. Together with hammermen, squaremen, tailors, weavers, skinners and glovers, and fleshers, shoemakers made up the Seven Trades of Dumfries.

'Something is learned about the shoemakers so far back as the time when Flodden was fought, from a Seal of Cause granted to them by the Town Council [on this day]. That document tells us that the market for leather and made work was held in "the Cowgate, fra the New Well to the Greyfriars"; that the goods were to be exposed from seven o'clock in summer, and nine in winter, till twelve at noon; that searchers were authorised to overhaul the goods, and to bring any found insufficient to the magistrates for confiscation; that no unfreemen were allowed to purchase leather in the market till eleven o'clock; nor to sell boots or shoes of their own make except at the market on Mondays; the freemen being, of course, permitted to dispose of their wares on any day of the week, in their own booths, "when gude", Sundays excepted.' (McDowall, William, *History of Dumfries* (2nd Edn., 1873))

⁓ December 2nd ⁓

1830: On this day, Dumfries gave 'a hearty adhesion to the Reform cause', by way of a meeting held in the Court House that 'was the greatest political gathering that had ever … taken place in the town, at least in modern times. It was densely crowded, comprised most of the principal burgesses, and, to give it increased influence and éclat, the Provost, Mr. John Fraser, though a Conservative, presided – seemingly not unwilling to be carried with the current of the prevailing tide. The resolutions … declared the dissatisfaction of the inhabitants with the existing mode of election, as not affording "a full, free, and equal representation of the people" in the Commons House of Parliament; and they especially pointed out the defective nature of the Scottish representative system … All the resolutions, with a petition to the House of Commons based upon them, were unanimously adopted. Mr. Adam Rankine, a gentleman noted for his fervid temperament and public spirit, was so pleased with the meeting that he forwarded an account of it by express to Lord Advocate Jeffrey, the substance of which was communicated to a great Edinburgh Reform meeting, and elicited from it a round of cheers in honour of "the judicious resolutions and patriotic example of the citizens of Dumfries".'(McDowall, William, *History of Dumfries* (2nd Edn., 1873))

~ December 3rd ~

1822: On this day, the *Dumfries and Galloway Courier* reported a calamity at sea, involving a local vessel: 'We are sorry to announce the loss of the Queen Charlotte, of this port (John Heuchan, master) a stout seaworthy brig, of at least 150 tons burthen. This brigantine sailed from Limerick for Hull on the 28th Ult., and after weathering the tremendous gales of the beginning of the month, and escaping the many perils of the Pentland Firth, had to flee for safety to the port of Aberdeen. From this place she again sailed, the weather appearing a little more calm and settled; but she had hardly put to sea when the prospect changed. When nearly opposite Newcastle, the vessel fairly upset (probably from the shifting of her cargo, rape-seed), and in less than fifteen minutes sunk in twenty fathoms of water. The situation of the crew ... was one of great peril. So sudden was the disaster, that they expected every moment to be washed from their insecure footing on the broadside of the vessel, when they were most providentially picked up by the Friendship of Grangemouth, and carried into Hull. The Queen Charlotte, we are sorry to add, was not insured.'

– DECEMBER 4TH –

1793: On this day, Miss Fontenelle, a leading popular actress of her time, was given a Benefit Night at the town's Theatre Royal. It would prove to be an evening of extremely varied entertainment. 'Cobb's comic opera, "The Haunted Tower", was performed in Dumfries for the first time. At the end of Act Two, a new Scots Air called "The Banks of the Nith", the words written by Mr. Burns and the music composed by Robert Riddle of Glenriddle Esq., was sung by Miss Fontenelle. At the end of the play, [she gave] a New Occasional Address, written by Mr. Burns … The last item of the evening was a Grand Spectacle called "The Siege of Valenciennes", founded on a series of events in the late operations of the combined armies on the Continent, accompanied by Machinery and Action, [and giving] whatever is most striking in the progress and termination of the siege, particularly the working of the Trenches, the Preparation and Explosion of a Mine, and the Manner of effecting and entering a breach, [and concluding] with a General View of the Storming Party, their getting possession of, and the consequent Capitulation and Surrender of the Town.' (*Dumfries Weekly Journal*)

~ December 5th ~

1851: On this day, the *Dumfriesshire and Galloway Herald and Register* ran the following report: 'Bloomerism – For one night only, on Wednesday next, at the Theatre Royal, Miss Julia Lester, Member of the Female Convention and Dress Reform Association of New York (President, Mrs. Bloomer), will deliver a lecture on this important subject. During the lecture, she will appear in full Bloomer costume, and exhibit the Bloomer wedding dress and walking costume."'

1865: Also on this day, the *Dumfries and Galloway Courier* remarked that 'the cattle plague continues to prove very fatal in this neighbourhood and, in the past few days, has broken out at several farms near Dumfries previously free from the disease, indicating that it partakes more of the epidemic character than was at first supposed. We regret to learn that it has also appeared in the Stewartry, on the farm of Lincluden Mains, where the stock consists of 12 cows, 6 calves, 2 two year-old queys [heifers], and four one year-old queys, all Ayrshires, and 15 two year-old Galloway bullocks. On Saturday, a one year-old Ayrshire quey, which had been ailing, presented an appearance which led to the suspicion of Rinderpest, and on Mr. McIntosh – Vetinerary Surgeon at Dumfries, and Inspector for the Maxwelltown district under the Privy Council Orders – being called in, he at once saw that the animal was suffering from that disease. Yesterday, the disease was found to have attacked another Ayrshire quey, a two year-old, on the same farm.'

─ December 6th ─

1848: On this day, during an outbreak of cholera in the town, 'Dr. Sutherland, on a mission from the Central Board of Health, met with the Committee of the Dumfries Parochial Board, and the Medical staff, for the purpose of giving them advice in the present emergency.

Dr. Sutherland, after remarking on the great number of cholera cases in Dumfries that had been reported, said it was so far a fortunate circumstance that nearly all the cases had a well-marked premonitory stage. In Edinburgh, for instance, it was a common thing for individuals to be struck with the poison at once, and hurried without warning to the very verge of the grave. Here in Dumfries, however, timely warning was generally afforded, and he was very desirous of pressing on all the necessity of attending to the slightest symptoms of the disease's approach ... Once ascertained, medical assistance should be instantly procured.

To obtain the required information, a system of visitation was necessary. Voluntary agents were to be preferred, and he thought none were so well-fitted for the work as ministers of congregations with their elders or deacons. Let them visit from house to house, and enquire into the health of every inmate.' (*Dumfries and Galloway Standard*)

~ DECEMBER 7TH ~

1802: On this day, the *Dumfries Weekly Journal* announced that 'Mr. O'Brien, the celebrated Irish Giant, has now arrived in this town, on his road to Glasgow and Edinburgh. His stupendous height is nearly nine feet, and he weighs upwards of five hundredweight. His stay in Dumfries will be till Wednesday evening. This Phenomenon of Nature has never appeared in Scotland before, and he has lately been represented in all the public papers as being deceased.'

1813: Also on this day, the newspaper published the following report: 'Dumfries Subscription Assemblies: At a General Meeting of the Subscribers, held on Wednesday last, the Annual Subscription for the ensuing year was fixed at One Guinea for each Gentleman, and Half-a-Guinea for each Lady. The Subscription Paper lies with Mrs. McClure.

The next Assembly will be held on Thursday the 16th of December current – the dancing to commence, during the season, at eight o'clock; and if twelve dancing Ladies be not present at that hour, the lights will be immediately extinguished, and no Assembly will take place. This resolution the Subscribers are resolved to adhere to in the strictest manner.' (*Dumfries Weekly Journal*)

⌣ December 8th ⌣

On this day, the following notices appeared in the *Dumfries Weekly Journal*:

1801: 'I, Marion Austin, daughter of Robert Austin, in Terreagles-town, do hereby acknowledge, that I, about twelve or fifteen months ago, scandalized and defamed Janet Kirkpatrick, late servant in Terreagles-town, now in Shaws of Closeburn, and daughter of James Kirkpatrick in Shaws aforesaid, by saying that she had stolen some clothes out of my father's house; that I had no other cause for impeaching the said Janet Kirkpatrick, except the information or saying of a Woman who pretended to tell Secrets, by the turning of a Sieve or Riddle, and was thereby led foolishly into such rash Slander. I do hereby declare, upon cool thoughts, that I did scandalize her improperly, and that I believe she is innocent of the theft; and I am extremely sorry for what I said of Janet Kirkpatrick. This I mark with my usual mark, declaring I cannot write.'

———

1818: 'M. Constable Maxwell Esq., of Nithsdale, has given instructions that every person will be prosecuted with the utmost rigour of the law, who shall be found taking away either STONES or RUBBISH from Lincluden College, as Mr. Maxwell is determined to preserve the remains of this ancient structure. Mr. Woodburn, his Factor, will handsomely reward any person who will inform him, and their names will be kept secret.'

~ December 9th ~

1836: On this day, it was reported that 'information having been given to the Dean on Saturday morning, that an individual was selling potatoes with weights which were not properly stamped, he immediately granted warrant to Mr. Haugh, Inspector for the Burgh, to examine the weights, and seize the same if light. The person complained of, having been brought before the Dean and Bailie McGowan in the afternoon, and the Inspector having reported that he had seized four weights, which were not authenticated in terms of the recent Act of Parliament, besides being considerably lighter than required by law; and the party having admitted that he had sold with them, the Dean proposed (there being some strong circumstances in mitigation), that the full fine should not be exacted, but that a moiety thereof should be taken, and that the weights which were seized should be forfeited and destroyed.

This is the second time within these last four months, that conviction has followed upon a similar charge, and we earnestly recommend all persons who have not attended to the regulations of the Act of Parliament, instantly to do so; because the moment a complaint is made to the Magistrates, they are resolved to put the law into due execution ...' (*Dumfriesshire and Galloway Herald and Advertiser*)

– December 10th –

1909: On this day, the *Dumfries and Galloway Standard* reported that, following a sudden thaw of lying snow and the onset of heavy rain, flooding occurred at Whitesands: 'On this occasion the lower part of the Whitesands was completely submerged, the water washing against the New Bazaar Hotel, Grapes Inn, and other houses in line with them. The water flowed up Friars' Vennel almost to the Victoria Inn. At the lower end the houses at Waterloo Place were cut off by the waters. Nith Place was flooded for half its length, the approaches to the suspension bridge being submerged. At the New Bridge a depth of twelve feet and a half was registered.

In the course of the forenoon little groups of bystanders were seen about the head of the Whitesands, and they watched with interest the progress of milk-carts and other vehicles through the shallow side of the water. Some amusement was caused shortly after ten o'clock by the exit of the dues collector from the upper storey of his house near the Dumfries Arms. He dropped from the window on to a van which had been brought alongside, and was driven through the water to terra-firma, after which he was able to resume his duties.'

~ DECEMBER 11TH ~

1924: On this day, the *Dumfries and Galloway Standard* reported that 'Sir James M. Barrie, Bart., O.M., L.L.D., was presented with the Freedom of Dumfries, in admiration of his great gifts as a literateur and dramatist, and in recognition of his having spent the formative years of his life in Dumfries. It was an expression of the gratitude of the citizens for the honour which he had brought to the town and to his old school, the Academy of Dumfries.

The Freedom ceremony was held in the Lyceum Theatre and was attended by about two thousand citizens. Provost McGeorge, in presenting Sir James with the Burgess Ticket enclosed in a silver casket, gave expression in an elegant and dignified speech to the admiration of the townspeople for the new Burgess. Sir James had won, the Provost said, new triumphs in a new field, for he was the first great Scottish dramatist, and had enriched and ennobled the literature of Scotland. He had given the children a friend and companion besides Cinderella and Robinson Crusoe. As the creator of Peter Pan the world was his debtor.

In a characteristic reply, alternating between sadness and humour, the new Burgess revealed that he had written a novel of Dumfries while at the Academy, and had "gently torn it up" but a year ago. His second revelation was that the fairy fantasy "Peter Pan", had its genesis in a Dumfries garden.'

— December 12th —

1848: On this day, the following notice appeared in the *Dumfries and Galloway Courier*: 'We regret deeply to state that cholera was very severe in Dumfries during the last week. The total number of cases which have been reported ... since the first occurrence of the disease, now nearly three weeks ago, is 180; of these 65 have proved fatal.'

———

1914: Also on this day, it was reported that 'during the past week, recruiting for the 5th Reserve Battalion of the K.O.S.B. at Dumfries has been quieter than usual. It was expected that, following upon the Martinmas term, a large number of the agricultural class would come forward, but the number of recruits from that class has been disappointingly small. It is expected that today a draft of fifty-four men, who have completed their musketry training at Conhuith, will be sent to join the service battalion at North Queensferry, and that a similar number will arrive in Dumfries from the service battalion to complete their musketry course. Dumfries is proving an admirable centre for the training, as the training area, the drill fields, and places for entrenching practice in the vicinity are of the very finest description. In addition, the extended range at Conhuith is highly suitable for musketry practice.' (*Dumfries and Galloway Courier and Herald*)

~ DECEMBER 13TH ~

1825: On this day, the following notice appeared in the *Dumfries Weekly Journal*: 'An opinion having been entertained, that passengers travelling by the Galloway Mail were entitled to seats in the Edinburgh Mail, to the exclusion of the inhabitants of Dumfries, the contractors hereby intimate that, while they have every wish to accommodate the public, no preferences are given, excepting where seats are previously secured by written notice. This intimation has become necessary in consequence of the misunderstandings that have arisen lately.'

1899: Also on this day, it was reported that 'the fifth annual supper of the coachmen and grooms of Dumfries and Maxwelltown, took place in the White Hart Hotel on Thursday night ... Mr. A.C. Penman, coachbuilder, presided. After an excellent dinner ... the loyal and patriotic toasts were duly honoured, then the Chairman proposed the toast of the evening, that of "Coachmen and Grooms". In doing so, he spoke of the qualities requisite for the perfect coachman, as a trainer, caretaker, and driver of horses, and as a keeper of carriages. The younger members of the company he advised to make themselves above all competent, reminding them that no matter how much a trade might be crowded, there was always room at the top.' (*Dumfries and Galloway Standard*)

~ December 14th ~

1840: On this day, the arrival of a novel entertainment was announced: 'Marshall's splendid new moving PANORAMA of the Grand Tournament and Passage of Arms at Eglinton Castle, will open on Friday in the New Assembly Rooms. Brilliantly lighted with gas, and seen to equal advantage both day and night, the Panorama – painted on 16,000 feet of square canvass, with figures as large as life and accompanied by music – displays the whole of the magnificent Procession, including the Queen of Beauty, Lady Archeresses, Maids of Honour, Lady Visitors mounted upon their Plumed Steeds, the Knights in magnificent Suits of Armour, their steeds barbed with frontlets of steel, their lances borne by their different Esquires, the Ancient Bowmen of England, with their Cloth Yard Shafts and Round Targets, the Herald of the Tournament and Trumpeters, the Irvine Archers, in their suits of Forest Green, the gallant train of the youthful and handsome Pages in their antique-cut Doublets and Tunics, the Clansmen of Athol, fierce and brave as the band of Rhoderic Dhu, the Men-at-Arms in their Ancient Garb and Half Armour, the wooded scene around, and the Towering Battlements of the Castle &c. Mr. Marshall, ever anxious to gratify the Nobility and Public of Dumfries, regardless of expense, had Mr. Danson from London to witness and make Drawings of this splendid and unique Pageant, the correctness of which will be gratifying to all who were present.' (*Dumfries and Galloway Courier*)

~ DECEMBER 15TH ~

1778: On this day, the *Dumfries Weekly Journal* printed the following notice: 'Whereas William Hutchison of Dalkeith was at Dumfries on 1st October, and had the misfortune of losing his Pocket Book, which contained Two Bills both accepted by George Maxwell Esq., of Munches, one dated 4th September 1777, for two hundred pounds sterling, and the other dated 22nd August 1777, for four hundred pounds sterling ... made payable, or intended to be made payable to Thomas Hutchison of Dalkeith, but to which bills, it is believed, the said Thomas Hutchison has not figured his name as drawer; and in which Pocket Book were contained several other papers of no use to any other person but the owner. It is therefore requested that if any person has found this Pocket Book, and Papers therein contained, they will deliver up the same to the said William or Thomas Hutchison, or to Mr. William Kirkpatrick, junior, merchant in Dumfries, by whom they will receive a reward of Three Guineas ... In case any person should presume to offer to pass these bills, it is requested that notice thereof may be given to the said Messrs. Hutchison, or the above Mr. William Kirkpatrick.'

— DECEMBER 16TH —

1686: On this day, a letter was sent to the Magistrates and Town Council by the Privy Council in Edinburgh: 'All the persons underwritten should be nominat and appointed Magistrates and other Councillors for the Burgh of Dumfreise, as being such whom his Majestie judges most loyall and ready to promote his Royall Service. Therefore the Lords of his Majesties Privy Councill ... do hereby nominate and appoint John Maxwell of Barncleugh to be Provost of the said Burgh of Dumfreise, John Irving to be Baillie in place of Baillie Fingass deceased, John Rome, present Baillie, and John Irving, present Baillie, to continue Baillies; John Crosbie, present Deacon of the Trades to be Convener, and the four new merchant councillors which are yearly elected with the Dean Treasurer and the rest of the Deacons of Trades, to be elected by the advice of the Magistrates aforesaid. And the said Lords ordain the persons above named to meet at the Toun Councill House ... upon the 11th day of January nixt, and there to enter to their respective offices ...' (Quoted in Edgar, Robert, (Ed. Reid, R.C.), *An Introduction to the History of Dumfries* (J. Maxwell & Sons, Dumfries, 1915))

— DECEMBER 17TH —

1792: On this day, a revolution in the tailoring industry was announced: 'The town's master tailors met, and "having taken into consideration that the prices charged by them for work done to their customers has been nearly the same for a hundred years past, although all other mechanics have increased their wages, they resolved to form their 'log' according to the following rate of charges, English money: Making a gentleman's suit of clothes, 10*s*; making a gentleman's greatcoat, 5*s* 6*d*; mechanics' and livery servants' clothes, 8*s*; boy's first suit, 3*s*; mending clothes, per hour, 2*d*; ladies' habits, 10*s* 6*d*; ladies' greatcoats, 5*s*. Anyone charging a lower figure, to be fined 10*s* 6*d* for each offence."' (McDowall, William, *History of Dumfries* (2nd Edn., 1873))

———

1834: A General Election was on the horizon, and the *Dumfries Times* assessed the local candidates.

'Mr. H. Johnston (Whig), is to be opposed by Lord Viscount Stormont (Tory), who will have his father's influence and the more powerful interest of the Duke of Buccleuch. Whether Mr. Johnston will receive the votes of the reformers in the approaching contest must depend, in a great measure, on the terms of his address. Whatever he promises he will perform; but he must be specific in his promises. If he do not frankly avow his intention to oppose the Duke's government, we would advise the Liberal electors to leave him and his Tory opponents to fight their battles as best they can.'

— December 18th —

1833: On this day, a report appeared in the *Dumfries Times*: 'At a Public Meeting of the inhabitants of Dumfries and its vicinity, held in the New Church on Thursday, for the purpose of deliberating on the propriety of petitioning Parliament on the grievance of Patronage; and, also, of forming a society for the purpose of procuring the removal of that grievance, the following resolutions were agreed to:

That the right of individuals and of the Crown to nominate the spiritual instructors of the people, has no warrant in the Word of God.

That Church Patronage, which is alike opposed to the principles of the Reformation and to the practice of the Presbyterian Church in the days of its greatest purity, has long been productive of results most baneful to a Christian community. Patronage, which is the source of so much evil, cannot be too speedily abolished, that thereby the hearers of the Word of God may be reconciled to their ministers; and that ministers may deserve and enjoy a due influence over the people, for the promotion of sound scripture truth And the meeting is further of opinion that, to secure such blessings, it is alike right and expedient that the power of electing parish ministers should be vested in all parishioners, being hearers and in full communion with the Church.'

~ December 19th ~

1888: On this day, the following indignant reader's letter appeared in the *Dumfries and Galloway Standard*: 'Sir, I am astonished at the proposition to again erect a public urinal in beautiful Queensberry Square. Some years ago a similar erection stood in the same place, but it soon became such an eyesore and unmitigated nuisance that it had to be removed, in answer to the outcry of an indignant community ... Some time ago the Monument was burnished up, and in several matters its surroundings were improved; and now it is proposed to set down a hideous erection at its base. Are not such places usually put up in rather out-of-the-way corners, or where they are as much hidden from the public view as possible? And that, I think, is just where they should be. Shame upon those Councillors, then, who are attempting to outrage common decency by planting down such a nuisance in such a public and exposed place. When the former one was there, how often was the eye offended by men adjusting their dress when far on to the street. Raise your voice like a trumpet and protest against the erection of the abomination.'

~ December 20th ~

1873: On this day, the *Dumfries and Galloway Standard* reported that 'on Tuesday afternoon, a lot of fat pigs were being driven from the Auction Mart to the railway station, but were taken to the watering-place, opposite the foot of Bank Street, to quench their thirst. One of the lot, a large pig, entered the river ... and he was borne down by the current. The high quay wall prevented any attempt at rescue, but the animal repeatedly breasted the flood ... At Nith Place, he was too far out in the stream to effect a landing, and was borne downwards, at times seeming as if he must succumb to the flood. At the ferry, the boat was crossing and he passed so close to it that an attempt was made to seize him by the ears, but it failed. A boat was procured and proceeded after the animal, but the pig turned towards the Galloway shore, and after a gallant struggle reached the bank near the Nithsdale Woollen Mills. After being allowed a short time to recover breath, the animal was driven quietly up the river's side, and in due time rejoined its companions little the worse for its adventure.'

— DECEMBER 21ST —

1745: On this day, 'the rulers and other leading men of the town met in the Presbytery house attached to the New Church, for the purpose of considering a renewed demand upon them for money. [Prince Charles Edward, with troops of his Jacobite army, had descended on Dumfries.] Provost Bell was not present to preside over them, he having been seized as a hostage that the burgh would keep good faith with its captors. A sad meeting it must have been; which conviction is deepened as we read the following record of its proceedings. "Mr. John Hay represented that he had a commission from his Royal Highness, Prince Charles ... to demand of the said burgh a contribution of two thousand pounds sterling, to be paid tomorrow, against eight o'clock at night, and to deliver to him, for the use of their army, one thousand pair of shoes together with all their arms, public and private, that are to be found in town, against the same time, and that as they would redeem their houses and families from destruction and ruin."' (McDowall, William, *History of Dumfries* (2nd Edn., 1873))

― December 22nd ―

1745: On this day, the effect of the arrival of Prince Charles and his army is brought vividly to life in the diary of Revd George Duncan: 'A melancholy day – the rebels in Dumfries, about 4,000 – with the Pretender's son at their head, in great rage at the town for carrying off their baggage from Annandale and for raising volunteers, and calling out the militia of the country in defence of the Government. Demanded £2,000 sterling of contributions, and that they [the inhabitants] convey their carts, with their carriages after them, to their headquarters. They were most rude in the town – pillaged some shops – pulled shoes off gentlemen's feet in the street. In most of the churches for some miles about Dumfries, no sermon. God be blessed! We had public worship. I lectured 1 Sam. IV.; Mr. John Scott, minister of Dumfries, (there being no sermon there), preached. Much confusion in all the neighbouring parishes – rebels robbing people's stables – pillaging some houses. They came to the border of our parish, but God be thanked! came no further, and we suffered no loose usage.' (Quoted in McDowall, William, *History of Dumfries* (2nd Edn., 1873))

~ December 23rd ~

1800: The *Dumfries Weekly Journal* reported on a possible solution to a long-running issue: 'The Earl of Dalkeith, his Majesty's Lieutenant for this County, in pursuance of a Letter from his Grace the Duke of Portland, requests a Meeting of the Deputy Lieutenants, Justices of the Peace, Commissioners of Supply, and Heritors of the County of Dumfries, within the Court-house, Dumfries, at 12 noon on Wednesday next, to consider the most effectual mode of carrying into execution his Majesty's late Proclamation respecting the Scarcity of Grain.'

1828: Also on this day, the same newspaper announced that 'now exhibiting at 13 High Street, Dumfries, [was] The Wonder of the World Alive, that beautiful Race Mare, "Pincushion Jenny", with seven legs, shod and stands on six feet. The seventh leg is far advanced and an eighth is growing! With extra hocks, fetlocks, thigh bones, sinews and tendons, the main bones of the extra legs are set from the hips and shoulders, and have beautiful muscular shape. At three years old her new formation began, after running nine races! She is descended from "Sorcerer" out of "Slim"; grand-dam, "Brown Charlotte", from the breed of "Eclipse". In her racing career, "Jenny" proved herself a superior racer and a winner.

This beautiful and astonishing animal, which has excited the admiration of the Royal Family, and the Nobility, was bred at Belgrave Hall, by Mr. Checketts, a celebrated Breeder and Agriculturist.

Admittance: Noblemen and Gentlemen, 1s. Working persons, 6d. Servants and Children, Half Price.'

~ December 24th ~

1688: On this day, a communication was sent to the Magistrates and Town Council from the Privy Council in Edinburgh. This extract reflects the anti-Catholic atmosphere of the time: 'There being this day a representation made to the Council of your care and diligence to prevent tumults, and suppressing any insurrection that might have been in your town, and by apprehending ... Papists, suspected priests or others of that persuasion amongst you, and detaining them from joining any who may have been in arms ... the Council have desired me in their name to give you hearty thanks for your care and timely intelligence given them in this matter, and do approve of your procedure in this affair, and look upon it as good and acceptable service at such a dangerous juncture as this is; and allows you to detain as prisoners in your Tolbooth those persons apprehended by you. Your care and diligence for the future to prevent troubles, and to keep peace amongst yourselves, and keeping your Town in a condition of defence for the Protestant Religion and security of the Kingdom is expected.' (Quoted in Edgar, Robert, (Ed. Reid, R.C.), *An Introduction to the History of Dumfries* (J. Maxwell & Sons, Dumfries, 1915))

~ December 25th ~

1585: William McDowall refers to a specific incident on this date that caused a great deal of controversy: 'The progress of the Reformation in Dumfries was impeded by the Maxwells. They still clung to the old faith; and in 1584 the fifth Lord Herries was accused of openly defying the law by causing mass to be publicly celebrated in the town ... His kinsman, Lord Morton, or Maxwell, as we prefer calling him, on the Christmas which followed the receipt of the royal amnesty ... summoned a meeting of followers and ecclesiastics for the purpose of making a defiant show of his religion ... and [on this day], after those composing it had been arranged as a procession, they marched to the College of Lincluden ... On arriving at the College, mass was performed in the ancient fane with unusual splendour and effect. For six hundred years Lincluden, first as an abbey and next as a collegiate institution, had been the scene of such religious rites; but the choral swell with which the venerable walls rang on this occasion was as the dying requiem of the ancient faith – mass never having been since said or sung in the house of Uchtred.' (McDowall, William, *History of Dumfries* (2nd Edn., 1873))

− December 26th −

1928: On this day, 'very serious damage was caused to the Dumfries Town Hall, by a disastrous outbreak of fire which occurred. Sergeant Service, who was on duty at the police office, immediately summoned the fire brigade, and then, along with Mr. Kerr, janitor at the Sheriff Court-house, rushed up to the Town Council Chamber, where there were a number of valuable paintings on the walls. Their efforts were directed towards the salvage of these pictures, which include examples of the art of Landseer and Raeburn, and also to the famous "Siller Gun", presented by James VI of Scotland to the Incorporated Trades … The recovery of the smaller pictures did not present much difficulty, and they were soon taken from the walls, but the large Landseer and the Raeburn portrait were of such size that their salvage could only be undertaken with considerable labour. The portraits of former Provosts, and documents, were removed from the Provost's room, but the Landseer and Raeburn pictures could not be removed from the building, and were placed in a corner of the Town Hall which was likely to be untouched by the flames.' (*Dumfries and Galloway Standard*)

~ December 27th ~

1803: On this day, the *Dumfries Weekly Journal* reported that the following resolution was passed at a meeting held by the Dumfriesshire Lieutenancy: 'In every town and parish within the County, a proportion of the inhabitants – taken either from the lists or from those who have voluntarily offered to serve, (but have not yet been enrolled in the Volunteer Companies), or from among the other able-bodied men willing to come forward on the present occasion – shall be enrolled, formed into Companies, and mustered from time to time.'

1815: This day marked the third centenary of the Dumfries Kilwinning Lodge No. 61 (originally denominated the Old Lodge of Dumfries) and, as the *Dumfries and Galloway Courier* subsequently reported: 'The brethren held a lodge in the New Assembly Rooms in celebration of the event. About nine o'clock, they proceeded in Masonic order to the Ballroom, and the Master having … stated the object of the meeting, opened the ball with the assistance of his officers. The splendour of the rooms had a most imposing effect; the excellence of the entertainment received the most marked approbation, and the decorum and propriety, hitherto so characteristic of the Old Lodge and with which everything was regulated, excited the admiration of all.'

— December 28th —

1678: On this day, John Graham of Claverhouse, ruthless pursuer of Covenanters in south-west Scotland, wrote to his commander, the Earl of Linlithgow: 'My lord, I came here [Moffat] last night with the troop, and am just going to march for Dumfries, where I resolve to quarter the whole troop … I am informed since I came that this county has been very loose. On Tuesday was eight days, and Sunday, there were great field conventicles [assemblies of Covenanters] just by here, with great contempt of the regular clergy; who complain extremely that I have no orders to apprehend anybody for past demeanours … Besides that, my lord, they tell me that the end of the bridge of Dumfries is in Galloway, and that they may hold conventicles at our nose [and] we dare not dissipate them, seeing our orders confine us to Dumfries and Annandale. Such an insult as that would not please me; and, on the other hand, I am unwilling to exceed orders, so that I expect from your lordship orders how to carry in such cases.' (Quoted in McDowall, William, *History of Dumfries* (2nd Edn., 1873))

— December 29th —

1824: On this day, the renowned actor Edmund Kean gave the first of several nights' performances at the town's Theatre Royal. 'This celebrated tragedian made his first appearance here these two years, in the arduous character of Richard III. Never did we hear a more affectionate welcome given to any performer than that with which he was honoured. A burst of acclamation testified the interest which the audience felt on his return to Dumfries, and the enthusiastic applause was renewed at every instance of those striking and emphatic passages in which this accomplished artist so particularly excels, and which give to his representation of this grand part an effect which no rival has produced. His style of acting is, if we may use the expression, more magnificent – more pregnant with meaning – more varied and alive in every part than any we have ever witnessed. It is wonderful that, so little assisted by voice, he should give such animation and vigour to his every accent.

On the nights following this opening performance, Kean played Sir Giles Overreach in Philip Massinger's "A New Way to Pay Old Debts", the title role in "Othello", and Shylock in "The Merchant of Venice".' (*Dumfries Weekly Journal*)

— December 30th —

1778: On this day, the *Dumfries Weekly Journal* reported that 'whereas the Magistrates and Commissioners of Police of the town of Dumfries, having for years past observed than an "Act for the Regulation of Carters, Carriages, and Loaded Horses, and for removing obstructions and nuisances upon the Streets and Highways", has not been attended to, hereby give public notice that they are determined to see the same put into force, to the utmost extent, within this borough and its privileges, from and after the first day of January next.'

The clauses of the act were many and various, and included 'that fines would be levied against every chaise driver found sitting in his chaise without another person sitting on one of the horses; and every carter found riding on his carriage, without a proper personage on foot to guide it'. Also, 'no drivers of carriages shall drive alongside other carriages, so as to obstruct the free passage of streets and highways, but shall follow one after another, and have bridles or halters on every horse, which the driver shall have in his hand; and that the drivers of carts etc. shall not leave their vehicles upon any street or highway unyoked.'

— DECEMBER 31ST —

1822: On New Year's Eve, the *Dumfries Weekly Journal* announced the arrival in town of 'Cook's Grand Exhibition, under the Immediate Patronage of the Royal Family, and containing three of the Greatest Curiosities in the World. The first grand prominent feature is the Gigantic Youth, only 16 years of age and weighs Thirty-Five stones. He is 24 inches round the Calf of the Leg, 56 round the Chest and twelve-and-half round the wrist. The second is Mr. John Bucknall, a native of Staffordshire, an Astonishing Dwarf. At seventeen years of age, he stands only 27 inches high and weighs only 24lbs. This wonderful little gentleman is allowed by every connoisseur to be a most elegant, perfect and interesting little person, for his pleasing vivacity, perfect symmetry of form, and beauty of features.

Also, just arrived from Ireland, General O'Brian, twenty-eight years of age, stands only two feet high, and has a wife and three small children. He will be pleased to recite the particulars of his ancestors, wife and family on request.

Admittance: Ladies and Gentlemen, 1*s*. Servants, 6*d*.'